D1567455

[These pages are reserved for Official Pronouncements by the Chancellor of the A∴ A∴]

Persons wishing for information, assistance, further interpretation, etc., are requested to communicate with

THE CHANCELLOR OF THE A∴ A∴

c/o THE EQUINOX,

33 Avenue Studios,

76 Fulham Road,

South Kensington, S.W.

Telephone: 2632, KENSINGTON,

or to call at that address by appointment. A representative will be there to meet them.

THE Chancellor of the A∴ A∴ wishes to warn readers of THE EQUINOX against accepting instruction in his name from an ex-Probationer, Captain J. F. C. Fuller, whose motto was "Per Ardua." This person never advanced beyond the Degree of Probationer, never sent in a record, and has presumably neither performed practices nor obtained results. He has not, and never has had, authority to give instructions in the name of the A∴ A∴.

THE Chancellor of the A∴ A∴ considers it desirable to make a brief statement of the financial position, as the time has now arrived to make an effort to spread the knowledge to the ends of the earth. The expenses of the propaganda are roughly estimated as follows—

Maintenance of Temple, and service . .	£200 p.a.
Publications	£200 p.a.
Advertising, electrical expenses, etc. . .	£200 p.a.
Maintenance of an Hermitage where poor Brethren may make retirements . .	£200 p.a.
	£800 p.a.

As in the past, the persons responsible for the movement will give the whole of their time and energy, as well as their worldly wealth, to the service of the A∴A∴.

Unfortunately, the sums at their disposal do not at present suffice for the contemplated advance, and the Chancellor consequently appeals for assistance to those who have found in the instructions of the A∴A∴ a sure means to the end they sought. All moneys received will be applied solely for the purpose of aiding those who have not yet entered the circle of the light.

The Chancellor wishes to express his gratitude to those who have so generously come forward with assistance. The full amount is, however, not yet guaranteed, and he hopes that those interested will make a special effort without delay.

Owing to the unnecessary strain thrown upon Neophytes by unprepared persons totally ignorant of the groundwork taking the Oath of a Probationer, the Imperator of A∴A∴, under the seal and by the authority of V.V.V.V.V., ordains that every person wishing to become a Probationer of A∴A∴ must first pass three months as a student of the Mysteries.

He must possess the following books :—

1. THE EQUINOX, from No. 1 to the current number.
2. "Raja Yoga," by Swami Vivekananda.
3. "The Shiva Sanhita," or "The Hathayoga Pradipika."
4. "Konx Om Pax."
5. "The Spiritual Guide," by Miguel de Molinos.
6. "777."
7. "Rituel et Dogme de la haute Magie," par Eliphaz Levi, or its translation, by A. E. Waite.
8. "The Goetia of the Lemegeton of Solomon the King."

9. "Tannhäuser," by A. Crowley.
10. "The Sword of Song," by A. Crowley.
11. "Time," by A. Crowley.
12. "Eleusis," by A. Crowley.
      [These four last items are to be found in his
            Collected Works.]
13. "The Book of the Sacred Magic of Abra-melin
      the Mage."
14. The Tao Teh King and the Writings of Kwang
      Tzu (Sacred Books of the East, Vols. XXXIX,
      XL).

An examination in these books will be made. The Student
is expected to show a thorough acquaintance with them, but
not necessarily to understand them in any deeper sense. On
passing the examination he may be admitted to the grade of
Probationer.

———————

With the publication of No. X of THE EQUINOX in
September next the Official Pronouncements of the A ∴ A ∴
will cease, according to the Rule of the Order, which pre-
scribes Five Years of Silence alternating with Five Years of
Speech. This Silence was maintained from the year O to the
year IV of this era. Speech followed, from the year V to the
year IX. Silence will, therefore, be maintained from the year
X to the year XIV. After this September, therefore, there
will be no further open publications made by the Executive
until March 1918 o.s.

I.N.R.I.

BRITISH SECTION OF THE
ORDER OF ORIENTAL TEMPLARS
O.T.O.

M ∴ M ∴ M ∴

[The Premonstrator of the A ∴ A ∴ permits it to be known that there is not at present any necessary incompatibility between the A ∴ A ∴ and the O. T. O. and M ∴ M ∴ M ∴, and allows membership of the same as a valuable preliminary training.]

[This Order in no way conflicts with, or infringes the just privileges of, the United Grand Lodge of England.]

ORDER OF ORIENTAL TEMPLARS

MYSTERIA MYSTICA MAXIMA

PREAMBLE

DURING the last twenty-five years, constantly increasing numbers of earnest people and seekers after truth have been turning their attention to the study of the hidden laws of Nature.

The growth of interest in these matters has been simply marvellous. Numberless societies, associations, orders, groups, etc., etc., have been founded in all parts of the civilized world, all and each following some line of occult study.

While all these newly organized associations do some good in preparing the minds of thoughtful people for their eventually becoming genuine disciples of the One Truth, yet there is but ONE ancient organization of Mystics which shows to the student a Royal Road to discover the One Truth. This organization has permitted the formation of the body known as the " ANCIENT ORDER OF ORIENTAL TEMPLARS." It is a modern School of Magi. Like the ancient Schools of Magi it derived its knowledge from Egypt and Chaldea. This knowledge is never revealed to the profane, for it gives immense power for either good or evil to its possessors.

It is recorded in symbol, parable and allegory, requiring a Key for its interpretation.

The symbols of Freemasonry were originally derived from the more ancient mysteries, as all who have travelled the burning sands know. The ritual and ceremonies, signs and passwords have been preserved with great fidelity; but the Real Key has been long lost to the crowds who have been initiated, advanced and raised in Masonry.

The KEY to this knowledge can, however, be placed within the reach of all those who unselfishly desire, study and work for its possession.

The Symbols of Ancient Masonry, the Sacred Art of the Ancient Chemi (Egyptians), and Homer's Golden Chain are but different aspects of the One Great Mystery. They represent but different degrees of initiation. By the Right Use of the " Key " alone the " Master Word " can be found.

In order to afford genuine seekers after Hermetic Truth some information on the aims of the Ancient Order of Oriental Templars, we now print the preliminary instruction issued by the Fratres of this Order.

FIRST INSTRUCTION

To all whom it may concern—

Let it be known that there exists, unknown to the great crowd, a very ancient order of sages, whose object is the amelioration and spiritual elevation of mankind, by means of

viii

conquering error, and aiding men and women in their efforts of attaining the power of recognizing the truth. This order has existed already in the most remote and prehistoric times; and it has manifested its activity secretly and openly in the world under different names and in various forms; it has caused social and political revolutions, and proved to be the rock of salvation in times of danger and misfortune. It has always upheld the banner of freedom against tyranny, in whatever shape this appeared, whether as clerical or political, or social despotism or oppression of any kind. To this secret order every wise and spiritually enlightened person belongs by right of his or her nature; because they all, even if they are personally unknown to each other, are one in their purpose and object, and they all work under the guidance of the one light of truth. Into this sacred society no one can be admitted by another, unless he has the power to enter it himself by virtue of his own interior illumination; neither can any one, after he has once entered, be expelled, unless he should expel himself by becoming unfaithful to his principles, and forget again the truths which he has learned by his own experience.

All this is known to every enlightened person; but it is known only to few that there exists also an external, visible organization of such men and women who, having themselves found the path to real self-knowledge, are willing to give to others, desirous of entering that path, the benefit of their experience and to act as spiritual guides to those who are willing to be guided. As a matter of course, those persons who are already sufficiently spiritually developed to enter into conscious communion with the great spiritual brotherhood will be taught directly by the spirit of wisdom; but those who still need external advice and support will find this in the external organization of that society. In regard to the spiritual aspect of this secret order, one of the Brothers says—

"Our community has existed ever since the first day of creation when the gods spoke the divine command: 'Let there be light!' and it will continue to exist till the end of time. It is the Society of the Children of Light, who live in the light and have attained immortality therein. In our school we are instructed directly by Divine Wisdom, the Celestial Bride, whose will is free and who selects as her disciples those who are devoted to her. The mysteries which we are taught embrace everything that can possibly be known in regard to God, Nature and Man. Every sage that ever existed in the world has graduated at our school; for without wisdom no man can be wise. We all study only one book, the Book of Nature, in which the keys to all secrets are contained, and we follow the only possible method in studying it, that of experience. Our place of meeting is the Temple of the Holy Spirit pervading the universe; easily to be found by the elect, but for ever hidden from the eyes of the vulgar. Our secrets cannot be sold for money, but we give them free to every one capable to receive them."

As to the external organization of that society, it will be necessary to give a glance at its history, which has been one and the same in all. Whenever that spiritual society manifested itself on the outward plane and appeared in the world, it consisted at its beginning of a few able and enlightened people, forming a nucleus around which others were

x

attracted. But invariably, the more such a society grew in numbers, the more became attracted to its elements, such as were not able to understand or follow its principles; people who joined it for the purpose of gratifying their own ambition or for making the society serve their own ends obtained the majority over those that were pure. Thereupon the healthy portion of it retired from the field and continued their benevolent work in secrecy, while the remaining portion became diseased and disrupted, and sooner or later died disgraced and profaned. For the Spirit had departed from them.

For this reason the external organization of which we speak has resolved not to reveal its name or place to the vulgar. Furthermore, for the same reason, the names of the teachers and members of this society shall remain unknown, except to such as are intimately associated with them in their common work. If it is said that in this way the society will gain only few members, it may be answered that our society has a spiritual head, and that those who are worthy of being admitted will be guided to it by means of their intuition; while those who have no intuition are not ripe for it and not needed. It is better to have only a comparatively small number of capable members than a great many useless ones.

From the above it will be clear that the first and most necessary acquirement of the new disciple is that he will keep silent in regard to all that concerns the society to which he is admitted. Not that there is anything in that society which needs to be afraid of being known to the virtuous and good; but it is not necessary that things which are elevated and sacred should be exposed to the gaze of the vulgar, and be bespattered by them with mud. This would only impede the society in its work.

Another necessary requirement is mutual confidence between the teacher and the disciple; because a disciple who has no faith in his master cannot be taught or guided by him. There may be things which will appear strange, and for which no reasons can be given to the beginner; but when the disciple has attained a certain state of development all will be clear to him or her. The confidence which is required will also be of little service if it is only of a short duration. The way of the development of the soul, which leads to the awakening of the inner senses, is slow, and without patience and fortitude nothing will be accomplished.

From all this it follows as a matter of course that the next requisite is obedience. The purpose of the disciple is to obtain the mastery over his own lower self, and for this reason he must not submit himself to the will of his lower nature, but follow the will of that higher nature, which he does not yet know, but which he desires to find. In obeying the will of the master, instead of following the one which he believes to be his own, but which is in reality only that of his lower nature, he obeys the will of his own higher nature with which his master is associated for the purpose of aiding the disciple in attaining the conquest over himself. The conquest of the higher self over the lower self means the victory of the divine consciousness in man over that which in him is earthly and animal. Its object is a realization of true manhood and womanhood, and the attainment of conscious immortality in the realization of the highest state of existence in perfection.

xii

ORDER OF ORIENTAL TEMPLARS

These few preliminary remarks may be sufficient for those who desire information concerning our order; to those who feel themselves capable to apply for admission, further instructions will be given.

Address all communications to The Grand Secretary General, M∴M∴M∴, c/o THE EQUINOX, 33 Avenue Studios, 76 Fulham Road, South Kensington, S.W.

THE FOLLOWING

DISCOURSE

(Translated from the original French)

Was lately pronounced at Brunswick (Lower Saxony) where PRINCE . . . . is GRAND MASTER of M., by COUNT T., at the Initiation of his Son.

"I congratulate you on your admission into the most ancient, and perhaps the most respectable, society in the universe. To you the mysteries of M. are about to be revealed, and so bright a sun never shed lustre on your eyes. In this awful moment, when prostrate at this holy altar, do you not shudder at every crime, and have you not confidence in every virtue? May this reflection inspire you with noble sentiments; may you be penetrated with a religious abhorrence of every vice that degrades human nature; and may you feel the elevation of soul which scorns a dishonourable action, and ever invites to the practice of piety and virtue.

"These are the wishes of a father and a brother conjoined. Of you the greatest hopes are raised; let not our expectations be deceived. You are the son of a M. who glories in the profession; and for your zeal and attachment, your silence and good conduct, your father has already pledged his honour.

"You are now, as a member of this illustrious order, introduced a subject of a new country, whose extent is boundless. Pictures are opened to your view, wherein true patriotism is exemplified in glowing colours, and a series of transactions recorded, which the rude hand of Time can never erase. The obligations which influenced the first Brutus and Manlius to sacrifice their children to the love of their country are not more sacred than those which bind me to support the honour and reputation of this venerable order.

"This moment, my son, you owe to me a second birth; should your conduct in life correspond with the principles of M., my remaining years will pass away with pleasure and satisfaction. Observe the great example of our ancient masters, peruse our history and our constitutions. The best, the most humane, the bravest, and most civilized of men have been our patrons. Though the vulgar are strangers to our works, the greatest geniuses have sprung from our order. The most illustrious characters on earth have laid the foundation of their most amiable qualities in M. The wisest of princes, SOLOMON, planned our institution by raising a temple to the Eternal and Supreme Ruler of the Universe.

"Swear, my son, that you will be a true and faithful M. Know, from this moment, that I centre the affection of a parent in the name of a brother and a friend. May your heart be susceptible of love and esteem, and may you burn with the same zeal your father possesses. Convince the

xiv

world, by your new allegiance, you are deserving our favours, and never forget the ties which bind you to honour and to justice.

"View not with indifference the extensive connections you have formed, but let universal benevolence regulate your conduct. Exert your abilities in the service of your king and your country, and deem the knowledge you have this day attained the happiest acquisition of your life.

"Recall to memory the ceremony of your initiation; learn to bridle your tongue and to govern your passions: and ere long you will have occasion to say: 'In becoming a M., I truly became the man; and while I breathe will never disgrace a jewel that kings may prize.'

"If I live, my son, to reap the fruits of this day's labour, my happiness will be complete. I will meet death without terror, close my eyes in peace, and expire without a groan, in the arms of a virtuous and worthy M."

THE EQUINOX

THE EQUINOX

THE OFFICIAL ORGAN OF THE A∴A∴

THE REVIEW OF SCIENTIFIC ILLUMINISM

EDITED BY SOROR VIRAKAM

SUB-EDITOR : FRA. LAMPADA TRADAM

An IX   VOL. I. No. IX   ☉ in ♈

MARCH MCMXIII
O.S.

"THE METHOD OF SCIENCE—THE AIM OF RELIGION"

WIELAND & CO.
33 AVENUE STUDIOS, SOUTH KENSINGTON
LONDON, S.W.

The Equinox
The Review of Scientific Illuminism
Vol. I.   No. IX.

First published in London in 1913

An CXIV   ☉ in ♑

This edition copyright ©2018, Scott Wilde

Special thanks to Tony Iannotti
for providing images of the front cover, back, and spine

Digital edition available at:
https://keepsilence.org/the-equinox

Contents of this page
in the first edition:

RICHARD CLAY & SONS, LIMITED,
BRUNSWICK STREET, STAMFORD STREET, S.E.,
AND BUNGAY, SUFFOLK.

CONTENTS

[1] Rejected by *The English Review*.
[2] Reprinted from the *Daily Mail, Evening Times*, and *New York World*.
[3] Reprinted from *What's On?* by kind permission of Mr. Robert Haslam.
[4] Believed by Mr. Austin Harrison to be a true story ! ! ! but rejected.
[5] Not accepted by, or even offered to, the *Alpine Journal*.

EDITORIAL

WITH the issue of the next Number in September, the present series of the *Equinox* will close until March 1918, o.s., and no further open pronouncements from the A∴ A∴ may be expected until that date. The work will be carried on privately. The *Equinox* will, however, be replaced by another publication under the same Management, of smaller size, lower price, and more frequent appearance. It will be principally devoted to Mysteria Mystica Maxima, the extraordinary growth of which has surpassed the most sanguine expectations of its founders.

The first number of the new magazine will contain important pronouncements of this Body.

Full particulars will be given in the Editorial pages of No. X of the *Equinox*, which will appear on September 23, 1913.

Those readers who have not got complete sets are strongly advised to lose no time in making them up, as the demand is constantly increasing, and it will shortly be impossible to supply any more copies from this office. That we have been able to do so hitherto is only due to the enterprise of our agents in buying up second-hand copies all over the country.

Sets of the first eight numbers made up with such

second-hand copies have recently sold in America for forty dollars (£8).

What spectacle is more tragically pathetic than that of a man who has done good work reduced to beggary, his only remaining capital, his brain, in a state of hopeless decay? Poor Mathers never recovered from the exposure of his association with the Horos Gang.

Think of him as he is at present, laboriously copying out with his own hand the silly "Looking Glass" articles and sending them to the staff of the *Equinox*, who have all had their own copies for years, and were not particularly interested in them even at the time when the statements were fresh enough to be funny!

When one thinks that he could have had these articles reprinted for a few shillings a thousand, what a state of penury it reveals! His own followers appear to have abandoned him, or he could not be in such distress. Considering the debt which Occultism owes him for the translation of the "Key of Solomon," the "Kabbalah Unveiled," and the "Book of the Sacred Magic of Abra-melin," we have confidence in appealing to the generosity of the readers of the *Equinox* to form a Fund to enable the shattered mind and body to end its days in the comparative comfort of a *private* asylum.

Another blow to Morality; one more of our guardians has fallen. Mr. De Wend Fenton will be remembered as the gentleman who took exception to the Rites of Eleusis, though he was good enough to say after publishing the first of his articles attacking them, that he meant no harm, and would like to meet Mr. Crowley at dinner; presumably in the hope that mild and pious persuasion would induce him to amend his ways. An invitation which was *not* accepted. It is consequently with the greatest regret that we reprint the following cutting from the *Daily Mail.*

FINE ON "PINK 'UN" EDITOR

Mr. De Wend Fenton, editor of the *Sporting Times*, was fined £10 and £5 5s. costs at Mansion House by Alderman Sir John Knill on each of six summonses—£91 10s. in all—for sending through the post indecent articles contained in the paper.

Mr. George Raffalovich is in no way connected with *The Equinox.*

Mr. George Raffalovich has never been connected with *The Equinox* in any way but as an occasional contributor.

It cannot be too clearly understood that *The Equinox* has no connection with Mr. George Raffalovich.

We have much pleasure in stating that Mr. George Raffalovich is in no way connected with *The Equinox.*

We have no reason to anticipate that *The Equinox* will in any way be connected with Mr. George Raffalovich.

We trust that Mr. George Raffalovich will be satisfied with these statements of fact, to which we are prepared to testify on oath.

THE TEMPLE OF SOLOMON
THE KING

THE TEMPLE OF SOLOMON
THE KING

THE POET

WE left Frater P. at the end of 1906, acknowledged and admitted a Master of the Temple, and even more than this, as it were in perspective, and yet refusing to admit even to himself that he had obtained that Crown for which he had striven so earnestly since the beginning. Into these eight years had been concentrated the work not of one lifetime, but of many, but he felt that this work was in no sense complete. He might be entitled to the Grade without as yet being initiated into it, and we shall find that these eight years grew to eleven before this occurred.

We must now record how these three years were occupied. We learn that in September 1906, with Frater D. D. S., he had prepared a Ritual of the Augoeides, which might serve to initiate those who had not yet made any attainment on the path. We may again quote from the History Lection :—

19. Returning to England, he laid his achievements humbly at the feet of a certain adept D. D. S., who welcomed him brotherly and admitted his title to that grade which he had so hardly won.

20. Thereupon these two adepts conferred together, saying : May it not be written that the tribulations shall be

shortened? Therefore they resolved to establish a new Order which would be free from the errors and deceits of the former one.

21. Without Authority they could not do this, exalted as their rank was among adepts. They resolved to prepare all things, great and small, against that day when such Authority should be received by them, since they knew not where to seek for higher adepts than themselves, but knew that the true way to attract the notice of such was to equilibrate the symbols. The temple must be builded before the God can indwell it.

22. Therefore by order of D. D. S. did P. prepare all things by his arcane science and wisdom, choosing only those symbols which were common to all systems, and rigorously rejecting all names and words which might be supposed to imply any religious or metaphysical theory. To do this utterly was found impossible, since all language has a history, and the use (for example) of the word "spirit" implies the Scholastic Philosophy and the Hindu and Taoist theories concerning the breath of man. So was it difficult to avoid implication of some undesirable bias by using the words "order," "circle," "chapter," "society," "brotherhood," or any other to designate the body of initiates.

23. Deliberately, therefore, did he take refuge in Vagueness. Not to veil the truth to the Neophyte, but to warn him against valuing non-essentials. Should therefore the candidate hear the name of any God, let him not rashly assume that it refers to any known God, save only the God known to himself. Or should the ritual speak in terms (however vague) which seem to imply Egyptian, Taoist, Buddhist, Indian, Persian, Greek, Judaic, Christian, or Moslem philosophy, let him reflect that

4

this is a defect of language ; the literary limitation and not the spiritual prejudice of the man P.

24. Especially let him guard against the finding of definite sectarian symbols in the teaching of his master, and the reasoning from the known to the unknown which assuredly will tempt him.

We labour earnestly, dear brother, that you may never be led away to perish upon this point ; for thereon have many holy and just men been wrecked. By this have all the visible systems lost the essence of wisdom.

We have sought to reveal the Arcanum ; we have only profaned it.

25. Now when P. had thus with bitter toil prepared all things under the guidance of D. D. S. (even as the hand writes, while the conscious brain, though ignorant of the detailed movements, applauds or disapproves the finished work) there was a certain time of repose, as the earth lieth fallow.

26. Meanwhile these adepts busied themselves intently with the Great Work.

27. In the fullness of time, even as a blossoming tree that beareth fruit in its season, all these pains were ended, and these adepts and their companions obtained the reward which they had sought—they were to be admitted to the Eternal and Invisible Order that hath no name among men.

28. They therefore who had with smiling faces abandoned their homes, their possessions, their wives, their children, in order to perform the Great Work, could with steady calm and firm correctness abandon the Great Work itself : for this is the last and greatest projection of the alchemist.

In the spring of 1907 we consequently find Frater P.

living quietly his ordinary life as a man and engaged in no particular practices. His diary for this year 1907 has been lost, and we shall not be able to fill in the events of the year in any detail. We have, however, been able to inquire of those who had conversation with him during this period, and we hear of him as occupied mainly in reviewing the whole of his magical career—though why should we use an adjective, since every second of that career had been understood as part of the operation of the Magic of Light? It seems to him that this career was in some ways imperfect—as if he had jumped over some of the puddles in the path. He wished to explain to himself how this could be so, and, in particular, why. He found, for example, with regard to magical powers, that he was not able to exercise these in the way which he had originally conceived. He found, in short, that they were like all other powers, and could only be exercised as circumstance permitted. Even Herr Salchow could not cut his famous star unless there happened to be ice, and he was able to get to that ice with skates. Although he had performed so many wonders he perceived that his ability depended entirely upon some antecedent necessity. He was not a free agent. He was part of a universal scheme. Now the principal mark of the Master of the Temple was, in his opinion, that he could exercise these powers at will ; that he could enter Samadhi at will. He now saw that these words " At will " really meant at the will of the Universe, and he could only obtain this freedom through the coincidence of his will with the Universal Will. The active and the passive must be perfectly harmonious before free-will became intelligible. Only Destiny could exercise free-will. In order to exercise free-will he must,

6

therefore, become Destiny. He was then to know sooner or later the meaning of the Thirteenth Ether, to which subject we shall return in the proper place.

We are now to consider a further passage from the History Lection :—

29. Also one V. V. V. V. V. arose, an exalted adept of the rank of Master of the Temple (or this much He disclosed to the Exempt Adepts), and His utterance is enshrined in the Sacred Writings.

30. Such are Liber Legis, Liber Cordis Cincti Serpente, Liber Liberi vel Lapidis Lazuli and such others whose existence may one day be divulged unto you. Beware lest you interpret them either in the Light or in the darkness, for only in L. V. X. may they be understood.

Of V. V. V. V. V. we have no information. We do not know, and it is of no importance that we should know, whether he is an actual person or a magical projection of Frater P., or identical with Aiwass, or anything else, for the reasons previously given when discussing the utterance of Liber Legis, *Equinox VII*, pp. 384 and 385. It is sufficient to say that all the Class A publications of the A ∴ A ∴ should be regarded as not only verbally and liberally inspired by Him, but that this accuracy should be taken to extend even to the style of the letter. If a word is unexpectedly spelt with a capital letter, it must not be thought that this is a mistake ; there is some serious reason why it should be so. During this year 1907, therefore, we find a number of such books dictated by him to Frater P. Of the sublimity of these books no words can give expression. It will be noticed that they are totally different in style from Liber Legis, just as both of them are different from any of the writings of Frater P. We may turn for a moment to consider the actual conditions under which he received them. We find the hint of the nature of the communication in Liber LX and Liber VII. On one or two occasions the scribe introduced his thought upon the note, in particular Liber VII, Chapter I, Verse 30, where Verse 29 suggested Verse 30 to Frater P., who wrote it consciously and was corrected in Verse 31. Frater P. is, however, less communicative about this writing than about Liber Legis. It appears that during the whole period of writing he was actually in Samadhi, although, strangely enough, he did not know it himself. It is a question of the transference of the Ego from the personal to the impersonal. He, the conscious human man, could not say "I am in Samadhi"; he was merely conscious that "that which was he" was in Samadhi. This came to him as a sort of consolation for the disappointment which he was experiencing, for it was in his attempt to get into Samadhi that the writing of these books occurred. Yet the consolation itself was in a sense a disappointment. The transference of the human conscience to the divine, the partial to the universal, was no longer an explosion, a spasm, an orgasm. It was a passing into peace unaccompanied by any of the dazzling and overwhelming phenomena with which he was familiar. He did not realize that this was an immense advance. He did not see that it meant that he had become so attuned to Samadhi that its occurrence became hardly noticeable. He was still farther from understanding that that Samadhi is permament, eternal, entirely beyond accident of time or place ; that it was only necessary, as it were, to lean back into it to be there. He knew that by pronouncing the

8

Ineffable Name, the Universe dissolved in flame and earth-quake. He was far from the point at which by the utterance of a single sigh the universe slipped into dissolution. Like Elijah in the mountain, he expected to see the Lord in the tempest and the lightnings. He did not understand the still small voice. We shall find an increasing difficulty in writing of Frater P., because from this time he is increasing that nameless and eternal Nothing of which nothing true can be said, and it sometimes seems as if the conscious man was ever diminishing, ever less important, ever much nearer to the normal human being. In reality it is that he is much less confused. He does not allow the Planes to interfere with each other. He perceives that each Plane must work out its own salvation; that it is fatally wrong to appeal to the higher. He has identified himself with the will of the higher, and that will must extend downwards, radiating upon the lower. The lower may aspire to the higher, but not in order to get help from its troubles. It may wish as a whole to unite itself with the higher, to lose itself in the higher, but it should be very wary about asking the higher to rearrange its parts.

Apart from these writings, the years 1907 and nearly the whole of 1908 are quite uneventful. We do, however, find that he went into several Magical retirements, for in the spring of 1907 we hear of him at Tangier; in the winter in the English Lakes; but a great deal of his time must have been taken up by the personal matter referred to on page 44 of No. VIII of the *Equinox*. That cup of bitterness, at least, he drank to the dregs. In May 1908 he was at Venice while we find that he spent August and September on a long walk through Spain. We do not learn that he did anything particular during this period, but on the first of October, he began a serious Retirement of a really strenuous character of about a fortnight in duration, which has been recorded for us minute by minute in a book called *John St. John*, published in *Equinox I*. The ostensible object of this Retirement was to discover for certain whether by the use of the plain straightforward methods accessible to the normal man he could definitely attain Samadhi within a reasonable time. In other words, whether the methods themselves were valuable. This was a most important experiment, for a great many people had argued that he owed his Attainment to his personal genius; that any methods would have done for him ; that his methods might be useless for another. He was sufficiently satisfied with the efficacy of the methods to determine upon a course for which he had hitherto found no excuse—that of undertaking the gigantic task of the publication of all these methods on the basis of pure scepticism. There is, further, no doubt that by this Retirement he acquired a stock of magical energy which enabled him to carry out this work, to all intents and purposes without assistance, except of the most temporary and casual kind, from any other person. The mere quantity of this work in itself constitutes a miracle. The quality of this work is such that the word miracle is quite inadequate. It must be remembered that it was not only a question of writing down the details of this extraordinary knowledge, though that is surprising enough. For example, Book 777 from cover to cover was written down by him from memory in a single week, at a time when he was seriously ill and in constant pain. But in addition to this, he was compelled to waste his time in overseeing the mechanical details of printing and publishing. It is better to fight with beasts at Ephesus like

St. Paul than with printers in London as he did. He had, moreover, to furnish practically the whole of the funds required for the publication. He gave not only the remains of his great fortune, but all his hope of future fortune, and he issued his publications at cost price, often very much below it. In addition to this he was continually harassed and distressed by every form of domestic affliction. The ability to endure these five years following seems cheaply purchased at the cost of a fortnight's hard work.

From this moment, however, our own task becomes extremely simple. Hitherto Frater P. has been a private character, of whose life no one was competent to speak. Without his diaries it would not have been possible to write a single page of this book. But henceforward he is a public character, occupied in public work, and little, indeed, will be the content of his private life ; and yet there remains the most important event to be recorded : the dissolution of that life, the losing of his name.

(To be continued)

LINES TO A YOUNG LADY VIOLINIST ON HER PLAYING IN A GREEN DRESS DESIGNED BY THE AUTHOR

HER dress clings like a snake of emerald
And gold and ruby to her swaying shape;
In its constraint she sways, entranced, enthralled,
Her teeth set lest her rapture should escape
The parted lips—Oh mouth of pomegranate!
Is not Persephone with child of Fate?

What sunlit snows of rose and ivory
Her breasts are, starting from the green, great moons
Filling the blue night with white ecstasy
Of rippling rhythms, of tumultuous tunes.
Artemis tears the gauzes from her gorge,
And violates Hephæstus at his forge.

Then the mad lightnings of her magic bow!
They rave and roar upon the stricken wood,
Swift shrieks of death, solemnities too slow
For birth.   Infernal lust of dragon-hued
Devils, sublimest song of Angel choirs,
Echo, and do not utter, her desires!

I am Danae in the shower of gold
This Zeus flings forth, exhausted and possessed,

THE EQUINOX

Each atom of my being raped and rolled
Beneath her car of music into rest
Deeper than death, more desperate than life,
The agony of primæval slime at strife.

I am the ecstasy of infamy.
Tossed like a meteor when the Gods play ball,
Racked like Ixion, like Pasiphæ
Torn by the leaping life, with myrrh and gall
My throat made bitter, I am crucified
Like Christ with my dead selves on either side.

She stabs me to the heart with every thrust
Of her wild bow, the pitiless hail of sound ;
Her smile is murder—the red lips of lust
And the white teeth of death !   Her eyes profound
As hell, and frenzied with hell's love and hate,
Gleam grey as God, glare steadier than fate.

She gloats upon my torture as I writhe.
Her head falls back, her eyes turn back, she shakes
And trembles.   A sharp spasm takes the lithe
Limbs, and her body with her spirit aches.
The sweat breaks out on her ; there bursts a flood
Of shrieks ; she bubbles at the mouth with blood.

As Satan fell from heaven, so she crashes
Upon my corpse ; one long ensanguine groan
Ends her ; the soul has burnt itself to ashes ;
The spirit is incorporate with its own,
The abiding spirit of life, love, and light
And liberty, fixed in the infinite.

LINES TO A YOUNG LADY VIOLINIST

There is the silence, there the night.   Therein
Nor space nor time nor being may intrude;
There is no force to move, no fate to spin,
Nor God nor Satan in the solitude.
O Pagan and O Panic Pentecost!
Lost! lost eternally!—for ever lost!

ALEISTER CROWLEY.

ENERGIZED ENTHUSIASM

ENERGIZED ENTHUSIASM

A NOTE ON THEURGY

I

I A O the supreme One of the Gnostics, the true God, is the Lord of this work. Let us therefore invoke Him by that name which the Companions of the Royal Arch blaspheme to aid us in the essay to declare the means which He has bestowed upon us!

II

The divine consciousness which is reflected and refracted in the works of Genius feeds upon a certain secretion, as I believe. This secretion is analogous to semen, but not identical with it. There are but few men and fewer women, those women being invariably androgyne, who possess it at any time in any quantity.

So closely is this secretion connected with the sexual economy that it appears to me at times as if it might be a by-product of that process which generates semen. That some form of this doctrine has been generally accepted is shown in the prohibitions of all religions. Sanctity has been assumed to depend on chastity, and chastity has nearly always been interpreted as abstinence. But I doubt whether the relation is so simple as this would imply; for example, I find in myself that manifestations of mental creative force always concur with some abnormal condition of the physical powers of generation. But it is not the case that long periods of chastity, on the one hand, or excess of orgies, on the other, are favourable to its manifestation or even to its formation.

I know myself, and in me it is extremely strong; its results are astounding.

For example, I wrote *Tannhäuser*, complete from conception to execution, in sixty-seven consecutive hours. I was unconscious of the fall of nights and days, even after stopping; nor was there any reaction of fatigue. This work was written when I was twenty-four years old, immediately on the completion of an orgie which would normally have tired me out.

Often and often have I noticed that sexual satisfaction so-called has left me dissatisfied and unfatigued, and let loose the floods of verse which have disgraced my career.

Yet, on the contrary, a period of chastity has sometimes fortified me for a great outburst. This is far from being invariably the case. At the conclusion of the K 2 expedition, after five months of chastity, I did no work whatever, barring very few odd lyrics, for months afterwards.

I may mention the year 1911. At this time I was living, in excellent good health, with the woman whom I loved. Her health was, however, variable, and we were both constantly worried.

The weather was continuously fine and hot. For a period of about three months I hardly missed a morning; always on waking I burst out with a new idea which had to be written down.

ENERGIZED ENTHUSIASM

The total energy of my being was very high. My weight was 10 stone 8 lb., which had been my fighting weight when I was ten years younger. We walked some twenty miles daily through hilly forest.

The actual amount of MSS. written at this time is astounding; their variety is even more so; of their excellence I will not speak.

Here is a rough list from memory; it is far from exhaustive:

(1) Some dozen books of A ∴ A ∴ instruction, including Liber Astarte, and the Temple of Solomon the King for *Equinox VII*.

(2) Short Stories : The Woodcutter.
His Secret Sin.

(3) Plays : His Majesty's Fiddler
Elder Eel
Adonis   ⎫ written straight off, one
The Ghouls ⎭ after the other
Mortadello.

(4) Poems : The Sevenfold Sacrament
A Birthday.

(5) Fundamentals of the Greek Qabalah (involving the collection and analysis of several thousand words).

I think this phenomenon is unique in the history of literature.

I may further refer to my second journey to Algeria, where my sexual life, though fairly full, had been unsatisfactory.

On quitting Biskra, I was so full of ideas that I had to get off the train at El-Kantara, where I wrote " The Scorpion." Five or six poems were written on the way to Paris; " The

Ordeal of Ida Pendragon" during my twenty-four hours' stay in Paris, and "Snowstorm" and "The Electric Silence" immediately on my return to England.

To sum up, I can always trace a connection between my sexual condition and the condition of artistic creation, which is so close as to approach identity, and yet so loose that I cannot predicate a single important proposition.

It is these considerations which give me pain when I am reproached by the ignorant with wishing to produce genius mechanically. I may fail, but my failure is a thousand times greater than their utmost success.

I shall therefore base my remarks not so much on the observations which I have myself made, and the experiments which I have tried, as on the accepted classical methods of producing that energized enthusiasm which is the lever that moves God.

III

The Greeks say that there are three methods of discharging the genial secretion of which I have spoken. They thought perhaps that their methods tended to secrete it, but this I do not believe altogether, or without a qualm. For the manifestation of force implies force, and this force must have come from somewhere. Easier I find it to say "subconsciousness" and "secretion" than to postulate an external reservoir, to extend my connotation of "man" than to invent "God."

However, parsimony apart, I find it in my experience that it is useless to flog a tired horse. There are times when I am absolutely bereft of even one drop of this elixir. Nothing will restore it, neither rest in bed, nor drugs, nor exercise. On the other hand, sometimes when after a severe spell of work I have been dropping with physical fatigue, perhaps sprawling on the floor, too tired to move hand or foot, the occurrence of an idea has restored me to perfect intensity of energy, and the working out of the idea has actually got rid of the aforesaid physical fatigue, although it involved a great additional labour.

Exactly parallel (nowhere meeting) is the case of mania. A madman may struggle against six trained athletes for hours, and show no sign of fatigue. Then he will suddenly collapse, but at a second's notice from the irritable idea will resume the struggle as fresh as ever. Until we discovered "unconscious muscular action" and its effects, it was rational to suppose such a man "possessed of a devil"; and the difference between the madman and the genius is not in the quantity but in the quality of their work. Genius is organized, madness chaotic. Often the organization of genius is on original lines, and ill-balanced and ignorant medicine-men mistake it for disorder. Time has shown that Whistler and Gauguin "kept rules" as well as the masters whom they were supposed to be upsetting.

IV

The Greeks say that there are three methods of discharging the Leyden Jar of Genius. These three methods they assign to three Gods.

These three Gods are Dionysus, Apollo, Aphrodite. In English : wine, woman and song.

Now it would be a great mistake to imagine that the

Greeks were recommending a visit to a brothel. As well condemn the High Mass at St. Peter's on the strength of having witnessed a Protestant revival meeting. Disorder is always a parody of order, because there is no archetypal disorder that it might resemble. Owen Seaman can parody a poet; nobody can parody Owen Seaman. A critic is a bundle of impressions; there is no ego behind it. All photographs are essentially alike; the works of all good painters essentially differ.

Some writers suppose that in the ancient rites of Eleusis the High Priest publicly copulated with the High Priestess. Were this so, it would be no more "indecent" than it is "blasphemous" for the priest to make bread and wine into the body and blood of God.

True, the Protestants say that it is blasphemous; but a Protestant is one to whom all things sacred are profane, whose mind being all filth can see nothing in the sexual act but a crime or a jest, whose only facial gestures are the sneer and the leer.

Protestantism is the excrement of human thought, and accordingly in Protestant countries art, if it exist at all, only exists to revolt. Let us return from this unsavoury allusion to our consideration of the methods of the Greeks.

V

Agree then that it does not follow from the fact that wine, woman and song make the sailor's tavern that these ingredients must necessarily concoct a hell-broth.

There are some people so simple as to think that, when

they have proved the religious instinct to be a mere efflorescence of the sex-instinct, they have destroyed religion.

We should rather consider that the sailor's tavern gives him his only glimpse of heaven, just as the destructive criticism of the phallicists has only proved sex to be a sacrament. Consciousness, says the materialist, axe in hand, is a function of the brain. He has only re-formulated the old saying, " Your bodies are the temples of the Holy Ghost." !

Now sex is justly hallowed in this sense, that it is the eternal fire of the race. Huxley admitted that " some of the lower animalculæ are in a sense immortal," because they go on reproducing eternally by fission, and however often you divide x by 2 there is always something left. But he never seems to have seen that mankind is immortal in exactly the same sense, and goes on reproducing itself with similar characteristics through the ages, changed by circumstance indeed, but always identical in itself. But the spiritual flower of this process is that at the moment of discharge a physical ecstasy occurs, a spasm analogous to the mental spasm which meditation gives. And further, in the sacramental and ceremonial use of the sexual act, the divine consciousness may be attained.

VI

The sexual act being then a sacrament, it remains to consider in what respect this limits the employment of the organs.

First, it is obviously legitimate to employ them for their natural physical purpose. But if it be allowable to use them ceremonially for a religious purpose, we shall find the act hedged about with many restrictions.

For in this case the organs become holy. It matters little to mere propagation that men should be vicious; the most debauched roué might and almost certainly would beget more healthy children than a semi-sexed prude. So the so-called "moral" restraints are not based on reason; thus they are neglected.

But admit its religious function, and one may at once lay down that the act must not be profaned. It must not be undertaken lightly and foolishly without excuse.

It may be undertaken for the direct object of continuing the race.

It may be undertaken in obedience to real passion; for passion, as its name implies, is rather inspired by a force of divine strength and beauty without the will of the individual, often even against it.

It is the casual or habitual—what Christ called "idle"— use or rather abuse of these forces which constitutes their profanation. It will further be obvious that, if the act in itself is to be the sacrament in a religious ceremony, this act must be accomplished solely for the love of God. All personal considerations must be banished utterly. Just as any priest can perform the miracle of transubstantiation, so can any man, possessing the necessary qualifications, perform this other miracle, whose nature must form the subject of a subsequent discussion.

Personal aims being destroyed, it is *à fortiori* necessary to neglect social and other similar considerations.

Physical strength and beauty are necessary and desirable

for æsthetic reasons, the attention of the worshippers being liable to distraction if the celebrants are ugly, deformed, or incompetent. I need hardly emphasize the necessity for the strictest self-control and concentration on their part. As it would be blasphemy to enjoy the gross taste of the wine of the sacrament, so must the celebrant suppress even the minutest manifestation of animal pleasure.

Of the qualifying tests there is no necessity to speak ; it is sufficient to say that the adepts have always known how to secure efficiency.

Needless also to insist on a similar quality in the assistants ; the sexual excitement must be suppressed and transformed into its religious equivalent.

VII

With these preliminaries settled in order to guard against foreseen criticisms of those Protestants who, God having made them a little lower than the Angels, have made themselves a great deal lower than the beasts by their consistently bestial interpretation of all things human and divine, we may consider first the triune nature of these ancient methods of energizing enthusiasm.

Music has two parts ; tone or pitch, and rhythm. The latter quality associates it with the dance, and that part of dancing which is not rhythm is sex. Now that part of sex which is not a form of the dance, animal movement, is intoxication of the soul, which connects it with wine. Further identities will suggest themselves to the student.

By the use of the three methods in one the whole being of man may thus be stimulated.

The music will create a general harmony of the brain, leading it in its own paths; the wine affords a general stimulus of the animal nature; and the sex-excitement elevates the moral nature of the man by its close analogy with the highest ecstasy. It remains, however, always for him to make the final transmutation. Unless he have the special secretion which I have postulated, the result will be commonplace.

So consonant is this system with the nature of man that it is exactly parodied and profaned not only in the sailor's tavern, but in the Society ball. Here, for the lowest natures the result is drunkenness, disease and death; for the middle natures a gradual blunting of the finer feelings; for the higher, an exhilaration amounting at the best to the foundation of a life-long love.

If these Society "rites" are properly performed, there should be no exhaustion. After a ball, one should feel the need of a long walk in the young morning air. The weariness or boredom, the headache or somnolence, are Nature's warnings.

VIII

Now the purpose of such a ball, the moral attitude on entering, seems to me to be of supreme importance. If you go with the idea of killing time, you are rather killing yourself. Baudelaire speaks of the first period of love when the boy kisses the trees of the wood, rather than kiss nothing. At the age of thirty-six I found myself at Pompeii, passionately kissing that great grave statue of a woman that stands in the avenue of the tombs.   Even now, as I wake in the morning, I sometimes fall to kissing my own arms.

It is with such a feeling that one should go to a ball, and with such a feeling intensified, purified and exalted, that one should leave it.

If this be so, how much more if one go with the direct religious purpose burning in one's whole being! Beethoven roaring at the sunrise is no strange spectacle to me, who shout with joy and wonder, when I understand (without which one cannot really be said ever to see) a blade of grass. I fall upon my knees in speechless adoration at the moon ; I hide my eyes in holy awe from a good Van Gogh.

Imagine then a ball in which the music is the choir celestial, the wine the wine of the Graal, or that of the Sabbath of the Adepts, and one's partner the Infinite and Eternal One, the True and Living God Most High!

Go even to a common ball—the Moulin de la Galette will serve even the least of my magicians—with your whole soul aflame within you, and your whole will concentrated on these transubstantiations, and tell me what miracle takes place!

It is the hate of, the distaste for, life that sends one to the ball when one is old ; when one is young one is on springs until the hour falls ; but the love of God, which is the only true love, diminishes not with age; it grows deeper and intenser with every satisfaction. It seems as if in the noblest men this secretion constantly increases—which certainly suggests an external reservoir—so that age loses all its bitterness. We find "Brother Lawrence," Nicholas Herman of Lorraine, at the age of eighty in continuous enjoyment of union with God. Buddha at an equal age would run up and down the Eight High Trances like an acrobat on a ladder; stories not too dissimilar are told of Bishop Berkeley. Many persons have not attained union at all until middle age, and then have rarely lost it.

It is true that genius in the ordinary sense of the word has nearly always showed itself in the young. Perhaps we should regard such cases as Nicholas Herman as cases of acquired genius.

Now I am certainly of opinion that genius can be acquired, or, in the alternative, that it is an almost universal possession. Its rarity may be attributed to the crushing influence of a corrupted society. It is rare to meet a youth without high ideals, generous thoughts, a sense of holiness, of his own importance, which, being interpreted, is, of his own identity with God. Three years in the world, and he is a bank clerk or even a government official. Only those who intuitively understand from early boyhood that they must stand out, and who have the incredible courage and endurance to do so in face of all that tyranny, callousness, and the scorn of inferiors can do; only these arrive at manhood uncontaminated.

Every serious or spiritual thought is made a jest; poets are thought "soft" and "cowardly," apparently because they are the only boys with a will of their own and courage to hold out against the whole school, boys and masters in league as once were Pilate and Herod; honour is replaced by expediency, holiness by hypocrisy.

Even where we find thoroughly good seed sprouting in favourable ground, too often is there a frittering away of the forces. Facile encouragement of a poet or painter is far

30

worse for him than any amount of opposition. Here again the sex question (S.Q. so-called by Tolstoyans, chastity-mongers, nut-fooders, and such who talk and think of nothing else) intrudes its horrid head. I believe that every boy is originally conscious of sex as sacred. But he does not know what it is. With infinite diffidence he asks. The master replies with holy horror ; the boy with a low leer, a furtive laugh, perhaps worse.

I am inclined to agree with the Head Master of Eton that pæderastic passions among schoolboys " do no harm "; further, I think them the only redeeming feature of sexual life at public schools.

The Hindoos are wiser. At the well-watched hour of puberty the boy is prepared as for a sacrament ; he is led to a duly consecrated temple, and there by a wise and holy woman, skilled in the art, and devoted to this end, he is initiated with all solemnity into the mystery of life.

The act is thus declared religious, sacred, impersonal, utterly apart from amorism and eroticism and animalism and sentimentalism and all the other vilenesses that Protestantism has made of it.

The Catholic Church did, I believe, to some extent preserve the Pagan tradition. Marriage is a sacrament.[1] But in the attempt to deprive the act of all accretions which would profane it, the Fathers of the Church added in spite of themselves other accretions which profaned it more. They tied it to property and inheritance. They wished it to serve both God and Mammon.

[1] Of course there has been a school of devilish ananders that has held the act in itself to be " wicked." Of such blasphemers of Nature let no further word be said.

31

Rightly restraining the priest, who should employ his whole energy in the miracle of the Mass, they found their counsel a counsel of perfection. The magical tradition was in part lost; the priest could not do what was expected of him, and the unexpended portion of his energy turned sour.

Hence the thoughts of priests, like the thoughts of modern faddists, revolved eternally around the S.Q.

A special and Secret Mass, a Mass of the Holy Ghost, a Mass of the Mystery of the Incarnation, to be performed at stated intervals, might have saved both monks and nuns, and given the Church eternal dominion of the world.

IX

To return. The rarity of genius is in great part due to the destruction of its young. Even as in physical life that is a favoured plant one of whose thousand seeds ever shoots forth a blade, so do conditions kill all but the strongest sons of genius.

But just as rabbits increased apace in Australia, where even a missionary has been known to beget ninety children in two years, so shall we be able to breed genius if we can find the conditions which hamper it, and remove them.

The obvious practical step to take is to restore the rites of Bacchus, Aphrodite and Apollo to their proper place. They should not be open to every one, and manhood should be the reward of ordeal and initiation.

The physical tests should be severe, and weaklings should be killed out rather than artificially preserved. The same remark applies to intellectual tests. But such tests should be as wide as possible. I was an absolute duffer at school in all forms of athletics and games, because I despised them. I held, and still hold, numerous mountaineering world's records. Similarly, examinations fail to test intelligence. Cecil Rhodes refused to employ any man with a University degree. That such degrees lead to honour in England is a sign of England's decay, though even in England they are usually the stepping-stones to clerical idleness or pedagogic slavery.

Such is a dotted outline of the picture that I wish to draw. If the power to possess property depended on a man's competence, and his perception of real values, a new aristocracy would at once be created, and the deadly fact that social consideration varies with the power of purchasing champagne would cease to be a fact. Our pluto-hetairo-politicocracy would fall in a day.

But I am only too well aware that such a picture is not likely to be painted. We can then only work patiently and in secret. We must select suitable material and train it in utmost reverence to these three master-methods, or aiding the soul in its genial orgasm.

X

This reverent attitude is of an importance which I cannot over-rate. Normal people find normal relief from any general or special excitement in the sexual act.

Commander Marston, R.N., whose experiments in the effect of the tom-tom on the married Englishwoman are classical and conclusive, has admirably described how the vague unrest which she at first shows gradually assumes the sexual form, and culminates, if allowed to do so, in shameless masturbation or indecent advances. But this is a natural corollary of the proposition that married Englishwomen are usually unacquainted with sexual satisfaction. Their desires are constantly stimulated by brutal and ignorant husbands, and never gratified. This fact again accounts for the amazing prevalence of Sapphism in London Society.

The Hindus warn their pupils against the dangers of breathing exercises. Indeed the slightest laxness in moral or physical tissues may cause the energy accumulated by the practice to discharge itself by involuntary emission. I have known this happen in my own experience.

It is then of the utmost importance to realize that the relief of the tension is to be found in what the Hebrews and the Greeks called prophesying, and which is better when organized into art. The disorderly discharge is mere waste, a wilderness of howlings; the orderly discharge is a "Prometheus unbound," or a "L'age d'airain," according to the special aptitudes of the enthused person. But it must be remembered that special aptitudes are very easy to acquire if the driving force of enthusiasm be great. If you cannot keep the rules of others, you make rules of your own. One set turns out in the long run to be just as good as another.

Henri Rousseau, the douanier, was laughed at all his life. I laughed as heartily as the rest; though, almost despite myself, I kept on saying (as the phrase goes) "that I felt something; couldn't say what."

The moment it occurred to somebody to put up all his paintings in one room by themselves, it was instantly apparent that his *naïveté* was the simplicity of a Master.

Let no one then imagine that I fail to perceive or underestimate the dangers of employing these methods. The

34

occurrence even of so simple a matter as fatigue might change a Las Meninas into a stupid sexual crisis.

It will be necessary for most Englishmen to emulate the self-control of the Arabs and Hindus, whose ideal is to deflower the greatest possible number of virgins—eighty is considered a fairly good performance—without completing the act.

It is, indeed, of the first importance for the celebrant in any phallic rite to be able to complete the act without even once allowing a sexual or sensual thought to invade his mind. The mind must be as absolutely detached from one's own body as it is from another person's.

XI

Of musical instruments few are suitable. The human voice is the best, and the only one which can be usefully employed in chorus. Anything like an orchestra implies infinite rehearsal, and introduces an atmosphere of artificiality. The organ is a worthy solo instrument, and is an orchestra in itself, while its tone and associations favour the religious idea.

The violin is the most useful of all, for its every mood expresses the hunger for the infinite, and yet it is so mobile that it has a greater emotional range than any of its competitors. Accompaniment must be dispensed with, unless a harpist be available.

The harmonium is a horrible instrument, if only because of its associations; and the piano is like unto it, although, if unseen and played by a Paderewski, it would serve.

The trumpet and the bell are excellent, to startle, at the crises of a ceremony.

Hot, drubbing, passionate, in a different class of ceremony, a class more intense and direct, but on the whole less exalted, the tom-tom stands alone. It combines well with the practice of mantra, and is the best accompaniment for any sacred dance.

XII

Of sacred dances the most practical for a gathering is the seated dance. One sits cross-legged on the floor, and sways to and fro from the hips in time with the mantra. A solo or duet of dancers as a spectacle rather distracts from this exercise. I would suggest a very small and very brilliant light on the floor in the middle of the room. Such a room is best floored with mosaic marble; an ordinary Freemason's Lodge carpet is not a bad thing.

The eyes, if they see anything at all, see then only the rhythmical or mechanical squares leading in perspective to the simple unwinking light.

The swinging of the body with the mantra (which has a habit of rising and falling as if of its own accord in a very weird way) becomes more accentuated; ultimately a curiously spasmodic stage occurs, and then the consciousness flickers and goes out; perhaps breaks through into the divine consciousness, perhaps is merely recalled to itself by some variable in external impression.

The above is a very simple description of a very simple and earnest form of ceremony, based entirely upon rhythm.

It is very easy to prepare, and its results are usually very encouraging for the beginner.

XIII

Wine being a mocker and strong drink raging, its use is more likely to lead to trouble than mere music.

One essential difficulty is dosage. One needs exactly enough; and, as Blake points out, one can only tell what is enough by taking too much. For each man the dose varies enormously; so does it for the same man at different times.

The ceremonial escape from this is to have a noiseless attendant to bear the bowl of libation, and present it to each in turn, at frequent intervals. Small doses should be drunk, and the bowl passed on, taken as the worshipper deems advisable. Yet the cup-bearer should be an initiate, and use his own discretion before presenting the bowl. The slightest sign that intoxication is mastering the man should be a sign to him to pass that man. This practice can be easily fitted to the ceremony previously described.

If desired, instead of wine, the elixir introduced by me to Europe may be employed. But its results, if used in this way, have not as yet been thoroughly studied. It is my immediate purpose to repair this neglect.

XIV

The sexual excitement, which must complete the harmony of method, offers a more difficult problem.

It is exceptionally desirable that the actual bodily movements involved should be decorous in the highest sense, and many people are so ill-trained that they will be unable to regard such a ceremony with any but critical or lascivious

37

eyes; either would be fatal to all the good already done. It is presumably better to wait until all present are greatly exalted before risking a profanation.

It is not desirable, in my opinion, that the ordinary worshippers should celebrate in public.

The sacrifice should be single.

Whether or no . . .

XV

Thus far had I written when the distinguished poet, whose conversation with me upon the Mysteries had incited me to jot down these few rough notes, knocked at my door. I told him that I was at work on the ideas suggested by him, and that—well, I was rather stuck. He asked permission to glance at the MS. (for he reads English fluently, though speaking but a few words), and having done so, kindled and said : "If you come with me now, we will finish your essay." Glad enough of any excuse to stop working, the more plausible the better, I hastened to take down my coat and hat.

"By the way," he remarked in the automobile, "I take it that you do not mind giving me the Word of Rose Croix." Surprised, I exchanged the secrets of I.N.R.I. with him. "And now, very excellent and perfect Prince," he said, "what follows is under this seal." And he gave me the most solemn of all Masonic tokens. "You are about," said he, "to compare your ideal with our real."

He touched a bell. The automobile stopped, and we got out. He dismissed the chauffeur. "Come," he said, "we have a brisk half-mile." We walked through thick woods to an old house, where we were greeted in silence by a gentleman who, though in court dress, wore a very "practicable" sword. On satisfying him, we were passed through a corridor to an anteroom, where another armed guardian awaited us. He, after a further examination, proceeded to offer me a court dress, the insignia of a Sovereign Prince of Rose Croix, and a garter and mantle, the former of green silk, the latter of green velvet, and lined with cerise silk. "It is a low mass," whispered the guardian. In this anteroom were three or four others, both ladies and gentlemen, busily robing.

In a third room we found a procession formed, and joined it. There were twenty-six of us in all. Passing a final guardian we reached the chapel itself, at whose entrance stood a young man and a young woman, both dressed in simple robes of white silk embroidered with gold, red and blue. The former bore a torch of resinous wood, the latter sprayed us as we passed with attar of roses from a cup.

The room in which we now were had at one time been a chapel; so much its shape declared. But the high altar was covered with a cloth that displayed the Rose and Cross, while above it were ranged seven candelabra, each of seven branches.

The stalls had been retained; and at each knight's hand burned a taper of rose-coloured wax, and a bouquet of roses was before him.

In the centre of the nave was a great cross—a "calvary cross of ten squares," measuring, say, six feet by five—painted in red upon a white board, at whose edge were rings through which passed gilt staves. At each corner was a banner, bearing lion, bull, eagle and man, and from the top of their staves sprang a canopy of blue, wherein were figured in gold the twelve emblems of the Zodiac.

Knights and Dames being installed, suddenly a bell tinkled in the architrave. Instantly all rose. The doors opened at a trumpet peal from without, and a herald advanced, followed by the High Priest and Priestess.

The High Priest was a man of nearly sixty years, if I may judge by the white beard ; but he walked with the springy yet assured step of the thirties. The High Priestess, a proud, tall sombre woman of perhaps thirty summers, walked by his side, their hands raised and touching as in the minuet. Their trains were borne by the two youths who had admitted us.

All this while an unseen organ played an Introit.

This ceased as they took their places at the altar. They faced West, waiting.

On the closing of the doors the armed guard, who was clothed in a scarlet robe instead of green, drew his sword, and went up and down the aisle, chanting exorcisms and swinging the great sword. All present drew their swords and faced outward, holding the points in front of them. This part of the ceremony appeared interminable. When it was over the girl and boy reappeared ; bearing, the one a bowl, the other a censer. Singing some litany or other, apparently in Greek, though I could not catch the words, they purified and consecrated the chapel.

Now the High Priest and High Priestess began a litany in rhythmic lines of equal length. At each third response they touched hands in a peculiar manner ; at each seventh they kissed. The twenty-first was a complete embrace. The bell tinkled in the architrave ; and they parted. The High Priest

40

then took from the altar a flask curiously shaped to imitate a phallus. The High Priestess knelt and presented a boat-shaped cup of gold. He knelt opposite her, and did not pour from the flask.

Now the Knights and Dames began a long litany; first a Dame in treble, then a Knight in bass, then a response in chorus of all present with the organ. This Chorus was:

EVOE HO, IACCHE! EPELTHON, EPELTHON, EVOE, IAO!

Again and again it rose and fell. Towards its close, whether by "stage effect" or no I could not swear, the light over the altar grew rosy, then purple. The High Priest sharply and suddenly threw up his hand; instant silence.

He now poured out the wine from the flask. The High Priestess gave it to the girl attendant, who bore it to all present.

This was no ordinary wine. It has been said of vodki that it looks like water and tastes like fire. With this wine the reverse is the case. It was of a rich fiery gold in which flames of light danced and shook, but its taste was limpid and pure like fresh spring water. No sooner had I drunk of it, however, than I began to tremble. It was a most astonishing sensation; I can imagine a man feel thus as he awaits his executioner, when he has passed through fear, and is all excitement.

I looked down my stall, and saw that each was similarly affected. During the libation the High Priestess sang a hymn, again in Greek. This time I recognized the words; they were those of an ancient Ode to Aphrodite.

The boy attendant now descended to the red cross, stooped and kissed it; then he danced upon it in such a way that he seemed to be tracing the patterns of a marvellous rose of gold, for the percussion caused a shower of bright dust to fall from the canopy. Meanwhile the litany (different words, but the same chorus) began again. This time it was a duet between the High Priest and Priestess. At each chorus Knights and Dames bowed low. The girl moved round continuously, and the bowl passed.

This ended in the exhaustion of the boy, who fell fainting on the cross. The girl immediately took the bowl and put it to his lips. Then she raised him, and, with the assistance of the Guardian of the Sanctuary, led him out of the chapel.

The bell again tinkled in the architrave.

The herald blew a fanfare.

The High Priest and High Priestess moved stately to each other and embraced, in the act unloosing the heavy golden robes which they wore. These fell, twin lakes of gold. I now saw her dressed in a garment of white watered silk, lined throughout (as it appeared later) with ermine.

The High Priest's vestment was an elaborate embroidery of every colour, harmonized by exquisite yet robust art. He wore also a breastplate corresponding to the canopy; a sculptured "beast" at each corner in gold, while the twelve signs of the Zodiac were symbolized by the stones of the breastplate.

The bell tinkled yet again, and the herald again sounded his trumpet. The celebrants moved hand in hand down the nave while the organ thundered forth its solemn harmonies.

All the Knights and Dames rose and gave the secret sign of the Rose Croix.

It was at this part of the ceremony that things began to

happen to me. I became suddenly aware that my body had lost both weight and tactile sensibility. My consciousness seemed to be situated no longer in my body. I "mistook myself," if I may use the phrase, for one of the stars in the canopy.

In this way I missed seeing the celebrants actually approach the cross. The bell tinkled again; I came back to myself, and then I saw that the High Priestess, standing at the foot of the cross, had thrown her robe over it, so that the cross was no longer visible. There was only a board covered with ermine. She was now naked but for her coloured and jewelled head-dress and the heavy torque of gold about her neck, and the armlets and anklets that matched it. She began to sing in a soft strange tongue, so low and smoothly that in my partial bewilderment I could not hear all; but I caught a few words, Io Paian! Io Pan! and a phrase in which the words Iao Sabao ended emphatically a sentence in which I caught the words Eros, Thelema and Sebazo.

While she did this she unloosed the breastplate and gave it to the girl attendant. The robe followed; I saw that they were naked and unashamed. For the first time there was absolute silence.

Now, from an hundred jets surrounding the board poured forth a perfumed purple smoke. The world was wrapt in a fond gauze of mist, sacred as the clouds upon the mountains.

Then at a signal given by the High Priest, the bell tinkled once more. The celebrants stretched out their arms in the form of a cross, interlacing their fingers. Slowly they revolved through three circles and a half. She then laid him down upon the cross, and took her own appointed place.

43

The organ now again rolled forth its solemn music.

I was lost to everything. Only this I saw, that the celebrants made no expected motion. The movements were extremely small and yet extremely strong.

This must have continued for a great length of time. To me it seemed as if eternity itself could not contain the variety and depth of my experiences. Tongue nor pen could record them ; and yet I am fain to attempt the impossible.

1. I was, certainly and undoubtedly, the star in the canopy. This star was an incomprehensibly enormous world of pure flame.

2. I suddenly realized that the star was of no size whatever. It was not that the star shrank, but that it ($= I$) became suddenly conscious of infinite space.

3. An explosion took place. I was in consequence a point of light, infinitely small, yet infinitely bright, and this point was *without position.*

4. Consequently this point was ubiquitous, and there was a feeling of infinite bewilderment, blinded after a very long time by a gush of infinite rapture (I use the word " blinded " as if under constraint ; I should have preferred to use the words "blotted out " or " overwhelmed " or " illuminated ").

5. This infinite fullness—I have not described it as such, but it was that—was suddenly changed into a feeling of infinite emptiness, which became conscious as a yearning.

6. These two feelings began to alternate, always with suddenness, and without in any way overlapping, with great rapidity.

7. This alternation must have occurred fifty times—I had rather have said an hundred.

44

ENERGIZED ENTHUSIASM

8. The two feelings suddenly became one. Again the word explosion is the only one that gives any idea of it.

9. I now seemed to be conscious of everything at once, that it was at the same time *one* and *many*. I say "at once," that is, I was not successively all things, but instantaneously.

10. This being, if I may call it being, seemed to drop into an infinite abyss of Nothing.

11. While this "falling" lasted, the bell suddenly tinkled three times. I instantly became my normal self, yet with a constant awareness, which has never left me to this hour, that the truth of the matter is not this normal "I" but "That" which is still dropping into Nothing. I am assured by those who know that I may be able to take up the thread if I attend another ceremony.

The tinkle died away. The girl attendant ran quickly forward and folded the ermine over the celebrants. The herald blew a fanfare, and the Knights and Dames left their stalls. Advancing to the board, we took hold of the gilded carrying poles, and followed the herald in procession out of the chapel, bearing the litter to a small side-chapel leading out of the middle anteroom, where we left it, the guard closing the doors.

In silence we disrobed, and left the house. About a mile through the woods we found my friend's automobile waiting.

I asked him, if that was a low mass, might I not be permitted to witness a High Mass?

" Perhaps," he answered with a curious smile, "if all they tell of you is true."

In the meanwhile he permitted me to describe the ceremony and its results as faithfully as I was able, charging me only to give no indication of the city near which it took place.

I am willing to indicate to initiates of the Rose Croix degree of Masonry under proper charter from the genuine authorities (for there are spurious Masons working under a forged charter) the address of a person willing to consider their fitness to affiliate to a Chapter practising similar rites.

XVI

I consider it supererogatory to continue my essay on the Mysteries and my analysis of *Energized Enthusiasm.*

THE "TITANIC"

FORTH flashed the serpent streak of steel,
　Consummate crown of man's device ;
Down crashed upon an immobile
　And brainless barrier of ice.
Courage !
The grey gods shoot a laughing lip :—
Let not faith founder with the ship !

We reel before the blows of fate ;
　Our stout souls stagger at the shock.
Oh ! there is Something ultimate
　Fixed faster than the living rock.
Courage !
Catastrophe beyond belief
Harden our hearts to fear and grief !

The gods upon the Titans shower
　Their high intolerable scorn ;
But no god knoweth in what hour
　A new Prometheus may be born.
Courage !
Man to his doom goes driving down ;
A crown of thorns is still a crown !

THE *TITANIC*

No power of nature shall withstand
　　At last the spirit of mankind :
It is not built upon the sand ;
　　It is not wastrel to the wind.
Courage !
Disaster and destruction tend
To taller triumph in the end.

ALEISTER CROWLEY.

A LITERATOORALOORAL
TREASURE-TROVE

A LITERATOORALOORAL
TREASURE-TROVE

The happiest of literary discoveries would presumably be the complete works of Sappho.   In the meantime we have got along wonderfully well with the masterpiece of "G. Ragsdale M'Clintock" which Mark Twain unearthed in his matchless "Cure for the Blues."   (He does not specify Oxford or Cambridge.)   The phrase that chiefly sticks in my memory is one of which Mark Twain makes especial fun : "the topmast topaz of an ancient tower."   But this is not funny, it is superb ; it is pure early Maeterlinck, and better than the Belgian imitation at that.   I admit, however, that the rest of the book is quite as absurd as Mark Twain makes out.

But after all this is no funnier than the "St. Irvine ; or, The Rosicrucian," and the "Zastrozzi" of Percy Bysshe Shelley ; and I may modestly claim recognition as the finder of a rarer and more exquisite treasure.   Modestly, for my treasure-trove was not the result of research ; I followed up no clues ; I deciphered no cryptogram.   I claim only this degree of insight and moral courage : the minute I found it, I stole it.

I feel sure it was the author's own copy ; for I cannot believe that any one else would have had one.   My atonement be to give him belated recognition !

On the approved principles, let me describe my booty.   It is a small 4to about $6\frac{1}{2}'' \times 4\frac{1}{2}$, quietly bound in black cloth. It is printed on very bad paper, and the edges have been cut and marbled.

Unassuming, indeed, is this slim booklet of 207 pages. But the author knew his business; for on the front cover appear these words—it is like an obscure grey battleship suddenly belching her broadside—

SONNETICAL
NOTES ON
PHILOSOPHY
By WM. HOWELL WILLIAMS.

The first shot struck me between wind and water. Sonnetical! There's glory for you! A beautiful new adjective; a perfect adjective; so simple, and yet nobody ever thought of it before. Get smoked glasses and look at it! No good; one cannot comment or criticize or weave a word picture (as the D—— M—— might say) about it. One can only bow down in reverent silence and adore.

But that is not all. That is only external barbaric splendour. There is more behind. Think of all the things that *might* be sonnetical—why, there isn't one. Nothing is sonnetical but a sonnet. Aha! that is where your great mind droops; where you stop, Wm. Howell Williams begins.

Notes on Philosophy are to be sonnetical. Now one can think of many things about which sonnets have been written; there is just one which you would never think of—Philosophy. That is where Wm. Howell Williams has you every time.

In a stunned manner one opens the book. The author pours in his second broadside, and leaves you but a laughter-logged derelict. What *might* these Sonnetical Notes on Philosophy be? It suggests Rousseau and Shelley, in a kind

52

of way.   One might think of Bertram Dobell—a mildly athe-istic set of sonnets.   Oh dear no !

There is one thing that could not be there—and there it is.   It is a reproduction of Holman Hunt's picture of the Saviour with a stable lantern trying to look like Nana Sahib in his more cynically cruel moments.

(I understand that the original of this picture has been acquired by Manchester ; and from what I am told of Manchester, the penalty fits the crime.)

And opposite that is the text, " Behold, I stand at the door and knock," etc.

You now begin to wonder if two books have not got mixed up ; but no.

The title-page then appears.

SONNETICAL

NOTES

ON

PHILOSOPHY

BY

WM. HOWELL WILLIAMS.

No date ; no publisher ; no price.   But on the reverse we find, very small—

Copyrighted by
Wm. Howell Williams
April 1901.

(It was in May 1906 that I stole this copy.)

THE EQUINOX

Now one would have liked a preface, something to explain the astounding choice of form, and so on. Or to give some idea of the scope and purpose of the treatise. No; nothing of the sort. He butts right in with

INTRODUCTION.

And no sooner does this begin than you see what the author is driving at. He is out to prove that no matter how simple language may seem, in his master hands it can be made absolutely unintelligible. He begins:

> " Philosophy must knowledge be,
> Hence knowledge is philosophy."

Ponder that " hence." At least it must lead to something else. No. He continues :

> "It matters not what savant say
> If somehow knowledge comes man's way."

You now see the beginning of his first great rule of grammar: " Never inflect a verb ! "

But wait ! he is going to lay a trap for the unwary. He is going to give us three couplets which seem consecutive, and possess a meaning—

> "Supposing can be only fun,
> And knowledge never so begun.
> With supposition's wand laid by
> Hume, Berkley (*sic*), Kant and Hegel fly.
> Nay ! single, several, or all,
> Together taken they appall."

The spelling of "appall" is perhaps intended to spur the relaxed attention ; for the next couplet wants it.

> " Philosophers need not agree,
> Still is philosophy to be."

A LITERATOORALOORAL TREASURE-TROVE

The comma is a very subtle weapon! And when you discover (by and by) that his Seventh great Rule is " Never use relative pronouns!" a return to this sublime Sphinx-verse leaves you worse off than you are at the first reading.

> " All knowledge is on being cast:
> The being first and knowledge last."

Quite so : you must *be* before you can know.   Wait.

> " But note—'The first shall be the last
> And last shall be the first' ere cast."

How's that, umpire?

Perhaps the next couplet will clear things up.   No : it only serves to introduce a point—of etiquette rather than of law —which deprecates sentences containing a principal verb.

> " Such knowledge only consciousness
> In case of being under stress."

White resigned.

Wm. Howell Williams, however, has now got on to his mashie.   Every couplet within a foot of the hole.

> " All other were mere vanity,
> Save, sadly, 'tis profanity."

And, a little later, for I cannot quote the whole twenty-three pages of this lucid introduction :

> " In consciousness experience
> Is manifesting prescience.
> In prescience experience
> Establishes thought permanence.
> Nor need eventuation solve
> All prescience assume to prove.
> Beginning nor the end of time
> Eventuation need not chime.
> Time being but persistency
> Of some conditionality."

THE EQUINOX

These, as Sherlock Holmes would say, are indeed deep waters, Watson.

However, Wm. gets irritated, I think, on page 13, when he says:

> "Each perfectly see it is so
> And yet the fool to logic go."

But in the next verse he explains:

> "He only taking in as sent
> Away will reason increment."

Still on the bullying tack! Still using words of three syllables to hide his meaning in! But the master will rise to the heights yet.

> "Not faith but knowledge would lead man,
> Did he himself but see as can."

There's the true gold. Until the very last word you think it's going to mean something: and then—smash!

Very rarely, however, he tries a simpler method yet. He writes you a couplet which does mean something, though of course out of all connection with the context, and that something is the maddest nonsense.

> "To give mankind a consciousness
> Lived Jesus Christ of Nazareth."

This sentence is not written merely to show off his ability as a rimester; no, the master wants you to think, "Well, Wm. means something else when he writes 'consciousness.'" Then he has you. Because never will he give you a glimmer of his meaning. He will unsettle you about simple terms in this way, and then leave you to perish miserably.

56

A LITERATOORALOORAL TREASURE-TROVE

Again :

> " Ere was condition manifest,
> The unconditioned was at rest."

Yes, certainly. That I did know before.

> " Relations of rest with unrest
> Hence did conditions manifest."

Um. Seems to skate over the difficulty a little. But go on.

> "To such relation specify
> We use the word velocity."

Do we ?

> "Velocity sole history
> Of uncondition's mystery."
>   ! . . ! . . !

We may leave the introduction with the surmise :

> "Specific trouble history
> Of introduction's mystery."

I think I have fairly caught the style !

But this is only introduction; this is all mere mashie chips on the green : come and see what he can do with a wooden club, this plus four Wm. Howell Williams.

On page 24 he just gives you one more flick of the mashie, and reprints four couplets of the Introduction— not consecutive, and of course not coherent. Then comes the half-title " Sonnetical Notes on Philosophy" and the Magnum Opus starts. There are One Hundred and Eighty-two " Sonnets, " and the master rapidly introduces some important and novel rules.

The Octet *must* end with a colon.

A sonnet should if possible contain one sentence only.

That sentence should have no subject, predicate or object. But the reader should be led to think that they are there, and gently undeceived as the sonnet unfolds.

THE EQUINOX

Sonnet I exhibits these qualities in maddening perfection. I must quote it in full. Another writer might have led one up to this, might have feared a falling-off. But not so Wm. Howell Williams. Just as the Introduction went calmly on, never hesitating, never turning aside, rolling over the difficulties as if they were not there, so he begins and so he ends, never one seed of doubt in his mind.

> "While man trains up the child in way men go,
> It goes without the saying that man's way
> In life convention only will display,
> As each one by himself can surely know;
> Hence may these notes that light of rush-light throw
> Where glares so-called, civilization's day,
> Without night's darkness chasing once away,
> Perchance as simple truth for some one glow."

Now I have studied Wm. as reverently as Mr. Frank Harris has studied the other Wm. and I would almost swear I know what these lines mean. The secret is that line 8 belongs to line 5. The "Hence" is my real difficulty. Education leads to conventionality (lines 1–4), therefore these notes may glow as simple truth for some one.

I'm afraid

> "Each perfectly see it is so
> And yet the fool to logic go"

is one on me. But all speculations are futile, for the sonnet continues as follows :

> "If seen the curse, if be a curse, on man
> Is taxing self to understand, amid
> Environment that ever keeps its place,
> What shape may take his life, if any can,
> That haunting foolishness alone not bid
> Him to endure, with pain, but for disgrace."

58

A LITERATOORALOORAL TREASURE-TROVE

Where's your subject now? Where's your principal sentence? Where's any vestige of connection with anything? You can find a meaning of sorts if you pick out any line or two, and are allowed to supply all sorts of those cheap and nasty little words that the master has discarded : *e. g.*—

If (it be) seen (that) the curse, if (it) be a curse, on man is (that he is obliged to be) taxing (him) self to understand (the universe) amid (his) environment that ever keeps its place——

There's enough conjecture there to endear me more than ever to my dear old tutor, Dr. A. W. Verrall (since I wrote this article, alas! he has joined Agamemnon)—but anyhow, there it stops. I cannot imagine in my wildest moments any nexus with the last three lines of the sestet. I cannot see the merest germ of an apodosis for that majestic protasis.

The second sonnet is not quite equal to this, in my opinion. The method is not the same—perhaps, though, this is the master's plan, to give us the same effect in a totally different fashion. But I call it sheerly meretricious to *spoil* the sonnet by a full stop after four lines.

> "Man's place is truth that makes no sign, but is,
>   Which man, who seek a sign where is no sign
>   Will ever overlook till forced repine
> In dumb despair since nothingness is his."

Put " seeks " for " seek," and " to " before " repine," and it makes sense. Ah! but there's a " for " coming!

> " For other than what is may not say 'tis
>   But to impose on blind a fool's design
>   As thorns about the brow of Christ define
> Not him, but those who mock, with emphasis :
>   Less puncto see and pundit silent pass
>   Mankind from truth will ever wander on—"

and so on, almost intelligibly,   With a single word he knocks down our castle of cards.   Who or what is "puncto"?

I'm not sure about "less," it may be Wm.ese for lest.   It occurs again in line 13.

"Less absolute, as absolute, be gone——"

There is a fine passage in Sonnet III :

"Whence knowledge once a sensibility
Of a present conditionality,
Must helpless self-persistence enterprise."

These lines are rather important, as they bunch the Dramatis Personæ of these sonnets.   He rings the changes on Sensibility Sahib and Count Conditionality and Sir Self-Persistence all through the book.   But the Principal Boy is called "propositional"; he is introduced to us in the wonderful 29th sonnet.

"A proposition : propositional
To imagery of presence in sense felt
Of actuality : is ever spelt,
By consciousness as abstract actual,
Persisting unperceived as well, withal,
As when perceived : an image nothing pelt
Against without itself is backward dealt
As if by something quite perpetual :
Whence seen non-actual relation come
As mystery unveiled to simulate
In imagery that actual won't deal :
And budding thence has blossomed forth till dome
Of all creation cannot estimate
Imaginary being that existence steal."

I regard this as one of the very finest sonnets in the book. I like "pelt"; it baffles conjecture entirely.   And the final "steal," which suddenly checkmates the aspiring intellect that thought the last three lines were going to mean something, is a supreme touch of Wm.'s art.

But one cannot select ; the whole is so stupendous a piece of perfection. The absolute balance of phrases which mean something (if taken in watertight compartments) with those which mean nothing, and can mean nothing ; the miraculous skill shown in avoiding even a suggestion of a subject, the expectation of which is so compelled by the beginning " A proposition " : the admirable steam-roller obsquatulation of grammar and syntax—all these things and many more make this sonnet unique in the language. I am afraid the rest of our investigations (said I) will be anti-climax. Dear, no ! Wm. Howell Williams is not so poor in pride. Whenever you stop, whenever you think he must stop, just there he begins. In Sonnet XXXV, for example :

> " A propositional abstractional
>   Remain, that proposition may include
>   An indisputable, as well exclude
> Disputable, in sphere provisional
> To stand immovable conditional,
>   Whence comprehension never to conclude
>   But ever know what thereto did intrude
> Lest venturing become habitual :
> As in imaginary personage
>   Usurp the functionality bestowed
>   On creature by a providential hand,
> And rashly venturing themselves engage
> To journey through their lives without a road
>   That they can see or guide they can command."

This is sublime art. To the last five lines one could put a beginning to make sense ; and it seems to refer to the fear (of Providence) lest venturing should become habitual. With one single line " as in imaginary personage " the whole idea is reduced to ruin. That line is a mammoth.

Note ; it is the first line of the sestet. And the first line of the octet is that dinosaur

" A propositional abstractional "

with the lovely verb " remain " following it, lest any " habitual venturer " should conjecture that one or both of the adjectives was a noun.

He is evidently pleased with it himself; for XXXVI begins :

" Abstractional, as propositional."

Here is another very charming method. It consists of repeating words with different verbs and things, a sort of weaving. The only limitation of course is that of meaning. Try Sonnet LXX :

> " Philosophy, as quantity, be less
>   When knowledge as a quantity be more
>   Than quantity, philosophy can score ;
> Hence quantity less quality possess,
> Sensation never can put under stress ;
>   Since semblance of condition cannot store
>   Shades protean as quality before
> Proportionate of quantity duress :
> Since semblance of condition unity
>   Possess by holding unit under stress,
>   As quantity, however, change will stay ;
> While quality as mere diversity,
>   Stress more or less of quality, more or less
>   Enforced, with dying force will melt away."

One can only say Look ! Ecce Wm. !

Another very pretty plan is to use constantly words which

may be either nouns or verbs, and "that" where it may be either relative or demonstrative.

In Sonnet X, for example, he begins :

> "Though aggregation form, as semblance place,
>   Where mere sensation will substantial find
>   Unseen relation force conditioned mind
> Form aggregation ever set to face
> Perception shall be as fixed for the case."

Remember that Wm. has suppressed prepositions. Then "form," "place," "find," "Unseen," "force," "mind," "Form," may any of them be either nouns or verbs ; and of course in no case can sense be made of the sentence.

Take also the passage in Sonnet CIX :

> "*Example :* Huxley nihil bonum screen ;
>   How :"

Parse screen !

And what can it mean, this Fragment of Ozymandias ? It stands there, absolutely isolated from any reference to Huxley ; as an "example," but of what who can say ? on all sides, boundless and bare, the lone and level sonnets stretch far away.

Did Huxley put a screen on the market called the nihil bonum ?

Did he give shelter to "nothing good"? or did "nothing good" save him from exposure ?

Or was Huxley's screen no good ? Or it is no good to screen Huxley ?

It makes me feel what he feels in No. CXIII :

THE EQUINOX

"Creation absolute by absolute
Of absolute for absolute imply
What self-pride primes mere mortals to deny;
Nor other fluting for its fluting flute,
But idle tooting idle fancy toot
That never any being satisfy
But leaves all hungering,—— "

And in his last sonnet, CLXXXII, he most surely utters the supreme wish of every would-be reader:

"O Lord, arise, help and deliver us
For Thy name's sake."

But it was time to stop: his eagle pinions droop; the last quatrain of the octet becomes sense, grammar, almost poetry.

"O Lord, arise, help and deliver us
From pride and foolish faith and idle fears
That baseless phantom Hope in man uprears
Since Eos woke his eons dolorous."

It is his first slip; but he accepts Nature's warning, and retires into private life.   This

"henchman stout
To blow imagination's windy flute
That aggregations wantoning en route
To thin Attenuation whistles out:

returns to his propositional abstractional unconditioned absolute consciousness quality less quantity require like a mere Newton temple Rimmon "To be or not to be" "Fools, liars, hypocrites" brigade flut, and leaves us who have certainly "stood at the door, and knocked" long enough to our dormant deride aggregated imagination eradicate; until "attenuation properly, withal, Semblantic manifestation repossess," "all sensation notes is vacancy."

LEMUEL S. INNOCENT.

64

THRENODY

Poets die because they find
    Words too petty to express
All the things they have in mind.
    Rime and rhythm only dress
    All their naked loveliness.

Poets die because their love
    Grows too great for life to stem;
Death alone can soar above
    Limits that encircle them.

Poets die because—but why
    Should divine ones be divined?
Let the sleeping secret lie!
It suffices—poets die.

DISCHMATAL BY NIGHT

THERE is a dirge of cataracts that fall
   Far far away up in the shadowed glen.
   A faint wind moans among the pines, and then
Shudders away to silence.   The deep pall
Of snow lies chill and voiceless over all.
   And through the mist the moon peers down as when
   By the veiled light of lanthorns speechless men
Gaze on some sheeted corpse's funeral.

Savagely mute ; remotely merciless,
   There is a Presence here that awes and chills,
      A Stillness aged and inviolate.
It is the Spirit of the wilderness,
   The everlasting Silence of the hills
      Who shroud themselves in Solitude : and wait.

A QUACK PAINTER

A QUACK PAINTER

ALGERNON AGRIPPA DOOLEY was the Only-begotten Son of the Reverend Archibald Agrippa Dooley. The unusual capitals are intended to indicate the importance of this fact to our petty cosmos. The Reverend Archibald was a fussily feeble old soul who would have been in his place in a hunting shire; his purchase of a fat metropolitan living was a tragic joke for his parishioners. Utterly incapable of intellectual movement himself, he bitterly resented intellect in others, regarding not only its display but its reputed possession as a direct insult to himself. "A fine morning, Mr. Dooley!" was met by an action described in the family circle as "pluffing," which resembled the gathering rage of the turkey, with purpler effects. It culminated in a splutter, "You're a very impudent young fellow." And why? Because the freely expressed contempt of his son and heir had in the course of years drilled into him that very stupid people spoke of the weather. Ergo, when a reputedly clever person spoke to him of it, the implication was that it was a shaft of satire.

Individuals, unlike nations, do not always get the government they deserve. Nothing in Mr. Dooley's character called for such punishment as the wife the gods had given him. A secret drinker and a cunning adulteress, she concealed both defects and the infinite malignity of a hell-hound under the most odious and consummate hypocrisy of conduct and the most saintly and venerable exterior. She was perhaps in all this not blameworthy. Her entire family was epileptic, her sister Amelia a hopeless melancholic whom—it is a characteristic trait of the family—they imprisoned in the house rather than face the publicity of a certificate, despite of the young children who were thus brought up in earshot of her screams. Original taints weaken if the stock survive; and what in one sister was insanity, and the other vice, became in one daughter dipsomania, in another viraginity, and in our hero *petit mal* and a taste for art.

Algernon gave no early sign of his eventual P.R.A.; he passed scatheless through dame's school and Harrow. It was the talk made in undergraduate circles by the decadents that caught his puberty, and thrust it in that direction. And of original genius or capacity he had none. Of all essentials he had none. But, on the other hand, of inessentials, of all superficial qualities, he had all. His mimetic faculty was fine, almost incredibly fine. Fortunately for my credit, my collection comprises not only borders and initials of which probably no expert would care to swear that they were not the work of William Morris, but pencil sketches of Rossetti girls and Burne-Jones girls done with equal excellence and Beardsleyesque drawings imitating even the miraculous fineness of that great draughtsman's execution. Some one had said to him that Beardsley's line showed no rough edge under a glass. He satisfied himself of the fact, and in a few weeks came near to rival the master.

But there was a limitation. He could copy these masters —the only masters, except Watts, of whom he had not yet heard—only by copying their work directly. He could not sketch from Nature at all, only from the reproductions that he possessed, and from imagination. Nor could he treat a Beardsley subject in a Rossetti style, or *vice versa*.

This faculty of imitation possessed his mind in every detail. He projected a press "*like* the Kelmscott Press," a periodical "*like* the Yellow Book." He could not even get near enough to originality to propose a Morris periodical !

Of course something very like this stage is common to all artists. Nothing is more pitiable and slavish than Shelley's early plagiarisms of Mrs. Aphra Behn, Keats's efforts to reproduce Moore at his worst—by "Moore at his worst" I do not here seek a euphemism for "George Moore." In fact, the sensitiveness and receptivity which is one side of genius makes this inevitable. So that one might have hoped to see the stem of Dooley spring from roots which drew sustenance from these many masters.

It was some three years before I had another opportunity of observing this youth ; but no stem had yet appeared ; it was the tangle still. Here was a fan painted exquisitely on silk in Conder's own technique, though (with a better artist as his model) Dooley had not made quite such a success. It was not Conder at his best ; but it was not Conder plus anything or anybody. Such as it was, it was pure Conder. On an easel was the portrait of a girl by Rembrandt-Dooley ; against the wall another girl by Whistler-Dooley ; the big easel held a vast Velasquez-Dooley which was not going very well.

By this time (observe !) Dooley had learnt to paint from Nature, but he could not reach the Velasquez-conception, the

Whistler point-of-view ; and to this extent he failed—and oh! how glaring and how ghastly was the failure !—to reproduce their style. But in all the inessentials he was there all the time. Theme, brush-work, treatment, tone, composition, all that was imitable he imitated admirably ; and he had none of his own.

It was very amusing to hear him explain his failure— which he occasionally realized, for in some ways he was a fine critic, though with no real standard of balance. Painting he declared to be a lost art, in the same sense as the manufacture of gunpowder might be. He thought the old masters had "amber in their varnish." He bought a truck-load of books on chemistry to find out what was wrong with his colours ; a task joyfully undertaken and rigorously prosecuted with that degree of success which might have been prognosticated by any scientific person who happened to be cognizant of the fact that he knew absolutely no chemistry—or even any other exact science to help him a little with the terminology. However, he made endless experiments ; he ground up his own colours and used all kinds of oils, and in every other way exhibited the indomitable perseverance which does indeed bring one to the top of a Sunday-school, but is unfortunately useless to the alchemist of silk-purse from sow's ear.

He tried many another plan. No draughtsman, he photographed his models with the assistance of a bald ratcatcher in a Norfolk jacket who had a perpetual snuffle and was named Mowles ; pantagraphed the photo on to a canvas "Double Bishop," and proceeded to paint it in ! I do not think that many geniuses do this at twenty-five !

A QUACK PAINTER

He had, too, a great deal of trouble with his Whistler, because of Whistler's "low tone." As he had no real idea of harmony and balance, this was quite beyond him. But somebody told him that Whistler used black as a harmonizer; so he mixed everything with black. I saw him mix paint the colour of London mud for the high light on the cheek of a blonde. These pictures were scarcely discernible in the light of day, especially after—in spite of chemistry!—the paint had sunk in. In fact he told me himself a year ago that he started to paint over an old canvas, thinking it was only a background, to recognize (too late!) his favourite portrait of the Honourable Mavourneen Jones.

Any real advance that he may have made at this time was due to various friends who really could paint, or rather, who had something to paint, and couldn't paint it to their liking. (Dooley had nothing to paint; "there never was a Dooley.") But the only visible result was a number of very creditable J. W. Morrice landscapes. And, unfortunately, there was an American among these good folk of Paris; like Gilbert, "his name I shall not mention," but he really was a discontented sugar broker, if ever there was one. He was Pinkerton of *The Wrecker* come to life. He started with newspapers in the gutters of Chicago, and was earning £2,000 a year by his gift of suggesting an American girl to any person who had never seen one by a representation of a spider's web struck by lightning. This youth fell under the influence of Dooley, whose manner was bluster and bounce *à l'Americaine*, but more so, and thus eminently calculated to subjugate the Yank, who cannot suspect an effete European of drawing two cards to three little clubs. Dooley inspired him with a higher mawrl code, and in three weeks he was trying to imitate Dooley! So admirably did he succeed that nobody could tell the difference—each being always mud—and the supreme jest was that he exhibited the picture in the Salon, on the strength of his name!

His gratitude to Dooley was great, and he pointed out, just like Pinkerton, that artists must advertise, and proceeded to boom him in the Transatlantic press.

Another evil influence was a very old friend, a surgeon whose sole claim to distinction was his beautiful bedside manner, and his deference to the heads of his profession. I remember Dooley criticizing him one night in Lavenue's for this very fault. "When you see him with the big man," he said, "it's—damn it, it's almost like this." With his perfect art of mimicry, he gave the smile and the hand-rub of the shop-walker. In twelve months, he was doing the same thing himself!

Yet a third; a medical failure who fancied himself as 'a playwright, and by adapting 15-year old Palais Royal farces captured the English stage. He also had the impudence to publish novels page after page of which was stolen almost verbatim from various other books. His only other qualifications were his stutter, and his incapacity to conceive of greatness of any kind. That Dooley should have taken this creature seriously, even thought him an artist, exhibits the melancholy ruin into which his critical faculty had followed his aspirations. I am sorry about this: Dooley had always been a gentleman of high ideals. He had honestly wished to achieve art, and toiled like a man to attain. Now he began to criticize Milton:

74

A QUACK PAINTER

"Fame is no plant that grows on mortal soil
Nor in the glistering foil
Set off to the world, nor in broad rumour lies,
But lives and sits aloft in those pure eyes
And perfet witness of all-judging Jove:
As He pronounces lastly on each deed
Of so much fame in Heaven accept thy meed."

He found that there was "no money in France"; "England is the market"; so to England he went, and sat down to paint in an atmosphere which would have turned Titian into a maker of coloured illustrations for society novels. Ultimately even he revolted, and furnished a studio in the most fashionable part of the West End at the cost of some thousand pounds or so with works of art of every nation. But still no Dooleys.

In default of these, he set seriously to work to obtain commissions, through the social influence of his family and his friends. The seats of the mighty, he learnt, were amicably stirred by the titillation of a tongue; the brush became a secondary instrument in his armoury. His very conversation forgot art; he began to prate of "gentlemen" and "his social position." He began to reproach me one day for knowing painters who could paint. "There are bad painters who are gentlemen," he said, "and there are bad painters who are not gentlemen. Now *my* friends are gentlemen." I had humbly to confess that I did know one bad painter who was not a gentleman!

His ideals were by now wholly commercial. He no longer asked himself "Who are the greatest painters? Let me paint like they did!" but "What is the most paying branch of Art?" and being answered on all hands "Portrait painting," continued, "Who are the best-paid portraitists to-day? Let me

75

paint like they do!" He then proceeded to produce Sargents and Shannons, so as to deceive the very elect. His attitude to his older friends was now very beautiful. "Yes," he would say, "I'm painting rubbish. I'm painting pot-boilers, frankly. But no artist attains complete mastery of his method till he is sixty; by then I shall have made a fortune, and can afford to paint what I like!" This from the owner of No. 1, Vanderbilt Studios, Astor Place, Rockefeller Street, Park Lane!

Another typical tragedy is the Affair of Lady X. This excellent lady was of such blood that she could afford to regard the Plantagenet part of her ancestry as rather a blot on her 'scutcheon. Dooley cadged a commission, and made her look like her own housekeeper. This circumstance attracting comment, the great Dooley suddenly shifted his ground. It now appeared that he was not painting the particular, but the general. It was not Lady X.; it was "The Perfect Lady," or "Quite the Lady." Not a camel, but a whale—and oh! how like a whale!

When a man reaches this state, he is beyond hope. You cannot call the righteous, but sinners to repentance. "Why is your face so dirty?" "Do you cast stones at the poor?" "Then why do you wear a frock coat?" "I hope I am a gentleman." Dooley had discovered the secret of epithets, that you can make any one of them sound praise or dispraise as you will. He was therefore beyond criticism.

"Quel est le philosophe français qui disait, 'Je suis un dieu qui ai mal diné'?"—'Cette ironie ne mordrait pas sur un esprit enlevé par le haschisch,' il répondrait tranquillement. 'Il est possible que j'ai mal diné, mais je suis un dieu.'"

Dooley's vanity could give a stroke a hole to hashish; he

would reply that he had dined badly in order to mortify his flesh.

Such degradation can hardly go further ; it only remains to set the seal upon it. As valour is not increased, but only recognized, by the Victoria Cross, so nothing can be done for Dooley but to make him A.R.A.

A. QUILLER, JR.

AT SEA

As night hath stars, more rare than ships
    In ocean, faint from pole to pole,
So all the wonder of her lips
    Hints her innavigable soul.

Such lights she gives as guide my bark ;
    But I am swallowed in the swell
Of her heart's ocean, sagely dark,
    That holds my heaven and holds my hell.

In her I live, a mote minute
    Dancing a moment in the sun :
In her I die, a sterile shoot
    Of nightshade in oblivion.

In her my self dissolves, a grain
    Of salt cast careless in the sea ;
My passion purifies my pain
    To peace past personality.

Love of my life, God grant the years
    Confirm the chrism—rose to rood !
Anointing loves, asperging tears
    In sanctifying solitude !

AT SEA

Man is so infinitely small
    In all these stars, determinate.
Maker and moulder of them all,
    Man is so infinitely great!

ALEISTER CROWLEY.

CANCER ?

CANCER?

A STUDY IN NERVES

BERTIE BERNARD, Sociétaire of the Salon des Beaux Arts, and officer of the Légion d'Honneur, looked at the world from the window of his favourite café. In front, behold the hideous façade of the Gare Montparnasse and the clattering devastation of the Place de Rennes! It was a chill summer morning; a thin rain fell constantly. Great columns of ice came into the restaurant on men's backs; waiters with napkins knotted round their necks sprinkled the sandy boards with water, laid the tables for lunch, bore great basins piled with slabs of sugar here and there; in short, began the day. Behind a small bar, perched, the lady cashier performed mysterious evolutions with a book of green tickets and counterfoils; a small blind puppy nestled into the crook of her elbow.

There was a greyness in everything. Without the good sun's kiss, or the glare of the lights and the kaleidoscope of the demi-monde, Paris is a sad city. Nowhere, I think, are the distances so great, the communications so bad. Nowhere do the pavements tempt so, and tire so.

Nor, as it happened, was Bernard full of that internal sunlight which transforms the world. For four months he had worked like a demon. Six pictures—'twas his right— hung on the walls of the Salon, excellent in a wilderness of mediocrity or worse —nay, nothing is worse! but one cannot live on a reputation alone, and the American Slump had hit the painters hard .

His was a solitary life at the best of times, and, when one works, that life offers indeed the best of times. But when work is over, when one has worked so hard that there is no longer energy to play—a gloomy world for the solitary!

So here he sat in the Café de Versailles and droned through the inanities of the Overseas (as distinguished from the Half-Seas-Over) *Daily Wail*. His eye caught a sudden paragraph : " Death of a Well-known Baronet." " He had been complaining, " said the paper, "of his throat for some time, but had not thought it worth while to consult a doctor. On Saturday last he saw Sir Herpes Zoster, who took so serious a view of the matter that he advised an immediate operation. Unhappily, pneumonia supervened, and death ensued early on Tuesday morning. . . ."

Cancer! read Bernard between the lines. At the word a whole cohort of ancient thoughts, armed and angry, swept up the glacis that defended his brain, and entering put the defenders to the sword.

Cancer! The one great memory of his boyhood; his mother's illness. They had shown him—idiots !—the dreadful tumour that was—uselessly, of course—to be cut away from the breast that, eight years before, had been his life. The bedside, the cold cleanliness of things, the false-smiling faces that failed to hide their fear, his mother's drawn face and staring eyes, the hideous disease itself—all this stood out in his mind, clear-cut and vivid as it had been yesterday; a violence done to his childhood.

84

CANCER ?

Then, his face already blanched, rose in his memory certain episodes of youth. Once in Switzerland, sleeping out on the mountains, a stone had bruised his side as he lay on it, and two days after, having forgotten the origin of the blue-brown stain, he had thought it cancer, and been laughed at by a medical friend in the hotel. But again the thought, " Is it hereditary?" leapt at him. Nobody knows—that is the trouble! Nobody knows anything at all about the cause of cancer. There are no precautions, no prognoses, no diathesis except (as some said) the negative one of incompatibility with tubercle.

Bernard would have liked a little tubercle. There's Luxor, Davos, Australia—but for cancer? Cancer is everywhere. Cancer takes no account of conditions.

Now Bernard was a brave man. For sheer devilment he had gone over and taken a hand in the Cuban mix-up. He had shot tigers on foot in Burmah, and was indeed so afraid of fear that he had always refused to take the least care of his health. Better die facing death! One must die. It is no good running away. One may as well live a man's life. So he fished for salmon without waders, and found by immunity that the doctors know as little about rheumatism as about anything else.

But on this morning at the Café de Versailles things went ill with his thoughts. All that he had ever read about cancer ; all the people he had ever heard of who had died of it ; all the false wicked bombast of the newspapers (once a week on an average) that an "eminent Scientist"—whatever a "scientist" may be—had discovered a perfect cure—puppy's livers, roseleaves, tomato-juice, strange serums,

85

anything and everything· All Ignorance ! Ignorance ! ! Ignorance ! ! !

He dropped the paper with listless anger, rapped on the marble, threw down his franc, and rose. And as he caught the sharp air of the street a little cough took his throat. "God! God!" he cried, "I have it at last!" And the precise parallelism between his symptoms and those of the dead baronet hit him, as it were a giant with a club.

He, too, had been troubled for a long while. He, too, had not thought it worth while to consult a doctor.

Then the healthy reaction surged up in him. "You're a hysterical fool, my lad, and I'll teach you a lesson. You shall go and see a doctor, and·be laughed at, and pay ten francs for your cowardice !"

Up sprang the assailing thought. "On Saturday he saw Sir Herpes Zoster, who took so serious a view of the matter that . . ."

"I daren't ! I daren't !" he cried inwardly, with bitter anguish. Bowed and old, his face wrinkled and blue-grey with fear, he faltered and turned back. He sat down on a little cane chair outside the café, and drove his nails into the palms of his hands.

Abject indecision had him by the throat. He would do this, he would do that. He would go to Italy, to New York, to ride horseback through Spain, to shoot in Morocco, to— half a hundred schemes. . . .

Each impulse was inhibited. He half rose from his chair again and again, and always fell back as the terrible reply beat him down. For New York he must have a new trunk, and the idea of going into a shop and buying one seemed as insanely impossible as if he had needed a live dodo. For Spain, the terrors of the Custom House on the frontier smote him back. Trifle after trifle, fierce and menacing, beat upon him, and the cry of his sane self: " Don't be a fool, it's only nerves, get away anywhere; eat, sleep, amuse yourself and you'll be all right in a day or so! " grew feebler and feebler as the dominant demon swung his fell spear, " Go away ? you've got cancer—cancer—cancer—you can't go away from cancer!" He knew, too, that did he but once decide to do anything, the cloud would clear. But decide he could not.

If only a good hearty stupid Briton had come along and taken him out of himself for a moment!

But he was a solitary ; and the early morning is not the time for meeting such few acquaintances as he possessed. He might have called on one or two friends, but he dared not. Laden with his terrible secret, he could not confront them.

At last he rose, still purposeless, driven by physical disquietude. The muscles, irritated by the anguish of the nerves, became uneasy, sent jerky, meaningless messages to the brain. He walked and walked, feebly and foolishly, everywhere and yet nowhere—the muscles of his back ached.

Cancer of the kidney! he thought, and was swept into a whirlpool of fear. He had once been supposed to have weak kidneys. "The seat of a previous lesion" was a likely spot. He put his hand to his neck to adjust his collar. There was a small "blackhead" half formed. Cancer !

He remembered how the previous evening—no! last week, last year—what did it matter ?—one of his friends had told of a man in South America who had died of a cancer on the neck, caused, he thought, by the irritation of his collar.

87

Bernard wrenched at his collar to tear it off. "Useless! too late!" cried one interior voice. "Nothing is known of the cause," whispered the consoler, common-sense. Then, louder: "My dear good ass, every man wears a collar; only one man in twenty-one dies of cancer, and probably not one in twenty-one of those have cancer of the neck." Louder, for the physical violence of his wrench had sent his blood faster, pulled him together a little.

In the new-found courage he began again to contemplate a change, for it was only too clear that his nerves were wrong. But the enemy had an answer to this: "One of the most painful features of the disease is the dreadful anxiety——" he remembered from some old medical book.

It had begun to rain more heavily; he was wet. The physical discomfort braced him; he looked up.

He was in the Rond-Point des Champs-Elysées, not a hundred yards from his doctor's house.

In a flash his mind was made up. He strode at six miles an hour to the physician, an old friend, one Dr. Maigrelette, and was shown into the consulting room. If the doctor had happened to see him as he entered, he would not have had to wait, as was the case.

Waiting, he could not tolerate the alleged amusing journals. He looked for the poison that was eating out his soul. Soon he happened on the *Lancet*, and found to his taste an authoritative article on " Cancer of the Ileum," urging speedy operation before—so he gathered—the appearance of any symptoms whatever. "Unfortunately," wrote the great surgeon, "cancer is a painless disease for many months."

CANCER?

God! God! *He, too, had no pain!* He did not know where the ileum might be; he never even knew that he *had* an ileum. And what an awakening! He had got cancer of it. For many, many months he had had no pain!

His perception of the absurd was utterly snowed under.

With clenched teeth, the sweat rolling from his brow, he rushed from the house.

What followed he never really knew. The agony of the mind had gone a step too far, and dropped below the human into a dull animal consciousness of fear. He was being hunted for his life. The instinct of flight became dominant. He found himself feverishly packing his bag; he found himself at the Gare de Lyon, with no very clear conception of how he came there.

Hunger brought him to. Luckily the restaurant of the station—one of the best in Paris—was full of the cheeriest memories. Time and again he had left the station for Italy, Switzerland, Algiers, always with high hope, good courage, pleasurable anticipation.

Almost himself again for the moment, he feasted superbly on a Caneton Rouennais au Sang, with a bottle of the ripe red Burgundy.

A peace stole over him. "I have had a bad attack of nerves;" he thought, "I will go away and rest. Worry and overwork, that's what it is. Where's the laziest place on earth? Venice."

And to Venice he went, almost gaily, in a wagon-lit.

Gaily? At the back of his consciousness was a dull sphere of some forgotten pain, some agony in abeyance.

The exhaustion of the day and the last benediction of the

good wine together drove him down the slopes of sleep into the Valley of deepest Anæsthesia. Almost trance.

II

The dull viewless journey up the Rhone Valley, with its everlasting hint of great things beyond, did Bernard good. More than a touch of mountain freshness in the air, nay! the very loathsomeness of the Swiss—that nation with the Frenchman's meanness without his insouciance, the German's boorishness without his profundity, the Italian's rascality without his picturesqueness, all these things reminded him of his happy youth spent among the glaciers. At lunch he ordered a bottle of Swiss champagne, drank that infamous concoction with a certain relish piercing through the physical disgust at its nauseousness, as remembering the joy of the opened bottle on some peak yet unclimbed by the particular ridge he had chosen. Life seemed very different now-a-days. He would hardly have taken the trouble to climb Mount Everest, had a Jinnee borne him to its foot upon a magic carpet. Fame, love, wealth, friendship—these things seemed valueless. He knew now what he wanted—rest—rest. Death would have pleased him. He thought of the Buddhist Nibbana, and almost determined to become an Arahat, or at least a Bhikkhu, the stage preliminary.

So the long day went by; at its end, Venice, a vulgar approach, a dead level of shapeless houses with insignificant church spires scarce visible.

Then the sudden wonder of the gondola, gliding between the tall jagged subtly coloured palaces, the surprise of the

90

CANCER?

moon, glittering down some unexpected alley. And again the sleep of utmost fatigue, only accentuated by the violent stimulus of the wonderful city, its undeniable romance, its air of dream, of enchantment.

In the morning he rose early. The Grand Canal was stirring, lively, with the pale gold of sunrise kindling it. He hailed a gondola, and until lunch-time drifted about in the narrow waterways, seeking to discover by some subtle mental process the secret which he imagined, as one is compelled to imagine, that each tall house contains.

Yet, lost as he was in the dream, there was ever present in the background of his mental picture, the waking life. What he conceived as the waking life was but that formless mass of horror, the disease whose fear was yet upon him.

In short, he was drugged with Venice, as with an opiate. There would come a reckoning. Life itself was poisoned. The mask matters little; the face behind the mask is all. And for Bernard, behind the mask of Venice, glittered the eyes of Cancer—Cancer—Cancer!

But as health came back, he consciously fought the demon.

One may as well die of cancer as anything else, he would think. He insisted on the word; he said it aloud, watching his voice to detect the tremor of fear. He would contemplate death itself—the worst (after all!) that would come, and discovered death to be but a baseless illusion. He made a dilemma for death. If consciousness ceases, he argued, there is no death, for one is not conscious of it, and nothing exists for the individual of which he is not conscious. If consciousness does not cease—why, that is life!

THE EQUINOX

And so on, making a brave show of the feeble weapon of intellect, as one sees a frightened insect try to appear terrible. Or as a guardsman struts with moustache and busby.

But this same bold analysis was, as he soon saw, but another shape of fear. It was courage, true! but courage implies fear. There was but one cure, absorption in work. So, as he rested, the capacity for work returned. He began, first sketches, then fair-sized pictures of the ever-changing, ever-identical beauty of Venice. He spent an altogether joyous morning buying materials for his art.

He met a charming child of Venice in black shawl, with Madonna's face and Venus's body; he painted her into all his foregrounds. In the evening, sitting together in the café of the Rialto Inn, he sketched her. He projected a large and sacred picture, full of the sensual strength of Rubens. His tired soul took her virgin vigour into itself; he became like a boy; he idealized, adored his mistress. He would learn a little Italian, so that they might talk together easily, no longer in broken French-Italian.

So one morning he strolled down to the old Dandolo Palace, glorious with memories of Georges Sand and de Musset, and consulted the jolly bearded blonde beautiful hall porter about lessons in Italian.

The porter gave him an address. Would he had added, "Venice is the most relaxing city in the five continents. A week will cure you, a fortnight kill you!"

So our friend was soon knocking at the door of the Signora who taught English.

She was a faded widow, her dyed blonde hair eked out with an improbable fringe, rouged and wrinkled, intensely respectable, Scotch, Presbyterian, sentimental, scented. The room was musty and ill-sized, an imported lodging-house from Ramsgate! The decorations in keeping. Undusted furniture, portraits of "Victoria the Good," and of the lady's "poor dear husband," a Bible, English and Italian novels and grammars. All frivolities, all dullnesses, all inessentials. The very piano had the air of an accident. Poor tired woman! Long since all hope, all purpose, is lost for you, he thought. And "Am I otherwise?" Vital scepticism tinged his disgust with the teacher as, mastering his repulsion, he arranged for a series of lessons.

It was on the third day of these lessons that he saw Germanica Visconti. She was a few minutes early at the teacher's, and intruded on his hour. Paler than death, and clad in deepest mourning, she had yet beauty rare and rich, a charm irresistible. The great sense of beauty that had made him the famous painter that he was allured him.

Voilà une belle idée—he scented intrigue. All night he dreamt of her, gliding as a gondola glides into the room. (For so do all Venetian women glide.)

The next day he began—the cunning fellow!—with a little apology. Had he overstayed his hour? She was rather a pretty girl (no Don Juan would openly say that; it was a clever subterfuge).

The old-young widow rose easily to the bait. The Visconti had just lost her father. Poor man, he had suffered terribly for two years. Smokers' cancer, they called it. You can operate twice, but the third time he must die. Oh, yes! it is very, very common in Venice.

The pipe in his pocket burnt him like a red-hot coal.

93

THE EQUINOX

The whole horror came flooding back, tenfold stronger for its week of abeyance. Good God! he had come to the very place of all places where he was sure to get it. Yet he was master of himself enough to sit out the lesson, to bow gracefully to Germanica as she came up the stairs. Thence he went shaking into Florian's, and thought filth of all the world.

The city, ever a positive impression, unlike most other cities, which one can ignore, hurt him. Very common here, he mused—and his throat, really a little irritated by the slackness and the sirocco, became dominant and menacing. He put his hand to his larynx, imagined a tumour. The word "induration" afflicted him, throbbed in his brain. He could not bear society: he got rid of his model, cruelly and crudely. Nothing but his stubborn courage saved him from throwing his pipe into the canal. By bravado, he smoked double his usual allowance. His throat naturally got worse, and his distress correspondingly increased.

He simply could not stand Venice any longer. Two days of speechless agony, and he went suddenly back to Paris, the dust of the journey aggravating his sore throat, and its misery dragging him ever lower into the abyss of despair. His indecision increased, invaded the smallest details of life. He walked miles, unable to find a restaurant to suit his whim. He would reach the door, perhaps enter, suddenly remember that the coffee was never good there, go out again, walk, walk, walk, repeat the folly again and again, until perhaps he would go to bed foodless. His sore throat (always a depressing influence on all of us) grew worse, and his soul sagged in sympathy.

94

CANCER?

He could not work, he could not read, he could do nothing. He went out to play Pelota at Neuilly one afternoon, and his very natural failure to play decently increased his misery. I am no more good, he thought, I am getting old. Thirty-six, he mused, and a sob came to his throat—the very age when cancer most begins to claim its prey.

He engaged a model, and discovered that he could no longer draw. He tried everything, and gave up after an ineffectual hour.

His throat grew worse: it pained him really very badly. The follicles of his tongue, too, inflamed sympathetically, and the horrid vision of a bottled cancerous tongue that he had once seen at the College of Surgeons stood luminous in his mind—an arched monstrous tongue of a hideous brown colour, with the ulcer just visible in the dorsum. It looked too big to be a human tongue at all, he had thought. Would his own tongue be bottled in a year from now?

He was afraid to go to a doctor; he could hear the diagnosis; the careful preparation to break it gently to him, the furtive eye that would assure itself of the presence of some necessary stimulant; the——

His thought shot on prophetic to the operation. Would he sink under it? He hoped so. "Early and successful operations afford a respite of from three to five years," he had read. Think of the waiting through those years for its recurrence! Think of Carrière—he, too, dead of throat-cancer—who had said after the operation, "If it comes back I'll shoot myself"—Carrière—his colleague—his friend.

He had once had an operation, a minor affair. He could picture everything — "extirpate the entire triangle," the surgeon would say—and do. He did not know what would be left of himself. Would he be able to speak, to swallow, during those horrible three, four, five years while he waited (in Hell !) for " recurrence " ?

Liability to recurrence ! he sneered angrily ; they know it means always, the dogs !

He thought of the title of a book he had seen advertised, " How Surgery blocks the way to the cure of cancer," and foamed against the folly of the surgeon, then against the blatant quackery of the alternatives. He hated mankind. He hated God, who had made such a world. Why not have ——? and discovered that it is not as easy as it sounds to devise a genuine undeniable improvement upon the universe.

He fought against the notion that his throat was cancerous, did it good with a simple gargle, made it worse again by smoking ; finally the shocking anxiety of the terror that he dared not reveal operated to make him really ill.

Only his magnificent constitution had saved him from being very ill indeed long before this.

As it was, the genuine physical suffering took his mind to some extent off his supposed disease, and in a fit of annoyance he determined to put an end of the matter one way or the other

He got into a fiacre, and drove off—idiot !—to the great Cancer Specialist, Dr. Pommery.

III

It was the very worst thing he—or any one—could have

done.   Dr. Pommery was famous as having — regardless of expense — grafted the skin of a pig's belly on to the face and hands of a negress, who was thereby enabled to marry a crazy Vicomte, whose parents objected to black blood in the family.   True, she had died.   He, too, had discovered the bacillus of cancer, the only flaw in his experiments being that the said bacillus was to be found in all known organic substances except sterilized agar-agar.   He had prepared a curative serum which killed cancer patients before the disease got half a chance, and he had received the record fee of £5,000 sterling for killing the actress wife of an English Duke—or so the Duke's friends laughed over his Grace's cigars and '47 port in his Grace's smoking-room.

He welcomed Bernard with a kindling eye.   " Dear me ! " (in his kindest professional manner) " Don't worry ! don't worry, my dear young friend !   I think we shall be able to help the little trouble.   At the same time, I must ask you to realize that it is somewhat serious, not at all a matter to neglect.   In fact, I ought to tell you—you are a man, and should be well able to bear a little shock—that—that——"

Bernard had heard him with set face, afraid no more but of showing the white feather.   Now as he caught the expression of the great specialist's eyes, the long strain broke. He burst into a torrent of glad tears, caught the doctor's hands in his, and wrung them hard.   " I know ! " he cried. " It's cancer—cancer !   Thank God !   Thank God ! "

His fear was over.

He sobered himself, arranged to go the next day to Dr. Pommery's private hospital for the treatment, and went off. His throat was better already.   Almost joyfully, he went about his affairs.   He bade good-bye to his one good friend at lunch, not wishing to sadden her by telling her the truth. He found a sombre pleasure in keeping the secret.   " The next she hears of me, I shall be dead. She will remember this lunch, think kindly of me that I would not spoil her pleasure." Then—" Poor girl, how will she live when I am gone ? "

Bernard had a small regular income ; he had no relations ; he would leave it to her.   So off he went to the Rive Droite to make his will.

The lawyer was an old friend, was grievously shocked at his story, made the usual attempts to minimize the affair, told a long story of how he too had been condemned to death by a doctor—" Twenty years ago, Herbert, and—well, I feel sure I shall die, you know, if I have to wait another forty years for it."

Bernard laughed duly, and was cheered ; yet the lawyer's sympathy jarred.   He detected a professionalism, an insincerity, in the good cheer.   He was quite wrong ; his friend did think him scared, and was honestly trying to give him courage.   He asked him to come back to tea.   Bernard accepted.

Now who should chance to drop in but Maigrelette, that same old medical friend of Bernard's, from whose consulting-room he had fled in terror a month before ! They were four at tea, Jobbs the lawyer and his wife, Maigrelette and the dying man.

At the proper moment Bernard began his sad story ; it was necessary to say farewell.

Maigrelette heard him with patient impatience. To his look, that asked for sympathy, he said but one explosive word, " Pommery ! "   It sounded like an oath !

98

CANCER?

"Come here!" he said, catching Bernard by the shoulder and dragging him to the window. He thrust a spoon, snatched from the tea-table, into his mouth. "Say R!"

"R-R-R-R-R," said Bernard obediently, wondering whether to choke or vomit.

"You d——d ass!" thundered Maigrelette, shaking him to and fro till his teeth chattered, "I beg your pardon, Mrs. Jobbs—what you've got is a very mild go of tonsillitis, and a very bad go of funk. What you're going to do is to go away with my brother Jack to-morrow morning for a month. He'll teach you what speed means. No nonsense, now! Hold up!"

But Bernard went limp, fainted.

While he lay unconscious, "You can tear up that will, Jobbs," said Maigrelette, "but it's a bad nervous case, as bad as I want to see. I don't think we'll trust him to go home alone, do you know?"

Bernard came to. The doctor took him back to his studio, packed his bag for him, carried him off to dinner. "Jack," he said to his brother, in a swift aside, "take the big Panhard, and L for leather all the way to Madrid! Let him out of your sight, day or night, for the next week, and I won't answer for it! After that, if he stop brooding—well, I'll have a look at him myself before you relax." Jack nodded comprehension, and after the cigars had been converted into ash and contentment, he went off with Bernard pounding through the night in the great journey to the south. Bernard, exhausted, dozed uneasily in the tonneau, the wind driving out of his brain the phantoms of its disorder. All day they raced through the haze and heat;

H 2   99 fed like giants here and there. The patient grew visibly sleek, his face got blood, his eyes brightness, the furtive inwardness of them sucked out by the good sun, the wild fresh air.

They stopped their headlong course at a small town in the Pyrenees. Bernard was honestly sleepy, as a tired man is, not as an exhausted man. As for Jack, he thought he could never get enough sleep. He had held the wheel nearly all day.

They dined, smoked, took a tentative walk cut short by the eagerness of the air and their own great fatigue. Bernard threw himself upon his bed, and slept instantly. Jack, with a glad sigh, "Safe till the morning!" imitated him.

So abode the utter stillness of the night upon them; so the dawn arose. A shaft of sunlight came through the mountain cleft, and fell obliquely upon Bernard's face. He half woke, wondered. His memory played him false. Where was he? The strange room baffled him. And suddenly his face whitened. "I have got cancer," he thought. And again: "It is I that have got cancer. It is I." The emphasis of egoity rose to a perfect shriek of nerve, dominated all other chords in the brain, once and for all.

He rose calm and smiling, like a little child, went on tip-toe to the window, kissed his hand to the sun, whose orb now rose clear of the mountain and looked full upon him. "What a ripping score off old Jack!" he said in a soft voice, laughing, and after a minute's search in his dressing-case, drew his razor with one firm sweep across his throat.

As he turned and fell, the bright blood sprang, a slim swift jet, and fell bubbling upon the face of the sleeper.

ALEISTER CROWLEY.

DUMB!

GABRIEL whispered in mine ear
    His archangelic poesie.
How can I write?   I only hear
    The sobbing murmur of the sea.

Raphael breathed and bade me pass
    His rapt evangel to mankind;
I cannot even match, alas!
    The ululation of the wind.

The gross grey gods like gargoyles spit
    On every poet's holy head;
No mustard-seed of truth or wit
    In those curst furrows, quick or dead!

A tithe of what I know would cleanse
    The leprosy of earth; and I—
My limits are like other men's.
    I must live dumb, and dumb must die!

THE VITRIOL-THROWER

To
Kathleen Scott.

THE VITRIOL-THROWER

THE Boulevard Edgar Quinet is convenient for life and death. There is squalid toil and squalid pleasure, represented by the Gare Montparnasse and the Rue de la Gaieté; at the other end is the exotic struggle of the quaint little colony of English artists. The boulevard itself hangs between these extremes; but, sinister and terrible omen! the whole of one side is occupied by that vast cemetery of Montparnasse which Charles Baudelaire has honoured by his bones.

I like to think that Baudelaire, brooding like an unquiet fiend above his carrion, may laugh, though it be but the laugh of hell, at this my tale.

A man who has deliberately taken human life on no responsibility but his own enjoys some of the immunities of a God. The habit of acting first and thinking afterwards is surely divine, or how can we explain the universe? Among civilized people few such men are to be found; they may be known by the grave courage of their steadfast eyes. Would you like to meet one? The first place to search is most certainly the Boulevard Edgar Quinet.

At least this is certain, that if you had been strolling down by the cemetery on Monday night before Mardi-Gras, twelve years ago, you would have had your opportunity.

Clement Seton was a tiny little man with a pale face.

105

One would have said that he suffered from a wasting illness. On his finger flashed a single ruby. Very unwise of you, young man! for the boulevard, deserted and leading no whither in particular, is the haunt of the greatest ruffians in Paris.

The two Apaches in the shadow laughed. Silent and swift, they leapt. But the Scot was swifter yet. Ten feet away he stood with a Colt levelled in the gloom, demanding "Your pleasure, gentlemen?"

They began some stammering excuse; the boy's light laugh trilled out, and he lightly replaced his weapon, turned on his heel, and left them to follow if they dared.

There is almost opposite the end of the boulevard an impasse miscalled the Rue Boissonade. A road it would have been, save for the obstinate leases in the midst thereof. A road it one day surely will be, but at present it is certainly trying that from No. N to No. N + 1 is a circuitous journey of near upon half a mile. On the right as you enter is a small low house, roofed for a studio, old-fashioned, with its ugly modern neighbours sneering over it. It had a bad name, too, even among the easy-going folk of Bohemian Paris.

Is your face the face of a cat or of a pig, strange dweller in that desolate house? Where did you get that shaggy mane of fire? Your face is covered with fine down, every tip whereof stings like a nettle. You have eyes that must devour the soul of a man ere they can sleep. You have long and heavy lips ever twitching; one thinks of an octopus waiting for its prey. Is that your blood that makes them scarlet, or the blood of all those who would not be warned in time?

How is it, too, that all men own you beautiful? How, surer test! that all women deny you beauty?

THE VITRIOL-THROWER

For beautiful you are. Your face is the face of some divine beast, adored of the Egyptians or the Mexicans.

What of your soul? Is that, too, the soul of a God and a beast? Does your face that warns us, and in vain, tell truth? People are afraid of you, Mirabelle! they cross the road to avoid passing over the pavements you have trod.

Who was that poor Hungarian boy that men cut down one morning from your gate? and the pianist who poisoned himself in Vienna?

What did the painter see in your eyes that he slashed your finished face from his canvas, and drew the second stroke across his throat?

Is there any gate of death, Mirabelle, that some man has not passed—for you?

Why, too, do you tire your hair so carefully to-night? You only lift your finger, and they die for you. Why, then, do you struggle? There is anxiety, not only pride, in the thrice-gazed-on mirror. You have swathed yourself close like a corpse; the amber silk clings to your beautiful body. After all, you have taken down your hair; it flows over your breasts like a river of hell.

How is it that you are waiting? Others should wait, surely; it is not for you to wait. You are in danger, Mirabelle; there is a God in heaven after all.

Yes, and you will have him in your arms.

II

Clement Seton shrugged his shoulders and threw his cigar away with a gesture of weariness. Life in Paris seemed tame after his exploits in Somaliland, where he had won the Victoria Cross standing over a wounded comrade half the day, while the survivors of what had been a very smart little outpost scrimmage tried in vain to come to terms with that waterless warrior.

"Most cowardly thing I ever did," he would explain. "The poor beggars couldn't get at us for the rocks. When a head appeared one put a bullet through it. Like bally clay pigeons, by Jove!" and then he would go on, in his talkative nonsensical way, with some absurd paradox in ethics or metaphysics.

Yet what good was to come of Paris? Bitter scorn of the sneaking Apaches ate up his soul. To come to grips with a devil were worth the pains. Murderers, he mused, are the salt of the earth. And lo! the salt hath lost its savour. And he laughed sourly.

At the gate of the lonely house he flung away his cigar, and his hand was on the latch.

Suddenly, a noiseless touch upon the arm, and a low, hurried, pleading voice. "Clement, my old friend, listen a moment." He turned, and saw dear, fat, good-natured old Miss Aitken. What was there in this woman to make her (as she had been) the friend of Swinburne, Carrière, and Verlaine?

Artists hate artists, not for envy, but because there can be no companionships among the Gods. Eternally silent in himself, a God sees all, knows all; yet nothing touches him. He can learn nothing from another such, while his study is mankind. So true friendship is their prize; Miss Aitken could not guess their detachment; she thought them human.

108

THE VITRIOL-THROWER

Maybe this flattered the poor Gods. In their weak hours they accept devotion gladly. Miss Aitken stood, white to the lips; her terror shining about her visibly. "That house is fatal, Clement," she moaned. "Go anywhere but there!" Patient and smiling, Clement heard her out. Half was he fain to put her off with a lie—some folly about God in heaven.

Then truth urged him to sing the song he had made of Mirabelle—

> "The world for a whore!
>   The sky for a harlot!
> All life—at your door—
>   For a Woman of Scarlet!
> A bitter exchange?
>   A bad bargain to strike? It
> May seem to you strange—
>   The fact is—I like it!
>
> You offer me gold,
>   Place, power, and pleasure
> To have and to hold—
>   Inexhaustible treasure!
> I'll give it and more
>   In this planet of boredom
> For a girl that's a whore
>   And is proud of her whoredom."

He reflected that such truth might seem to her but a sneer. So in the end he pressed her hand, thanked her, bade her be of good cheer, passed in.

III

Like a frail ghost, poor worn-out Sylvie glided from the graveyard, and confronted Clement Seton.

Three months had passed since his first visit to Mirabelle

109

the wonderful and beautiful, and still daily he strolled down the boulevard to his destiny. Thin and pale are you growing, my fine fool? Is it the air of Paris that robs you of your blood? We know better. Are you quite besotted? Or would you rather die thus than live otherwise?

This we cannot think; he cannot be absorbed body and soul in the contemplation of Mirabelle's perfections; for when poor worn-out Sylvie, with her harsh cough and hectic cheek, addresses him, he hears.

She took him to a corner of the graveyard, eagerly, with her worn face all fire, ever looking back. For he followed sedately. Clement would run nor to nor fro.

She paused by a low grave. "Here," she said, "lies Sergius, whom I loved—ah God! She took him from me; she threw him away, and laughed when he pistolled himself at her doorstep. You are her lover, monsieur. She will serve you so. I swear it. She lives for nothing else. God! God! to have these fingers but one moment at her throat."

She burst into a passion of weeping anger.

Seton lit a pipe. This Mirabelle! he mused. She leads me to Pisgah, he thought, she feeds me with milk and honey from the Promised Land. But to enter in and to possess it? No. She knows possession is but the prelude to the Captivity, the Exile to great Babylon. But who am I, to waste the months? I have said: Easy to write the curtain-raiser, but few who can pen five pungent acts. Yet, why should I wait? Why not make drama myself? Tragedy, no! for I am God, and must laugh at everything. Well! Well!

"I will kill her, kill her," sobbed the girl, kissing the cross upon the tomb.

THE VITRIOL-THROWER

Seton smiled, bent down caressingly, and whispered in her ear. Then swiftly turning he bent no undecided step towards the Gardens of his Armida.

*   *   *   *   *   *   *

Trembling in each other's arms with the violence of their repressed passion, Clement and Mirabelle still lay. Now he put forth all his force ; always she easily eluded it.

"For your sake, O goddess!" he exclaimed. "You are not utterly high, because you have not touched humanity. I sacrifice the splendour of our passion to initiate you."

"Not you then, but another!" she laughed wildly. "You are the only one that can play the Game ; I will not use you up."

He looked at her doubtfully ; then he knew she lied. Hers was a real prudery.

"Galilean!" he cried, "thou hast conquered!"

But so shocking was the irony of his voice that for a moment she feared him.

Then, rising up, they talked of many indifferent things ; yet, being gods, all language was hieroglyphic to their intimacy ; so that she marked a change.

"Am I adream?" she said ; "did not I win the bout?"

"At the odds," he said.

And again a chill passed over her.

Some premonition of things utterly forlorn?

Some intimate fear of the soul, struck bare and cold in the presence of its God?

"Tire yourself carefully to-night," wooed Clement in his velvet voice.

She thought of Jezebel, and a third time she shuddered.

Nevertheless, right comely was she, and golden in sheen of gossamer silk.

In the Boulevard Edgar Quinet the wear is not silk, O Mirabelle the beautiful! Rather a shroud. The desolate trees of the boulevard do not rustle like silk; rather do they whisper like murderers in league. The stones of the boulevard do not rustle like silk; they clatter foolishly. Is it not as the tears of your false passion on the adamantine hearts of men?

Mystic and doubtful, from behind a tree leaps out a ghost. With one hoarse word, poor worn-out Sylvie flings her vitriol, and speeds laughing down the boulevard.

Full in the face it splashed her; the great curse rose to a shriek and sank to a moan.

Clement Seton carried her back to the studio.

IV

Jolly fat old Miss Aitken! What a treasure you are in a world of sorrow!

Mirabelle's sins, which were many, were forgiven; especially as she could sin no more, thought she.

So she and Clement nursed her back to life; the face no more a face. One blind scar, more fearful to look upon than death. Her hands had escaped; one could judge by her hands what her beauty must have been.

But we are interested in her soul. In her weakness she grew human; and Clement, loving her through the flesh, loved her yet more. Why did he make her his mistress? You shall judge. But why did she comply? Who shall judge that? Judge not too easily; I myself, who am the great God who made these, dare not say.

So in the closest intimacy for more than a year they lived; and good-natured Miss Aitken like a mother to them.

Now was a new life stirred in Mirabelle; when Seton heard it, he called Miss Aitken aside privily, and said to her: "Dear friend, you may guess what she and I have always known: Love at its climax must decay thence. Such is the common lot; nothing escapes. I have given Mirabelle a child; let her seek there for new worlds to conquer. For me, I have studied her enough. Sylvie is dying; her consumption draws her to a close. I shall go live with her, and feast upon her end.

"She loves me, since I helped her vengeance; and hates me, since I have lifted her victim to such heights of joy. You never guessed? Yes, Sylvie loved Sergius, whom Mirabelle stole from her. 'Twas I that bade her throw the acid. Anon."

And he went whistling off. But to Miss Aitken, whose excellent memory broke this atrocious speech to Mirabelle, replied that expressionless mask of horror: "I knew it. I went to the death of myself that night; I went willingly, wittingly. It was Ananke and the Moirai. Moreover, I have had much joy of Clement; I leap with joy, breeding this child to him.

"Let him go to Sylvie: it is a woman's part to see her husband go away on strange errands. Was not Juno foolish, with her gadfly?"

In fact, when Sylvie died, Clement came back to her, brotherly. He had chosen the right moment to break off the

tie; Socrates suicide is finer than Socrates turned dotard.
So they remained fast friends.

The child was twelve years old last week. In him we see
the seeds of miraculous thoughts, things to transcend all
limitations mortal and immortal, common to man.

The Overman is surely come; in the second generation is
he established.

THE FAIRY FIDDLER

AWAY in the misty moorland glen
Where the Elf-Folk dance with the Wee Brown Men,
And the rowan-berry burns haughtily
As she tells of the wind's inconstancy—
'Tis there I am bound by the far faint rune
Of the Fairy Fiddler's silver shoon !

Where the harebell waves from the tufted grass,
There never the foot of a man may pass ;
For the painted fireflies glance and gleam
Like the golden thoughts in a goblin's dream,
And the ghostly coppice of oak and pine
Holds a legion of imps from the Moonbeam Mine.

When I lay me down in their wondrous car
I travel so quickly from star to star,
That the Earth and the Moon are as glowworm lights
That flash o'er the field of the blurred blue heights :
For it's there I am bound by the far faint rune
Of the Fairy Fiddler's silver shoon !

ETHEL ARCHER.

AN EVOCATION OF BARTZABEL
THE SPIRIT OF MARS

AN EVOCATION OF BARTZABEL
THE SPIRIT OF MARS

THE FORMULÆ OF THE MAGICK
OF LIGHT, let them be puissant in the
EVOCATION
of the
SPIRIT

ברצבאל

THE Ceremony consists of Five Parts :

1. The Banishings and Consecrations.
2. The Special Preparation of the Material Basis.
3. The Particular Invocations of the Forces of Mars.
4. The Dealings with Bartzabel, that mighty Spirit.
5. The Closing.

Gloria Deo Altissimo

Ra Hoor Khuit

in nomine Abrahadabra et in hoc signo

    The Circle has an inscribed Pentagon, and a Tau within that. Without are 5 pentagrams with 5 ruby lamps. There is an Altar with the Square of Mars and the Seal of Mars. The triangle has the names Primeumaton, Anaphaxeton,

Anapheneton and Mi-ca-el within. Also the Sigil of Bartzabel, and his name. About the Circle is the name ALHIM.

The Chief Magus wears the robe of a Major Adept, and the Uraeus crown and nemmes. He bears the Lamen of the Hiereus and the 1st Talisman of Mars. He bears as weapons the Spear and Sword, also the Bell.

The Assistant Magus wears the Robe of a Probationer and a nemmes of white and gold. He attends to the suffumigations of Art. He bears the 3rd Talisman of Mars (from the Key of Solomon), and the consecrated Torch. The Magus Adjuvant is robed as his brother, but wears the 5th Talisman of Mars. He attends to the Lustrations of Art. He bears the Book and Pen.

Upon the Altar is the Image of Ra Hoor Khuit, Isis is the East his Mother, Khem is the West facing him. In the South is the Censer, in the North the Cup.

The Material Basis is masked, and robed in red.

On the Altar are also the rope, the burin, the oil, and the Lamen of Mars for the Material Basis.

The Lamps are all alight.

PART I

C. M. *At altar, kneeling in humility.*

2 M. *With sword of C. M.*

3 M. *In other chamber with M. B.*

C.M. ⟩

2 M. Performs Banishing Rituals of Pentagram and Hexa-

gram around whole room, and replaces Sword on Altar.

3 M. Washes M. B. with pure water, saying :

Asperge${\{{eam \atop eum}\}}$Domine hyssopo et mundabitur ;

lavabis${\{{eam \atop eum}\}}$et super nivem dealbabitur.

He masks${\{{her \atop him}\}}$with the mask and robe of Mars, saying :

By the figurative mystery of these holy vestures of concealment, doth the Lord cloak thee in the Shroud of Mystery in the strength of the Most High ANCOR AMACOR AMIDES THEODONIAS ANITOR that our desired end may be effected through thy strength, Adonai, unto whom be the Glory in Saecula saeculorum A M E N.

He leads ${\{{her \atop him}\}}$to${\{{her \atop his}\}}$place in the Triangle.

The Chief Magus now rises from his knees, and takes the Spear from the Altar.

C.M. Hail unto Thee, Ra Hoor Khuit, who art the Lord of the Aeon !

Be this consecrated Spear

A thing of cheer, a thing of fear !

Cheer to me who wield it !—

My heart, its vigour shield it !

Fear to them who face it—

Their force, let fear disgrace it !

Be a ray from the Most High,
A glance of His unsleeping eye!
Arm me, arm me, in the fray
That shall be fought this dreadful day!

> *He hands Spear to 2nd Magus to hold.*
> *The Chief Magus takes the Sword.*

C.M. Hail unto Thee, Ra Hoor Khuit, who art the Lord of
the Aeon!

Be this consecrated Sword
Not abhorred before the Lord!
A guard of Steel, a tongue of flame
Writing in adamant His Name!
Puissant against the Hosts of Evil!
A mighty fence against the Devil!
A snake of lightning to destroy
Them that work Mischief and Annoy!
Arm me, arm me, in the fray
That shall be fought this dreadful day!

> *He hands Sword to 3rd Magus to hold.*
> *The Chief Magus raises his hands above the*
> *Altar.*

C.M. Hail unto Thee, Ra Hoor Khuit, who art the Lord of
the Aeon!

Be this consecrated Altar
A sign of sure stability!
Will and Courage never falter,
Thought dissolve in Deity!
Let thy smile divinely curving,
Isis, bless our dark device!

AN EVOCATION OF BARTZABEL

Holy Hawk, our deed unswerving
   Be thy favoured sacrifice !
Holy Khem, our vigour nerving,
   We have paid the priestly price.
Hail, Ra Hoor, thy ray forth-rolling
   Consecrate the instruments,
Thine Almighty power controlling
   To the Event the day's events !
Arm me, arm me, in the fray
   That shall be fought this dreadful day !

C.M.   *Takes Spear from 2nd M. and gives him the Censer and Torch ; Sword from 3rd M. and gives him the Cup, Book and Pen.*

C.M.   *Goes to apex of triangle. The others support him at the base. He takes the cord from the altar.*

C.M. {Frater/Soror} N !   As thou art blindfolded save for **that** light and sight which I can give thee, so do I now **bind** thee, so that thou mayst be for a space subject to my will and mine alone. (*Ties hands and feet. Takes Spear from altar.*) And since thou art without the circle in the place of the triangle, with this Spear do I invoke upon thee the protection of Ra Hoor Khuit, so that no force either of Heaven or of Earth, or from under the earth, may act upon thee, save only **that** force that I shall invoke within thee.

Bahlasti ! Ompehda !

So then, I being armed and exalted to the **Power** of the Most High, place upon thy head this drop of

123

consecrated oil, so that the ray of Godhead may illumine thee.

And I place this holy kiss upon thy neck, so that thy mind may be favourable unto us, open to our words, sensible of the power of our conjurations.

And with this burin do I draw from thy breast five drops of blood, so that thy body may be the Temple of Mars.

Wherefore also I command thee to repeat after me:

I submit myself to thee and to this operation; I invoke the Powers of Mars to manifest within me. *(done)*

(C. M. places about $\begin{Bmatrix} his \\ her \end{Bmatrix}$ *neck the Lamen of Mars.)*

Magi return to circle, face east.

C.M. Now, Brethren, since we are about to engage in a Work of so great danger, it is fitting that we make unto ourselves a fortress of defence in the name of the Most High, Elohim. Frater Adjuvant Magus, I command thee to purify the place with water.

(3rd M. sprinkles thrice around circle walking widdershins.)

C. M. Thus, therefore, first the Priest who governeth the works of Fire, must sprinkle with the waters of the loud-resounding sea.

Frater Assistant Magus, I command thee to consecrate the place with Fire.

(2nd M. censes the circle thrice around, walking widdershins.)

C. M. So when all the phantoms are vanished, and

124

through the Universe darts and flashes that holy
and formless Fire—Hear Thou the Voice of Fire!
    (*C. M. takes Sword.*)

The Lord is my fortress and my deliverer ; my God in
whom I will trust.

I will walk upon the lion and adder ; the young lion
and the scorpion will I tread under my feet.

Because he hath set his Love upon me, therefore will I
deliver him : I will set him on high, because he hath
known My Name.
    (*C. M. circumambulates thrice widdershins with
      sword.*)

Hail unto Thee, Ra Hoor Khuit, who art the Lord of
the Aeon !

    Be this consecrated Tower
    A place of power this fearful hour !
    May the Names of God that gird us
    Be our sign that he hath heard us !
    By the five unsleeping Stars
    Ward us from the wrath of Mars !
    By the rood of God erect
    Be He perfect to protect !
    Arm me, arm me, in the fray
    That shall be fought this dreadful day !
    (*He now conjures the Dog of Evil.*)

Arise, Dog of Evil, that I may instruct thee in thy
present duties.

In the name of Horus, I say unto thee, Arise.

Thou art imprisoned.

Confess thou that it is so.

THE EQUINOX

I have done this in the name and in the might of Horus.

Except thou set thy face in my defence, thou art blind, and dumb, and paralysed: but thou shalt hear the curses of thy Creator, and thou shalt feel the torments of my avenging wrath.

Therefore be thou obedient unto me, as a guard against them that hate me.

Let thy jaws be terrible as the storm-parted sky.

Let thy face be as a whirlwind of wrath and fury against the enemy.

Arise, I say, and aid and guard me in this Work of Art.

O thou! whose head is of coal-black fire!

Thou, whose eyes are as columns of smoke and flame!

Thou, from whose nostrils goeth forth the breath of destruction!

Thou whose body is of iron and brass, bound with exceeding strength: girt with the power of awful blind avenging force—under my control, and mine alone!

Thou, whose claws are as shafts of whirling steel to rip the very bowels of my adversaries.

Thee, thee, I summon to mine aid!

In the name of Horus: rise: move: appear:

And aid and guard me in this Work of Art!

Rise, Dog of Evil, to guard the Abyss of Height!

Rise, I say, to guard the Four Quarters: the Abyss of the North; the Abyss of the South; the Abyss of the East; the Abyss of the West.

Rise, I say, to guard the Abyss of the Great Deep.

Horus it is that hath given this commandment.

126

AN EVOCATION OF BARTZABEL

Be thou terrible against all them that hate me !

Be thou mighty to defend me from the Evil Ones !

At the confines of Matter : at the Threshold of the Invisible : be thou my Watcher and my Guardian ! Before the face of the Dwellers of the Abodes of Night !

As a flaming sword turning every way to keep the gates of my Universe : let thy teeth flash forth !

Nothing shall stop thee while thou settest thyself in my defence.

In the name of Horus : Rise, Move, and Appear : Be thou obedient unto me : for I am the Master of the Forces of Matter : the Servant of the Same thy God is my Name : true Worshipper of the Highest.

(Much incense is now burnt, and there is a pause.)

THE INVOCATIONS

(C. M. first performs the Invoking Ritual of Mars.)

(The Adepts stand at the points of the Tau.)

Even as of old there came three Magi from the ends of the earth to adore the Fivefold Star, so come we, O Lord, armed for the holy work of an Evocation of Bartzabel the spirit of Mars, that is obedient unto the Intelligence Graphiel, chosen from the Seraphim who follow Kamael the Great Archangel that serveth God under his name of Elohim Gibor, a spark from Thine intolerable light,

Ra Hoor Khuit !

Therefore hear Thou the Oath of the Obligation that we assume before Thee.

THE EQUINOX

(The Chief Magus points the Sword downward upon the apex of the Triangle of R. H. K. and the other Magi place their hands upon the hilt.)

We, Perdurabo, a Neophyte of the A∴A∴, All for Knowledge, a Probationer of A∴A∴, and Αγαθα, a Probationer of A∴A∴, swear unto Thee, O Lord God, by Thine own almighty power, by Thy force and fire, by Thy glittering Hawk's eye and Thy mighty sweeping wings: that we all here in this place and now at this time do utterly devote ourselves, mind, body, and estate, at all times and in all places soever to the establishment of Thy holy Kingdom.

And if we fail herein, may we be burnt and consumed by the Red Eye of Mars!

(Magi return to stations.)

And this our purpose is fivefold:

Firstly, that the Kingdom of Ra Hoor Khuit may be established in the Aeon.

Secondly, that we may succeed in that particular design of which it is not lawful to speak, even before Thee.

Thirdly, that we may have power to help the weak.

Fourthly, that we may be filled with the Courage and Energy of Mars for the Prosecution of the Great Work.

And, lastly, that we may obtain the service of Bartzabel that he may be obedient unto us thy servants, that between him and us there may be peace, and that he may always be ready to come whensoever he is invoked and called forth.

AN EVOCATION OF BARTZABEL

Now because in such a work it is not possible for us
to do anything at all of ourselves, we have humble
recourse unto Thine Almighty power, beseeching
upon our knees Thy favour and Thine aid.
    (*The Magi kneel at three sides of altar, all
    clasping spears in the proper manner.*)
I adore Thee in the Song :

> I am the Lord of Thebes, and I
>   The inspired forth-speaker of Mentu ;
> For me unveils the veilèd sky,
>   The self-slain Ankh-f-n-Khonsu
> Whose words are truth.   I invoke, I greet
> Thy presence, O Ra Hoor Khuit !
>
> Unity uttermost shewed !
>   I adore the might of Thy breath,
> Supreme and terrible God
>   Who makest the Gods and death
> To tremble before Thee :
> I, I adore Thee !
>
> Appear on the throne of Ra !
>   Open the ways of the Khu !
> Lighten the ways of the Ka !
>   The ways of the Khabs run through
> To stir me or still me !
> Aum ! let it fill me !

All say, repeatedly :
> A Ka dua
> Tuf ur biu

THE EQUINOX

Bi a'a chefu
Dudu ner af an nuteru!

*When the Chief Magus is satisfied with the
Descent of the God, let all rise and let C. M.
say:*

So that Thy light is in me; and its red flame is as a
sword in my hand to push thy order. There is a
secret door that I shall make to establish thy way
in all the quarters . . . as it is said:

The light is mine; its rays consume
    Me: I have made a secret door
Into the house of Ra and Tum,
    Of Khephra, and of Ahathoor.
I am thy Theban, O Mentu,
The prophet Ankh-f-n-Khonsu!

By Bes-na-Maut my breast I beat;
    By wise Ta-Nech I weave my spell.
Show thy star-splendour, O Nuith!
    Bid me within thine House to dwell,
O winged snake of light, Hadith!
Abide with me, Ra Hoor Khuit!

(Magus faces △, and others support him.)
Hail! Hail! Hail! Hail! Hail!
Send forth a spark of thine illimitable light and force,
    we beseech Thee, that it may appear in the Heaven
    of Mars as the God Elohim Gibor.
O winged glory of gold! O plumes of justice and
    stern brows of majesty! O warrior armed with

130

spear and shield! O virgin strength and splendour as of spring! That ridest in thy Chariot of Iron above the Storm upon the Sea! Who shootest forth the Arrows of the Moon! Who wieldest the Four Magick Weapons! Who art the Master of the Pentagram and of the blazing fury of the Sun!

Come unto me, thou great God Elohim Gibor, and send thy Angel Kamael, even Kamael the mighty, the Leader of thine Armies the fiery Serpents, the Seraphim, that he may answer my behests.

O purple flame that is like unto the whirling wheel of Life! O strong shoulders and virginal breasts and dancing limbs!

Kamael! Kamael! Kamael! Kamael!

I see thee before me, O thou great Archangel! Art thou not the Leader of the armies of the Lord? Of the grey snakes upon whose heads are triple crowns of spiritual light, and whose tongues are triply forked with judgment? Whose bodies are like the Sun in his strength, whose scales are of the adamant of Vulcan, who are slim and splendid and virginal as they rush flaming over the lashed sea?

Come unto me, Kamael, thou archangel almighty, and send to me Graphiel that great intelligence of thine, that he may answer my behest.

O moon, that sailest on the shoulders of the Sun! Whose warrior body is like white-hot steel! Whose virgin limbs and golden wings move like ripe corn at the caress of the thunderstorm!

O thou that wieldest the Sword and Balances of
    Power!

    Graphiel!   Graphiel!   Graphiel!

    Graphiel!   Graphiel!   Graphiel!

Come unto us, thou bright intelligence of Mars, and
    answer my behest.   In the name of Kamael thy
    Lord, I say: Compel the spirit Bartzabel that is
    under thy dominion to manifest within this triangle
    of Art, within the Ruach of the material basis that
    is consecrated to this work, within this pure and
    beautiful human form that is prepared for his
    habitation.

And now I see thee, O thou dull deceitful head, that I
    shall fill with wit and truth; thou proud heart that
    I shall humble and make pure; thou cold body that
    I shall fashion into a living flame of amethyst.
    Thou sexless being of whom I shall make the
    perfect child of Hermes and Aphrodite that is God;
    thou dull ox that I shall turn into the Bull of Earth;
    thou house of idleness wherein I shall set up the
    Throne of Justice.

    Bartzabel!   Bartzabel!   Bartzabel!

    Bartzabel!   Bartzabel!   Bartzabel!

Come forth, and manifest beyond the bars!
Forth from the palace of seraphic stars!
Come, O thou Bartzabel, the sprite of Mars!

Come: I unbind thee from the chains of Hell,
Come: I enclose thee in the invisible
To be my slave, thou spirit Bartzabel!

AN EVOCATION OF BARTZABEL

By the spear, the sword, the spell,
Come unto me, Bartzabel!
By the word that openeth Hell!
Come unto me, Bartzabel!

By the power o' th' panther's pell,
Come unto me, Bartzabel!
By the circling citadel,
Come unto me, Bartzabel!
By this mind of miracle
Come unto me, Bartzabel!

By Ra Hoor Khuit, by Elohim Gibor,
By Kamael and the Seraphim ; by Hoor,
Khem, and Mentu, and all the Gods of War,
Ares and Mars and Hachiman and Thor,
 And by thy master, Graphiel,
 Come unto me, Bartzabel!

And if he come not, let the Chief Magus and his assistants
humble themselves mightily, and repeat these holy invocations,
even unto thrice.

And if still he be obdurate and disobedient unto the
Words of Power, the Chief Magus shall assume the dignity
of Khem, and conjure him and curse him as his own ingenium
shall direct. Yet, if the rites have been duly performed, he
will assuredly have manifested before this.

And these will probably be the tokens of the manifestation:
 A ruddy light will play about the form of the Material
  Basis ; or even a dark lustre beetle-brown or black.
 And the Face thereof will be suffused with blood,

133

and the Heart beat violently, and its words will be swift and thick and violent. The voice thereof must be entirely changed; it may grow deep and hoarse, or at least strained and jerky, and it may be that it will suffer the torment of burning.

On the appearance of the Spirit much incense is thrown upon the Censer.

THE CHARGE

Hail, Bartzabel, and welcome, thou mighty spirit of Madim!

Welcome unto us art thou who comest in the name of Graphiel and of Kamael and of Elohim Gibor, and of Ra Hoor Khuit the Lord of the Aeon.

I charge thee to answer and obey.

1. How shall the Kingdom of the Aeon be established?

2. Will success attend that particular design of which it is not lawful to speak?

3. We shall obtain power to aid the weak; in what manner? Give us a sign.

4. Give us a sign of the Courage and Energy of Mars that floweth and shall ever flow through us by virtue of this ceremony.

5. Lastly, O thou Spirit Bartzabel, lay thine hands upon this sword, whose point I then place upon thine head, and swear faith and obedience unto me by Ra Hoor Khuit, the Lord of the Aeon, saying after me:

AN EVOCATION OF BARTZABEL

I, Bartzabel, the Spirit of Mars, do swear by the glory of Him that is Lord of the Aeon, and by the Might of Elohim Gibor, and by the Fear of Kamael and the Hosts of Fiery Serpents, and by Graphiel whose hand is heavy upon me—before which names I tremble every day—that I will punctually fulfil this present charge, not perverting the sense thereof, but obedient to the inmost thought of the Chief Magus ; that I will be ever the willing servant of thee and thy companions, a spirit of Truth in Force and Fire ; that in departing I will do no hurt to any person or thing, and in particular that the Material Basis shall not suffer through this ceremony, but shall be purified and fortified thereby ; that I will be at peace with thee and seek never to injure thee, but to defend thee against all thine enemies, and to work eternally for thy welfare ; finally, that I will be ready to come unto thee to serve thee whensoever I am invoked and called forth, whether by a word, or a will, or by this great and potent conjuration of Magick Art.

A M E N.

THE BENEDICTION

Let Ra Hoor Khuit bless thee !
Let His light shine perpetually in thy darkness !
Let His force eternally brace up thy weakness !
Let His blessing be upon thee for ever and for ever !
Yea, verily and Amen, let His blessing be upon thee for ever and ever !

THE LICENCE TO DEPART

Now, O thou Spirit Bartzabel, since thou didst come at my behest and swear faith and fealty unto me by the Lord of the Aeon,

> I license thee to depart in peace with the blessing of the Lord until such time as I have need of thee.

THE CLOSING

Let the Chief Magus perform the Banishing Ritual of Mars, give great Thanks unto the Lord of the Aeon, and perform the Lesser Rituals of the Pentagram and Hexagram.

THE TESTAMENT OF
MAGDALEN BLAIR

To
My Mother

THE TESTAMENT OF
MAGDALEN BLAIR

PART I

I

In my third term at Newnham I was already Professor Blair's favourite pupil. Later, he wasted a great deal of time praising my slight figure and my piquant face, with its big round grey eyes and their long black lashes; but the first attraction was my singular gift. Few men, and, I believe, no other women, could approach me in one of the most priceless qualifications for scientific study, the faculty of apprehending minute differences. My memory was poor, extraordinarily so; I had the utmost trouble to enter Cambridge at all. But I could adjust a micrometer better than either students or professor, and read a vernier with an accuracy to which none of them could even aspire. To this I added a faculty of sub-conscious calculation which was really uncanny. If I were engaged in keeping a solution between (say) 70° and 80° I had no need to watch the thermometer. Automatically I became aware that the mercury was close to the limit, and would go over from my other work and adjust it without a thought.

More remarkable still, if any object were placed on my

bench without my knowledge and then removed, I could, if asked within a few minutes, describe the object roughly, especially distinguishing the shape of its base and the degree of its opacity to heat and light. From these data I could make a pretty good guess at what the object was.

This faculty of mine was repeatedly tested, and always with success. Extreme sensitiveness to minute degrees of heat was its obvious cause.

I was also a singularly good thought-reader, even at this time. The other girls feared me absolutely. They need not have done so; I had neither ambition nor energy to make use of any of my powers. Even now, when I bring to mankind this message of a doom so appalling that at the age of twenty-four I am a shrivelled, blasted, withered wreck, I am supremely weary, supremely indifferent.

I have the heart of a child and the consciousness of Satan, the lethargy of I know not what disease; and yet, thank—oh! there can be no God!—the resolution to warn mankind to follow my example, and then to explode a dynamite cartridge in my mouth.

II

In my third year at Newnham I spent four hours of every day at Professor Blair's house. All other work was neglected, gone through mechanically, if at all. This came about gradually, as the result of an accident.

The chemical laboratory has two rooms, one small and capable of being darkened. On this occasion (the May term of my second year) this room was in use. It was the first week of June, and extremely fine. The door was shut. Within was a girl, alone, experimenting with the galvanometer.

I was absorbed in my own work. Quite without warning I looked up. "Quick !" said I, "Gladys is going to faint." Every one in the room stared at me. I took a dozen steps towards the door, when the fall of a heavy body sent the laboratory into hysterics.

It was only the heat and confined atmosphere, and Gladys should not have come to work that day at all, but she was easily revived, and then the demonstrator acquiesced in the anarchy that followed. "How did she know?" was the universal query; for that I knew was evident. Ada Brown (*Athanasia contra mundum*) pooh-poohed the whole affair; Margaret Letchmere thought I must have heard something, perhaps a cry inaudible to the others, owing to their occupied attention ; Doris Leslie spoke of second sight, and Amy Gore of "sympathy." All the theories, taken together, went round the clock of conjecture. Professor Blair came in at the most excited part of the discussion, calmed the room in two minutes, elicited the facts in five, and took me off to dine with him. " I believe it's this human thermopile affair of yours," he said. " Do you mind if we try a few parlour tricks after dinner?" His aunt, who kept house for him, protested in vain, and was appointed Grand Superintendent in Ordinary of my five senses.

My hearing was first tested, and found normal, or there-abouts. I was then blindfolded, and the aunt (by excess of precaution) stationed between me and the Professor. I found that I could describe even small movements that he made, so long as he was between me and the western window, not at all when he moved round to the other quarters. This is in conformity with the "Thermopile" theory; it was contradicted completely on other occasions. The results (in short) were very remarkable and very puzzling; we wasted two precious hours in futile theorizing. In the event the aunt (cowed by a formidable frown) invited me to spend the Long Vacation in Cornwall.

During these months the Professor and I assiduously worked to discover exactly the nature and limit of my powers. The result, in a sense, was *nil.*

For one thing, these powers kept on "breaking out in a new place." I seemed to do all I did by perception of minute differences; but then it seemed as if I had all sorts of different apparatus. "One down, t'other come on," said Professor Blair.

Those who have never made scientific experiments cannot conceive how numerous and subtle are the sources of error, even in the simplest matters. In so obscure and novel a field of research no result is trustworthy until it has been verified a thousand times. In our field we discovered no constants, all variables.

Although we had hundreds of facts any one of which seemed capable of overthrowing all accepted theories of the means of communication between mind and mind, we had nothing, absolutely nothing, which we could use as the basis of a new theory.

It is naturally impossible to give even an outline of the course of our research. Twenty-eight closely written note-books referring to this first period are at the disposal of my executors.

THE TESTAMENT OF MAGDALEN BLAIR

III

In the middle of the day, in my third year, my father was dangerously ill. I bicycled over to Peterborough at once, never thinking of my work. (My father is a canon of Peterborough Cathedral.) On the third day I received a telegram from Professor Blair, "Will you be my wife?" I had never realized myself as a woman, or him as a man, till that moment, and in that moment I knew that I loved him and had always loved him. It was a case of what one might call "Love at first absence." My father recovered rapidly; I returned to Cambridge; we were married during the May week, and went immediately to Switzerland. I beg to be spared any recital of so sacred a period of my life: but I must record one fact.

We were sitting in a garden by Lago Maggiore after a delightful tramp from Chamounix over the Col du Géant to Courmayeur, and thence to Aosta, and so by degrees to Pallanza. Arthur rose, apparently struck by some idea, and began to walk up and down the terrace. *I was quite suddenly impelled to turn my head to assure myself of his presence.*

This may seem nothing to you who read, unless you have true imagination. But think of yourself talking to a friend in full light, and suddenly leaning forward to touch him. "Arthur!" I cried, "Arthur!"

The distress in my tone brought him running to my side. "What is it, Magdalen?" he cried, anxiety in every word.

I closed my eyes. "Make gestures!" said I. (He was directly between me and the sun.)

He obeyed, wondering.

"You are——you are "——I stammered——"no! I don't know what you are doing. I am blind!"

He sawed his arm up and down. Useless; I had become absolutely insensitive. We repeated a dozen experiments that night. All failed.

We concealed our disappointment, and it did not cloud our love. The sympathy between us grew even subtler and stronger, but only as it grows between all men and women who love with their whole hearts, and love unselfishly.

IV

We returned to Cambridge in October, and Arthur threw himself vigorously into the new year's work. Then I fell ill, and the hope we had indulged was disappointed. Worse, the course of the illness revealed a condition which demanded the most complete series of operations which a woman can endure. Not only the past hope, but all future hope, was annihilated.

It was during my convalescence that the most remarkable incident of my life took place.

I was in great pain one afternoon, and wished to see the doctor. The nurse went to the study to telephone for him.

"Nurse!" I said, as she returned, "don't lie to me. He's not gone to Royston; he's got cancer, and is too upset to come."

"Whatever next?" said the nurse. "It's right he can't come, and I was going to tell you he had gone to Royston; but I never heard nothing about no cancer."

This was true; she had not been told. But the next morning we heard that my "intuition" was correct.

THE TESTAMENT OF MAGDALEN BLAIR

As soon as I was well enough, we began our experiments again. My powers had returned, and in triple force.

Arthur explained my "intuition" as follows: "The doctor (when you last saw him) did not know consciously that he had cancer; but subconsciously Nature gave warning. You read this subconsciously, and it sprang into your consciousness when you read on the nurse's face that he was ill."

This, farfetched as it may seem, at least avoids the shallow theories about "telepathy."

From this time my powers constantly increased. I could read my husband's thoughts from imperceptible movements of his face as easily as a trained deaf-mute can sometimes read the speech of a distant man from the movements of his lips.

Gradually as we worked, day by day, I found my grasp of detail ever fuller. It is not only that I could read emotions; I could tell whether he was thinking 3465822 or 3456822. In the year following my illness we made 436 experiments of this kind, each extending over several hours; in all 9363, with only 122 failures, and these all, without exception, partial.

The year following, our experiments were extended to a reading of his dreams. In this I proved equally successful. My practice was to leave the room before he woke, write down the dream that he had dreamt, and await him at the breakfast-table, where he would compare his record with mine.

Invariably they were identical, with this exception, that my record was always much fuller than his. He would nearly always, however, purport to remember the details supplied by me; but this detail has (I think) no real scientific value.

But what does it all matter, when I think of the horror impending?

V

That my only means of discovering Arthur's thought was by muscle-reading became more than doubtful during the third year of our marriage. We practised "telepathy" unashamed. We excluded the "muscle-reader" and the "super-auditor" and the "human thermopile" by elaborate precautions; yet still I was able to read every thought of his mind. On our holiday in North Wales at Easter one year we separated for a week, at the end of that week he to be on the leeward, I on the windward side of Tryfan, at an appointed hour, he there to open and read to himself a sealed packet given him by "some stranger met at Pen-y-Pass during the week." The experiment was entirely successful ; I reproduced every word of the document. If the "telepathy" is to be vitiated, it is on the theory that I had previously met the "stranger" and read from him what he would write in such circumstances! Surely direct communication of mind with mind is an easier theory !

Had I known in what all this was to culminate, I suppose I should have gone mad. Thrice fortunate that I can warn humanity of what awaits each one. The greatest benefactor of his race will be he who discovers an explosive indefinitely swifter and more devastating than dynamite. If I could only trust myself to prepare Chloride of Nitrogen in sufficient quantity. . . .

VI

Arthur became listless and indifferent. The perfection of love that had been our marriage failed without warning, and yet by imperceptible gradations.

My awakening to the fact was, however, altogether sudden. It was one summer evening; we were paddling on the Cam. One of Arthur's pupils, also in a Canadian canoe, challenged us to race. At Magdalen Bridge we were a length ahead—suddenly I heard my husband's thought. It was the most hideous and horrible laugh that it is possible to conceive. No devil could laugh so. I screamed, and dropped my paddle. Both the men thought me ill. I assured myself that it was not the laugh of some townee on the bridge, distorted by my over-sensitive organization. I said no more; Arthur looked grave. At night he asked abruptly after a long period of brooding, "Was that my thought?" I could only stammer that I did not know. Incidentally he complained of fatigue, and the listlessness, which before had seemed nothing to me, assumed a ghastly shape. There was something in him that was not he! The indifference had appeared transitory; I now became aware of it as constant and increasing. I was at this time twenty-three years old. You wonder that I write with such serious attitude of mind. I sometimes think that I have never had any thoughts of my own; that I have always been reading the thoughts of another, or perhaps of Nature. I seem only to have been a woman in those first few months of marriage.

VII

The six months following held for me nothing out of the ordinary, save that six or seven times I had dreams, vivid and terrible. Arthur had no share in these; yet I knew, I cannot say how, that they were his dreams and not mine; or rather that they were in his subconscious waking self, for one occurred in the afternoon, when he was out shooting, and not in the least asleep.

The last of them occurred towards the end of the October term. He was lecturing as usual, I was at home, lethargic after a too heavy breakfast following a wakeful night. I saw suddenly a picture of the lecture-room, enormously greater than in reality, so that it filled all space; and in the rostrum, bulging over it in all directions, was a vast, deadly pale devil with a face which was a blasphemy on Arthur's. The evil joy of it was indescribable. So wan and bloated, its lips so loose and bloodless; fold after fold of its belly flopping over the rostrum and pushing the students out of the hall, it leered unspeakably. Then dribbled from its mouth these words: " Ladies and gentlemen, the course is finished. You may go home." I cannot hope even to suggest the wickedness and filth of these simple expressions. Then, raising its voice to a grating scream, it yelled: " White of egg! White of egg! White of egg!" again and again for twenty minutes.

The effect on me was shocking. It was as if I had a vision of Hell.

Arthur found me in a very hysterical condition, but soon soothed me. " Do you know," he said at dinner, " I believe I have got a devilish bad chill?"

It was the first time I had known him to complain of his health. In six years he had not had as much as a headache.

I told him my "dream" when we were in bed, and he seemed unusually grave, as if he understood where I had failed in its interpretation. In the morning he was feverish; I made him stay in bed and sent for the doctor. The same afternoon I learnt that Arthur was seriously ill, had been ill, indeed, for months. The doctor called it Bright's disease.

VIII

I said "the last of the dreams." For the next year we travelled, and tried various treatments. My powers remained excellent, but I received none of the subconscious horrors. With few fluctuations, he grew steadily worse; daily he became more listless, more indifferent, more depressed. Our experiments were necessarily curtailed. Only one problem exercised him, the problem of his personality. He began to wonder *who he was*. I do not mean that he suffered from delusions. I mean that the problem of the true Ego took hold of his imagination. One perfect summer night at Contrexéville he was feeling much better; the symptoms had (temporarily) disappeared almost entirely under the treatment of a very skilful doctor at that Spa, a Dr. Barbézieux, a most kind and thoughtful man.

"I am going to try," said Arthur, "to penetrate myself. Am I an animal, and is the world without a purpose? Or am I a soul in a body? Or am I, one and indivisible in some incredible sense, a spark of the infinite light of God? I am going to think inwards: I shall possibly go into some form of trance, unintelligible to myself. You may be able to interpret it."

The experiment had lasted about half an hour when he sat up gasping with effort.

"I have seen nothing, heard nothing," I said. "Not one thought has passed from you to me."

But at that very moment what had been in his mind flashed into mine.

"It is a blind abyss," I told him, "and there hangs in it a vulture vaster than the whole starry system."

"Yes," he said, "that was it. But that was not all. I could not get beyond it. I shall try again."

He tried. Again I was cut off from his thought, although his face was twitching so that one might have said that any one might read his mind.

"I have been looking in the wrong place," said he suddenly, but very quietly and without moving. "The thing I want lies at the base of the spine."

This time I saw. In a blue heaven was coiled an infinite snake of gold and green, with four eyes of fire, black fire and red, that darted rays in every direction; held within its coils was a great multitude of laughing children. And even as I looked, all this was blotted out. Crawling rivers of blood spread over the heaven, of blood purulent with nameless forms —mangy dogs with their bowels dragging behind them; creatures half elephant, half beetle; things that were but a ghastly bloodshot eye, set about with leathery tentacles; women whose skins heaved and bubbled like boiling sulphur, giving off clouds that condensed into a thousand other shapes, more hideous than their mother; these were the least of the denizens of these hateful rivers. The most were things impossible to name or to describe.

I was brought back from the vision by the stertorous and strangling breath of Arthur, who had been seized with a convulsion.

From this he never really rallied. The dim sight grew

150

dimmer, the speech slower and thicker, the headaches more persistent and acute.

Torpor succeeded to his old splendid energy and activity; his days became continual lethargy ever deepening towards coma. Convulsions now and then alarmed me for his immediate danger.

Sometimes his breath came hard and hissing like a snake in anger; towards the end it assumed the Cheyne-Stokes type in bursts of ever-increasing duration and severity.

In all this, however, he was still himself; the horror that was and yet was not himself did not peer from behind the veil.

"So long as I am consciously myself," he said in one of his rare fits of brightness, "I can communicate to you what I am consciously thinking; as soon as this conscious ego is absorbed, you get the subconscious thought which I fear—oh how I fear!—is the greater and truer part of me. You have brought unguessed explanations from the world of sleep; you are the one woman in the world—perhaps there may never be another—who has such an opportunity to study the phenomena of death."

He charged me earnestly to suppress my grief, to concentrate wholly on the thoughts that passed through his mind when he could no longer express them, and also on those of his subconsciousness when coma inhibited consciousness.

It is this experiment that I now force myself to narrate. The prologue has been long; it has been necessary to put the facts before mankind in a simple way so that they may seize the opportunity of the proper kind of suicide. I beg my readers most earnestly not to doubt my statements: the notes of our experiments, left in my will to the greatest thinker now living, Professor von Bühle, will make clear the truth of my relation, and the great and terrible necessity of immediate, drastic, action.

PART II

I

THE stunning physical fact of my husband's illness was the immense prostration. So strong a body, as too often the convulsions gave proof; such inertia with it! He would lie all day like a log; then without warning or apparent cause the convulsions would begin. Arthur's steady scientific brain stood it well; it was only two days before his death that delirium began. I was not with him; worn out as I was, and yet utterly unable to sleep, the doctor had insisted on my taking a long motor drive. In the fresh air I slumbered. I awoke to hear an unfamiliar voice saying in my ear, "Now for the fun of the fair!" There was no one there. Quick on its heels followed my husband's voice as I had long since known and loved it, clear, strong, resonant, measured: "Get this down right; it is very important. I am passing into the power of the subconsciousness. I may not be able to speak to you again. But I am here; I am not to be touched by all that I may suffer; I can always think; you can always read my——" The voice broke off sharply to inquire, "But will it ever end?" as if some one had spoken to it. And then I heard the laugh. The laugh that I had heard by Magdalen Bridge was heavenly music beside that! The face of Calvin (even) as

152

he gloated over the burning of Servetus would have turned pitiful had he heard it, so perfectly did it express quintessence of damnation.

Now then my husband's thought seemed to have changed places with the other. It was below, within, withdrawn. I said to myself, " He is dead ! " Then came Arthur's thought, " I had better pretend to be mad. It will save her, perhaps ; and it will be a change. I shall pretend I have killed her with an axe. Damn it ! I hope she is not listening." I was now thoroughly awake, and told the driver to get home quickly. " I hope she is killed in the motor; I hope she is smashed into a million pieces. O God ! hear my one prayer ! let an Anarchist throw a bomb and smash Magdalen into a million pieces ! especially the brain ! and the brain first. O God ! my first and last prayer : smash Magdalen into a million pieces ! "

The horror of this thought was my conviction—then and now—that it represented perfect sanity and coherence of thought. For I dreaded utterly to think what such words might imply.

At the door of the sick-room I was met by the male nurse, who asked me not to enter. Uncontrollably, I asked, " Is he dead?" and though Arthur lay absolutely senseless on the bed I read the answering thought "Dead!" silently pronounced in such tones of mockery, horror, cynicism and despair as I never thought to hear. There was a something or somebody who suffered infinitely, and yet who gloated infinitely upon that very suffering. And that something was a veil between me and Arthur.

The hissing breath recommenced ; Arthur seemed to be

trying to express himself—the self I knew. He managed to articulate feebly, "Is that the police? Let me get out of the house! The police are coming for me. I killed Magdalen with an axe." The symptoms of delirium began to appear. "I killed Magdalen" he muttered a dozen times, then changing to "Magdalen with" again and again; the voice low, slow, thick, yet reiterated. Then suddenly, quite clear and loud, attempting to rise in the bed: "I smashed Magdalen into a million pieces with an axe." After a moment's pause: "a million is not very many now-a-days." From this—which I now see to have been the speech of a sane Arthur—he dropped again into delirium. "A million pieces," "a cool million," "a million million million million million million" and so on: then abruptly: "Fanny's dog's dead."

I cannot explain the last sentence to my readers; I may, however, remark that it meant everything to me. I burst into tears. At that moment I caught Arthur's thought, "You ought to be busy with the note-book, not crying." I resolutely dried my eyes, took courage, and began to write.

II

The doctor came in at this moment and begged me to go and rest. "You are only distressing yourself, Mrs. Blair," he said; "and needlessly, for he is absolutely unconscious and suffers nothing." A pause. "My God! why do you look at me like that?" he exclaimed, frightened out of his wits. I think my face had caught something of that devil's, something of that sneer, that loathing, that mire of contempt and stark despair.

THE TESTAMENT OF MAGDALEN BLAIR

I sank back into myself, ashamed already that mere knowledge—and such mean vile knowledge—should so puff one up with hideous pride. No wonder Satan fell! I began to understand all the old legends, and far more——

I told Doctor Kershaw that I was carrying out Arthur's last wishes. He raised no further opposition; but I saw him sign to the male nurse to keep an eye on me.

The sick man's finger beckoned us. He could not speak; he traced circles on the counterpane. The doctor (with characteristic intelligence) having counted the circles, nodded. and said: "Yes, it is nearly seven o'clock. Time for your medicine, eh?"

"No," I explained, "he means that he is in the seventh circle of Dante's Hell."

At that instant he entered on a period of noisy delirium. Wild and prolonged howls burst from his throat; he was being chewed unceasingly by "Dis"; each howl signalled the meeting of the monster's teeth. I explained this to the doctor. "No," said he, "he is perfectly unconscious."

"Well," said I, "he will howl about eighty times more."

Doctor Kershaw looked at me curiously, but began to count.

My calculation was correct.

He turned to me, "Are you a woman?"

"No," said I, "I am my husband's colleague."

"I think it is suggestion. You have hypnotized him?"

"Never: but I can read his thoughts."

"Yes, I remember now; I read a very remarkable paper in *Mind* two years ago."

"That was child's play. But let me go on with my work."

He gave some final instructions to the nurse, and went out.

The suffering of Arthur was at this time unspeakable. Chewed as he was into mere pulp that passed over the tongue of " Dis," each bleeding fragment kept its own identity and his. The papillæ of the tongue were serpents, and each one gnashed its poisoned teeth upon that fodder.

And yet, though the sensorium of Arthur was absolutely unimpaired, indeed hyperæsthetic, his consciousness of pain seemed to depend upon the opening of the mouth. As it closed in mastication, oblivion fell upon him like a thunderbolt. A merciful oblivion? Oh ! what a master stroke of cruelty ! Again and again he woke from nothing to a hell of agony, of pure ecstasy of agony, until he understood that this would continue for all his life ; the alternation was but systole and diastole, the throb of his envenomed pulse, the reflection in consciousness of his blood-beat. I became conscious of his intense longing for death to end the torture.

The blood circulated ever slower and more painfully ; I could feel him hoping for the end.

This dreadful rose-dawn suddenly greyed and sickened with doubt. Hope sank to its nadir ; fear rose like a dragon, with leaden wings. Suppose, thought he, that after all death does not end me !

I cannot express this conception. It is not that the heart sank, it had nowhither to sink ; it knew itself immortal, and immortal in a realm of unimagined pain and terror, unlighted by one glimpse of any other light than that pale glare of hate and of pestilence. This thought took shape in these words :

I AM THAT I AM.

THE TESTAMENT OF MAGDALEN BLAIR

One cannot say that the blasphemy added to the horror; rather it was the essence of the horror. It was the gnashing of the teeth of a damned soul.

III

The demon-shape, which I now clearly recognize as that which had figured in my last "dream" at Cambridge, seemed to gulp. At that instant a convulsion shook the dying man and a coughing eructation took the "demon." Instantly the whole theory dawned on me, that this "demon" was an imaginary personification of the disease. Now at once I understood demonology, from Bodin and Weirus to the moderns, without a flaw. But was it imaginary or was it real? Real enough to swallow up the "sane" thought!

At that instant the old Arthur reappeared. "I am not the monster! I am Arthur Blair, of Fettes and Trinity. I have passed through a paroxysm."

The sick man stirred feebly. A portion of his brain had shaken off the poison for the moment, and was working furiously against time.

"I am going to die.

"The consolation of death is Religion.

"There is no use for Religion in life.

"How many atheists have I not known sign the articles the sake of fellowships and livings! Religion in life is either an amusement and a soporific or a sham and a swindle.

"I was brought up a Presbyterian.

"How easily I drifted into the English Church!

" And now where is God ?

" Where is the Lamb of God ?

" Where is the Saviour ?

" Where is the Comforter ?

" Why was I not saved from that devil ?

" Is he going to eat me again ? To absorb me into him ?
O fate inconceivably hideous ! It is quite clear to me—I
hope you've got it down, Magdalen !—that the demon is made
of all those that have died of Bright's disease. There must be
different ones for each disease. I thought I once caught
sight of a coughing bog of bloody slime.

" Let me pray."

A frenzied appeal to the Creator followed. Sincere as it
was, it would read like irreverence in print.

And then there came the cold-drawn horror of stark
blasphemy against this God—who would not answer.

Followed the bleak black agony of the conviction—the
absolute certitude—" There is no God !" combined with a
wave of frenzied wrath against the people who had so glibly
assured him that there was, an almost maniac hope that
they would suffer more than he, if it were possible.

(Poor Arthur ! He had not yet brushed the bloom off
Suffering's grape ; he was to drink its fiercest distillation to
the dregs.)

" No ! " thought he, " perhaps I lack their ' faith.'

" Perhaps if I could really persuade myself of God and
Christ—— Perhaps if I could deceive myself, could make
believe——"

Such a thought is to surrender one's honesty, to abdicate
one's reason. It marked the final futile struggle of his will.

158

The demon caught and crunched him, and the noisy delirium began anew.

My flesh and blood rebelled. Taken with a deathly vomit, I rushed from the room, and resolutely, for a whole hour, diverted my sensorium from thought. I had always found that the slightest trace of tobacco smoke in a room greatly disturbed my power. On this occasion I puffed cigarette after cigarette with excellent effect. I knew nothing of what had been going on.

IV

Arthur, stung by the venomous chyle, was tossing in that vast arched belly, which resembled the dome of hell, churned in its bubbling slime. I felt that he was not only disintegrated mechanically, but chemically, that his being was loosened more and more into its parts, that these were being absorbed into new and hateful things, but that (worst of all) Arthur stood immune from all, behind it, unimpaired, memory and reason ever more acute as ever new and ghastlier experience informed them. It seemed to me as if some mystic state were super-added to the torment ; for while he was not, emphatically not, this tortured mass of consciousness, yet that was he. There are always at least two of us ! The one who feels and the one who knows are not radically one person. This double personality is enormously accentuated at death.

Another point was that the time-sense, which with men is usually so reliable—especially in my own case—was decidedly deranged, if not abrogated altogether.

We all judge of the lapse of time in relation to our daily

159

habits or some similar standard. The conviction of immortality must naturally destroy all values for this sense. If I am immortal, what is the difference between a long time and a short time? A thousand years and a day are obviously the same thing from the point of view of "for ever."

There is a subconscious clock in us, a clock wound up by the experience of the race to go for seventy years or so. Five minutes is a very long time to us if we are waiting for an omnibus, an age if we are waiting for a lover, nothing at all if we are pleasantly engaged or sleeping.[1]

We think of seven years as a long time in connection with penal servitude; as a negligibly small period in dealing with geology.

But, given immortality, the age of the stellar system itself is nothing.

This conviction had not fully impregnated the consciousness of Arthur; it hung over him like a threat, while the intensification of that consciousness, its liberation from the sense of time natural to life, caused each act of the demon to appear of vast duration, although the intervals between the howls of the body on the bed were very short. Each pang of torture or suspense was born, rose to its crest, and died to be reborn again through what seemed countless aeons.

Still more was this the case in the process of his assimila-

---

[1] It is one of the greatest cruelties of nature that all painful or depressing emotions seem to lengthen time; pleasant thoughts and exalted moods make time fly. Thus, in summing up a life from an outside standpoint, it would seem that, supposing pleasure and pain to have occupied equal periods, the impression would be that pain was enormously greater than pleasure. This may be controverted. Virgil writes: "Forsitan haec olim meminisse juvabit," and there is at least one modern writer thoroughly conversant with pessimism who is very optimistic. But the new facts which I here submit overthrow the whole argument; they cast a sword of infinite weight on that petty trembling scale.

tion by the "demon." The coma of the dying man was a phenomenon altogether out of Time. The conditions of " digestion " were new to Arthur, he had no reason to suppose, no data from which to calculate the distance of, an end.

It is impossible to do more than sketch this process ; as he was absorbed, so did his consciousness expand into that of the "demon"; he became one with all its hunger and corruption. Yet always did he suffer as himself in his own person the tearing asunder of his finest molecules ; and this was confirmed by a most filthy humiliation of that part of him that was rejected.

I shall not attempt to describe the final process ; suffice it that the demoniac consciousness drew away ; he was but the excrement of the demon, and as that excrement he was flung filthily further into the abyss of blackness and of night whose name is death.

I rose with ashen cheeks. I stammered: " He is dead." The male nurse bent over the body. " Yes !" he echoed, " he is dead." And it seemed as if the whole Universe gathered itself into one ghastly laugh of hate and horror, " Dead !"

V

I resumed my seat. I felt that I must know that all was well, that death had ended all. Woe to humanity ! The consciousness of Arthur was more alive than ever. It was the black fear of falling, a dumb ecstasy of changeless fear. There were no waves upon that sea of shame, no troubling of those accursed waters by any thought. There was no hope of any ground to that abyss, no thought that it might stop. So tire-less was that fall that even acceleration was absent; it was constant and level as the fall of a star. There was not even a feeling of pace; infinitely fast as it must be, judging from the peculiar dread which it inspired, it was yet infinitely slow, having regard to the infinitude of the abyss.

I took measures not to be disturbed by the duties that men —oh how foolishly!—pay to the dead: and I took refuge in a cigarette.

It was now for the first time, strangely enough, that I began to consider the possibility of helping him.

I analysed the position. It must be his thought, or I could not read it. I had no reason to conjecture that any other thoughts could reach me. He must be alive in the true sense of the word; it was he and not another that was the prey of this fear ineffable. Of this fear it was evident that there must be a physical basis in the constitution of his brain and body. All the other phenomena had been shown to correspond exactly with a physical condition; it was the reflection in a consciousness from which human limitation had fallen away of things actually taking place in the body.

It was a false interpretation perhaps; but it was his inter-pretation; and it was that which caused suffering so beyond all that poets have ever dreamt of the infernal.

I am ashamed to say that my first thought was of the Catholic Church and its masses for the repose of the dead. I went to the Cathedral, revolving as I went all that had ever been said—the superstitions of a hundred savage tribes. At bottom I could find no difference between their barbarous rites and those of Christianity.

162

THE TESTAMENT OF MAGDALEN BLAIR

However that might be, I was baffled. The priests refused to pray for the soul of a heretic.

I hurried back to the house, resumed my vigil. There was no change, except a deepening of the fear, an intensification of the loneliness, a more utter absorption in the shame. I could but hope that in the ultimate stagnation of all vital forces, death would become final, hell merged into annihilation.

This started a train of thought which ended in a determination to hasten the process. I thought of blowing out the brains, remembered that I had no means of doing so. I thought of freezing the body, imagined a story for the nurse, reflected that no cold could excite in his soul aught icier than that illimitable void of black.

I thought of telling the doctor that he had wished to bequeath his body to the surgeons, that he had been afraid of being buried alive, anything that might induce him to remove the brain. At that moment I looked into the mirror, I saw that I must not speak. My hair was white, my face drawn, my eyes wild and bloodshot.

In utter helplessness and misery I flung myself on the couch in the study, and puffed greedily at cigarettes. The relief was so immense that my sense of loyalty and duty had a hard fight to get me to resume the task. The mingling of horror, curiosity, and excitement must have aided.

I threw away my fifth cigarette, and returned to the death chamber.

VI

Before I had sat at the table ten minutes a change burst out with startling suddenness. At one point in the void the blackness gathered, concentrated, sprang into an evil flame that gushed aimlessly forth from nowhere into nowhere.

This was accompanied by the most noxious stench.

It was gone before I could realize it. As lightning precedes thunder, it was followed by a hideous clamour that I can only describe as the cry of a machine in pain.

This recurred constantly for an hour and five minutes, then ceased as suddenly as it began. Arthur still fell.

It was succeeded after the lapse of five hours by another paroxysm of the same kind, but fiercer and more continuous. Another silence followed, age upon age of fear and loneliness and shame.

About midnight there appeared a grey ocean of bowels below the falling soul. This ocean seemed to be limitless. It fell headlong into it, and the splash awakened it to a new consciousness of things.

This sea, though infinitely cold, was boiling like tubercles. Itself a more or less homogeneous slime, the stench of which is beyond all human conception (human language is singularly deficient in words that describe smell and taste ; we always refer our sensations to things generally known) [1] it constantly budded into greenish boils with angry red craters, whose

---

[1] This is my general complaint, and that of all research students on the one hand and imaginative writers on the other. We can only express a new idea by combining two or more old ideas, or by the use of metaphor ; just so any number can be formed from two others. James Hinton had undoubtedly a perfectly crisp, simple, and concise idea of the "fourth dimension of space" ; he found the utmost difficulty in conveying it to others, even when they were advanced mathematicians. It is (I believe) the greatest factor that militates against human progress that great men assume that they will be understood by others.

Even such a master of lucid English as the late Professor Huxley has been so vitally misunderstood that he has been attacked repeatedly for affirming propositions which he specifically denied in the clearest language.

jagged edges were of a livid white; and from these issued pus formed of all things known of man—each one distorted, degraded, blasphemed.

Things innocent, things happy, things holy! every one unspeakably defiled, loathsome, sickening! During the vigil of the day following I recognized one group. I saw Italy. First the Italy of the map, a booted leg. But this leg changed rapidly through myriad phases. It was in turn the leg of every beast and bird, and in every case each leg was suffering with all diseases from leprosy and elephantiasis to scrofula and syphilis. There was also the consciousness that this was inalienably and for ever part of Arthur.

Then Italy itself, in every detail foul. Then I myself, seen as every woman that has ever been, each one with every disease and torture that Nature and man have plotted in their hellish brains, each ended with a death, a death like Arthur's, whose infinite pangs were added to his own, recognized and accepted as his own.

The same with our child that never was. All children of all nations, incredibly aborted, deformed, tortured, torn in pieces, abused by every foulness that the imagination of an arch-devil could devise.

And so for every thought. I realized that the putrefactive changes in the dead man's brain were setting in motion every memory of his, and smearing them with hell's own paint.

I timed one thought: despite its myriad million details, each one clear, vivid and prolonged, it occupied but three seconds of earthly time.

I considered the incalculable array of the thoughts in his

well-furnished mind; I saw that thousands of years would not exhaust them.

But, perhaps, when the brain was destroyed beyond recognition of its component parts——

We have always casually assumed that consciousness depends upon a proper flow of blood in the vessels of the brain; we have never stopped to think whether the records might not be excited in some other manner. And yet we know how tumour of the brain begets hallucinations. Consciousness works strangely; the least disturbance of the blood supply, and it goes out like a candle, or else takes monstrous forms.

Here was the overwhelming truth; *in death man lives again, and lives for ever.* Yet we might have thought of it; the phantasmagoria of life which throng the mind of a drowning man might have suggested something of the sort to any man with a sympathetic and active imagination.

Worse even than the thoughts themselves was the apprehension of the thoughts ere they arose. Carbuncles, boils, ulcers, cancers, there is no equivalent for these pustules of the bowels of hell, into whose seething convolutions Arthur sank deeper, ever deeper.

The magnitude of this experience is not to be apprehended by the human mind as we know it. I was convinced that an end must come, for me, with the cremation of the body. I was infinitely glad that he had directed this to be done. But for him, end and beginning seemed to have no meaning. Through it all I seemed to hear the real Arthur's thought. "Though all this is I, yet it is only an accident of me; I stand behind it all, immune, eternal."

166

THE TESTAMENT OF MAGDALEN BLAIR

It must not be supposed that this in any way detracted from the intensity of the suffering. Rather it added to it. To be loathsome is less than to be linked to loathsomeness. To plunge into impurity is to become deadened to disgust. But to do so and yet to remain pure—every vileness adds a pang. Think of Madonna imprisoned in the body of a prostitute, and compelled to acknowledge " This is I," while never losing her abhorrence. Not only immured in hell, but compelled to partake of its sacraments; not only high priest at its agapae, but begetter and manifestor of its cult; a Christ nauseated at the kiss of Judas, and yet aware that the treachery was his own.

VII

As the putrefaction of the brain advanced, the bursting of the pustules occasionally overlapped, with the result that the confusion and exaggeration of madness with all its poignancy was superadded to the simpler hell. One might have thought that any confusion would have been a welcome relief to a lucidity so appalling; but this was not so. The torture was infused with a shattering sense of alarm.

The images rose up threatening, disappeared only by blasting themselves into the pultaceous coprolite which was, as it were, the main body of the army which composed Arthur. Deeper and deeper as he dropped the phenomena grew constantly in every sense. Now they were a jungle in which the obscurity and terror of the whole gradually overshadowed even the abhorrence due to every part.

The madness of the living is a thing so abominable and

167

fearful as to chill every human heart with horror; it is less than nothing in comparison with the madness of the dead!

A further complication now arose in the destruction irrevocable and complete of that compensating mechanism of the brain, which is the basis of the sense of time. Hideously distorted and deformed as it had been in the derangement of the brain, like a shapeless jelly shooting out, of a sudden, vast, unsuspected tentacles, the destruction of it cut a thousand-fold deeper. The sense of consecution itself was destroyed; things sequent appeared as things superposed or concurrent spatially; a new dimension unfolded; a new destruction of all limitation exposed a new and unfathomable abyss.

To all the rest was added the bewilderment and fear which earthly agaraphobia faintly shadows forth; and at the same time the close immurement weighed upon him, since from infinitude there can be no escape.

Add to this the hopelessness of the monotony of the situation. Infinitely as the phenomena were varied, they were yet recognized as essentially the same. All human tasks are lightened by the certainty that they must end. Even our joys would be intolerable were we convinced that they must endure, through irksomeness and disgust, through weariness and satiety, even for ever and for evermore. In this inhuman, this præterdiabolic inferno was a wearisome repetition, a harping on the same hateful discord, a continuous nagging whose intervals afforded no relief, only a suspense brimming with the anticipation of some fresh terror.

For hours which were to him eternities this stage continued as each cell that held the record of a memory underwent the degenerative changes which awoke it into hyperbromic purulence.

THE TESTAMENT OF MAGDALEN BLAIR

VIII

The minute bacterial corruption now assumed a gross chemistry. The gases of putrefaction forming in the brain and interpenetrating it were represented in his consciousness by the denizens of the pustules becoming formless and impersonal—Arthur had not yet fathomed the abyss.

Creeping, winding, embracing, the Universe enfolded him, violated him with a nameless and intimate contamination, involved his being in a more suffocating terror.

Now and again it drowned that consciousness in a gulf which his thought could not express to me; and indeed the first and least of his torments is utterly beyond human expression.

It was a woe ever expanded, ever intensified, by each vial of wrath. Memory increased, and understanding grew; the imagination had equally got rid of limit.

What this means who can tell? The human mind cannot really appreciate numbers beyond a score or so; it can deal with numbers by ratiocination, it cannot apprehend them by direct impression. It requires a highly trained intelligence to distinguish between fifteen and sixteen matches on a plate without counting them. In death this limitation is entirely removed. Of the infinite content of the Universe every item was separately realized. The brain of Arthur had become equal in power to that attributed by theologians to the Creator; yet of executive power there was no seed. The impotence of man before circumstance was in him magnified indefinitely, yet without loss of detail or of mass. He understood that The Many was The One without losing or fusing the conception of either. He was God, but a God irretrievably damned : a being infinite, yet limited by the nature of things, and that nature solely compact of loathliness.

IX

I have little doubt that the cremation of my husband's body cut short a process which in the normally buried man continues until no trace of organic substance remains.

The first kiss of the furnace awoke an activity so violent and so vivid that all the past paled in its lurid light.

The quenchless agony of the pang is not to be described ; if alleviation there were, it was but the exultation of feeling that this was final.

Not only time, but all expansions of time, all monsters of time's womb were to be annihilated ; even the ego might hope some end.

The ego is the "worm that dieth not," and existence the "fire that is not quenched." Yet in this universal pyre, in this barathrum of liquid lava, jetted from the volcanoes of the infinite, this "lake of fire that is reserved for the devil and his angels," might not one at last touch bottom? Ah! but time was no more, neither any eidolon thereof!

The shell was consumed ; the gases of the body, combined and recombined, flamed off, free from organic form.

Where was Arthur?

His brain, his individuality, his life, were utterly destroyed. As separate things, yes : Arthur had entered the universal consciousness.

And I heard this utterance : or rather this is my trans-

170

lation into English of a single thought whose synthesis is "Woe."

Substance is called spirit or matter.

Spirit and matter are one, indivisible, eternal, indestructible.

Infinite and eternal change!

Infinite and eternal pain!

No absolute: no truth, no beauty, no idea, nothing but the whirlwinds of form, unresting, unappeasable.

Eternal hunger! Eternal war! Change and pain infinite and unceasing.

There is no individuality but in illusion. And the illusion is change and pain, and its destruction is change and pain, and its new segregation from the infinite and eternal is change and pain; and substance infinite and eternal is change and pain unspeakable.

Beyond thought, which is change and pain, lies being, which is change and pain.

These were the last words intelligible; they lapsed into the eternal moan, Woe! Woe! Woe! Woe! Woe! Woe! Woe! in unceasing monotony that rings always in my ears if I let my thought fall from the height of activity, listen to the voice of my sensorium.

In my sleep I am partially protected, and I keep a lamp constantly alight to burn tobacco in the room: but yet too often my dreams throb with that reiterated Woe! Woe! Woe! Woe! Woe! Woe! Woe!

X

The final stage is clearly enough inevitable, unless we believe the Buddhist theories, which I am somewhat inclined to do, as their theory of the Universe is precisely confirmed in every detail by the facts here set down. But it is one thing to recognize a disease, another to discover a remedy. Frankly, my whole being revolts from their methods, and I had rather acquiesce in the ultimate destiny and achieve it as quickly as may be. My earnest preoccupation is to avoid the preliminary tortures, and I am convinced that the explosion of a dynamite cartridge in the mouth is the most practicable method of effecting this. There is just the possibility that if all thinking minds, all " spiritual beings," were thus destroyed, and especially if all organic life could be annihilated, that the Universe might cease to be, since (as Bishop Berkeley has shown) it can only exist in some thinking mind. And there is really no evidence (in spite of Berkeley) for the existence of any extra-human consciousness. Matter in itself may think, in a sense, but its monotony of woe is less awful than its abomination, the building up of high and holy things only to drag them through infamy and terror to the old abyss.

I shall consequently cause this record to be widely distributed. The note-books of my work with Arthur (Vols. I–CCXIV) will be edited by Professor von Buehle, whose marvellous mind may perhaps discover some escape from the destiny which menaces mankind. Everything is in order in these note-books ; and I am free to die, for I can endure no more, and above all things I dread the onset of illness, and the possibility of natural or accidental death.

THE TESTAMENT OF MAGDALEN BLAIR

NOTE

I am glad to have the opportunity of publishing, in a journal so widely read by the profession, the MS. of the widow of the late Professor Blair.

Her mind undoubtedly became unhinged through grief at her husband's death ; the medical man who attended him in his last illness grew alarmed at her condition, and had her watched. She tried (fruitlessly) to purchase dynamite at several shops, but on her going to the laboratory of her late husband, and attempting to manufacture Chloride of Nitrogen, obviously for the purpose of suicide, she was seized, certified insane, and placed in my care.

The case is most unusual in several respects.

(1) I have never known her inaccurate in any statement of veritable fact.

(2) She can undoubtedly read thoughts in an astonishing manner. In particular, she is actually useful to me by her ability to foretell attacks of acute insanity in my patients. Some hours before they occur she can predict them to a minute. On an early occasion my disbelief in her power led to the dangerous wounding of one of my attendants.

(3) She combines a fixed determination of suicide (in the extraordinary manner described by her) with an intense fear of death. She smokes uninterruptedly, and I am obliged to allow her to fumigate her room at night with the same drug.

(4) She is certainly only twenty-four years old, and any competent judge would with equal certainty declare her sixty.

(5) Professor von Buehle, to whom the note-books were

sent, addressed to me a long and urgent telegram, begging her release on condition that she would promise not to commit suicide, but go to work with him in Bonn. I have yet to learn, however, that German professors, however eminent, have any voice in the management of a private asylum in England, and I am certain that the Lunacy Commissioners will uphold me in my refusal to consider the question.

It will then be clearly understood that this document is published with all reserve as the lucubration of a very peculiar, perhaps unique, type of insanity.

V. ENGLISH, M.D.

ERCILDOUNE

A NOVEL

BY

ALEISTER CROWLEY

"A Red Star and a Waning Moon
Rede me this true rune;
A Gray Sun and a bastard loon
Ding doun Ercildoune."

ERCILDOUNE

CHAPTER I

THE GLACIER CAMP

MIDNIGHT on the Chogo Lungma La. Moonlight. The steady sweep of the icy blizzards of the north cuts through canvas and eiderdown and fur. Roland Rex, peering out for a moment from his tiny tent upon the stupendous beauty of the snows, almost wonders that the stars can stand before the blast. Yet, dimly and afar, a speck of life stirs on those illimitable wastes. How minute is a man in such solitudes! Yet how much man means to man! No avalanche, not the very upheaval of the deep-rooted mountains, could have held his attention so close as did that dot upon the wilderness of snow.

So far it was, so heavy the weight of the wind, so steep and slippery the slopes, that dawn had broken ere the speck resolved itself into a man. Tall and rugged, his black hair woven into a web over his eyes to protect them from the Pain of the Snows, as the natives call the fearful fulminating snow-blindness of the giant peaks, his feet wrapped round and round with strips of leather and cloth, he approached the little camp.

Patient and imperturbable are these men who face the

majesty of the great mountains : experience has taught them that it is useless to be angry with a snowstorm. A blizzard may persist for a week ; to conquer it one must be ready to persist for many weeks. So, quiet and at ease, just as if he had not made his two-and-twenty marches in six days, the messenger fumbled in his clothes and produced the mail.

Two years and more since Roland had been lost in the waste ; within a month of Skardu he had arrived, and sent forward a swift runner with a letter to the Tehsildar, the local official, and a budget for his friends at home. The wind had failed just after dawn, and the sun shone strongly on the glacier. Every particle of bedding was hung out to dry ; the coolies were right merry ; it would be easy to cook food to-day.

Roland had thawed his penultimate tin of sausages, and boiled up his chocolate. Seated on one of the leather-bound baskets which contained his few effects he was now enjoying the warmth, and his pipe, and the rapture of news from home. For though he could expect no letters, the thoughtful Tehsildar had sent him up a newspaper. Mr. Justice Billington had hay-fever ; Lord Wittle had obtained his decree nisi ; Consols had fallen a point ; Sir Julius Boot had left town for his country seat ; three pigs had been killed in Staffordshire, and a land-agent in Galway ; coal would probably soon be dearer ; Tariff Reform meant lower income-tax and work for all ; Peter Briggs, alias " Peter the Pounder," had got three years ; Buncombe's Bottlettes Cured Constipation ; Should Women Wear Braces ? and all the weariness of the daily drivel.

But the haunting unreality of the rubbish for a Londoner

gives place to a vivid brilliance and charm for one who is far off. Clearly the stuff that dreams are made of; therefore—strange paradox!—convincing. Lord Wittle became for the moment as real as Mr. Pickwick. Roland Rex was happy.

Nor was his satisfaction confined to the news of the world. After the starved brain has got every stupid phrase by heart, it turns, still eager, to the report of the Monthly Medal Competition at Little Piddlingborough, and the P. and O. sailings for next month. Even the dull personal column with its hairpin imbecilities and its bogus assignations gives a certain thrill. All is so deliciously fantastic; in the dreary maze of glaciers, in the grim silence of the rocks, in the splendour of the vast, sheathing as they did the iron of reality in the soul of the explorer, the fatuous piffle of the penny-a-liner is like a fairy story told for the first time to a child. Rather a shock to the child when it learns that its Cinderella is not true, but merely a lesson in humility and punctuality; so to the man should he find in his fairy newspaper a paragraph which directly concerns him. Roland Rex found two.

The first, in the memoriam column, read as follows:

"In memory of Lord Marcus Masters, who died—[a date two years earlier]—never forgotten by his affectionate wife. 'Blessed are the dead that die in the Lord.'"

He drew in his breath.

"Poor Marcus!" he exclaimed. And then—Roland Rex looked himself over. His hair and beard had been innocent alike of brush and scissors for three years; his skin was darker than that of his coolies; he would have been taken for a savage in any country of the world.

And he laughed. "If the Marquis dies to-morrow, I suppose I could hardly take my seat like this!"

Next his eye fell on the personal column. This time he started in genuine surprise.

The paragraph read :

"ss. 887. Austria to John. Come home. F."

Ronald translated thoughtfully. "Austria to John"? Now what the devil can he mean by that? I ought to know. But I suppose three years of wilderness dulls the intelligence. "Come home!" And the old boy has put that message in the paper 887 times!

Go home I will.

He called his headman, Salama. Laconic as ever. "Bas! Safar ho-gaya. Panch roz-ka dhal-bat bana'o; Askole-men jeldi jaebne." (Enough. The journey is over Take five days' provisions. We will go quickly to Askole.)

Right enough, in an hour's time, the whole caravan was hurrying down the slopes, tentless and on most meagre rations, if haply they might do fifteen days' march in four. At Askole he paid off the men; and with his gaunt old headman for sole companion, made headlong down the Bralduh valley to Skardu.

CHAPTER II

THE RIVER OF MUD

ROLAND REX had chosen the certain passage down the valley in preference to the dubious short cut over the Skoro La. Moreover, he wanted news pretty badly, and local rumour had it that a Sahib was now ascending the Bralduh on a sporting trip.

So down they slogged over the rough track.

About noon on the second day they met the servants of the sportsman in question preparing his lunch; learning from these that he was probably an hour behind, they pushed on, and found him sitting on the banks of that strange river of mud which flows into the Bralduh. Sluggish and even is its course; in normal weather of the consistency of very thick tar, it moves down inch by inch, until at last it oozes over into the pale amber froth of the grey Bralduh, and is lost.

Roland Rex had worn his English clothes threadbare long since; he wore the inevitable turban, that best of headgear against both heat and cold, and the rest of his costume was the handiwork of a Yarkand tailor. Small wonder if the natives failed to mark him as a Sahib, and salute; smaller that the Sahib sitting by the river equally mistook him. He called authoritatively to the travellers as they approached. Amused at the jest, Roland made his best salaam.

"Are there any Sahibs shooting or travelling in this nala?" he asked.

Roland said that he had heard of one or two.

"Is Rex Sahib in this district?"

Roland was startled, and showed it; but the spirit of mischief moved him to deny it. What should this stranger want with him?

"You are lying, son of a pig!"said the Englishman coolly, noticing the momentary confusion. It is easy to frighten the truth from an Asiatic by this simple plan. But Roland was really confused, and the stranger accordingly emboldened.

181

"You are his dak-runners!" he exclaimed. "Where have you left the Sahib?"

Roland's headman, Salama Tantra, took up the tale. An expert liar for over forty years, he was equal to the situation. Seeing that his master for some reason desired to deny his identity, the grey old hunter began a long tale of woe, beginning nowhere in particular, and ending up, after a series of magnificent falsehoods, with the statement that the Sahib had sent them on with letters, he himself having turned back up over the Hispar pass with the intention of visiting Hunza and returning by Gilgit. The stranger was apparently convinced.

"I am going to join him," he said. "My own dak-runners shall take the mail, and you shall return with me and take me to him. I am glad I have met you." And with truly royal generosity, he fished out some rupees of his shooting-coat, and bestowed them on the willing shikari.

Roland jumped to his meaning in a flash; it was the letters he wanted.

"It is not the order, Sahib," he explained, with an artistic cringe. "It is the order to take these letters to the Tehsildar of Skardu, and receive a paper from him."

"Nonsense!" said the stranger. "My own men can get this paper; I would not lose you for anything. See, I will give you each one hundred rupees."

"We cannot break an order, Sahib!" He assumed a gorgeous despair. "The master would punish us."

The stranger began to storm, but in vain. The travellers murmured the polite request for permission to leave the presence of the highness, and began to move toward the river, crossable in fairly dry weather by dint of many stones thrown in by gangs of villagers.

Suddenly out lashed the Englishman's revolver and a shot rang through the air. But he only pierced Roland in the thigh.

Long before his finger could press the trigger again, the huntsman had him by the waist; flung him far into the river of mud. Roland ran to save him, but in a trice he was tripped, and down, and the grey old ruffian kneeling on his chest.

"Useless, Sahib!" he hissed, "we have no ropes. He tried to kill you, Sahib, O my father and my mother."

The poor old fellow was in tears. Shriek after shriek came from the struggling murderer. "Allah has written it," the old man went on, "I saw the mark of death upon his brow."

In vain did Roland threaten, command, entreat. To all Salama answered, "The writing!" and kept his hold. The pain of his wound came home to Rex, and he half fainted.

Horrible were the curses of the wretch in the river. The whole valley shuddered. Yet he, too, ceased to struggle, slowly sucked in and down by the insidious mire. The lucid prologue of death's tragedy came upon him, of a sudden, at Roland's cry as he sat up, weak and bleeding, held now in his faithful servant's arms.

"Who are you, in God's name?" he shouted in English, "and what do you want with Roland Rex?"

"I am mad—I am dying—help! help!" cried the unhappy man. "How is it you seem to talk my tongue?"

"Why, I am Roland Rex; what do you want with me?"

"A curse on my wry shot," he shrieked, and fell back to

183

his old raving madness. The calm again. "I wanted the great reward—the great reward! For news of your death, you fool. So near! So near success!" and again his fury foamed; blood broke black at his lips. But now the mid-stream strength took him; looking over as he lay half-strangled in the slime, he could see the horror of the Bralduh fifty feet below. The roar of it drowned his choking yells. Then, with a last heave and gurgle through its oily mire, the river fell with him and mighty silence swallowed up the scene. Even as he fell, the storm rolled up the valley, and the blaze broke upon the wounded man and his companion.

By now the wound was staunched, for it was but a slight flesh-wound. Limping from the bullet, shaking from the dread mystery of the scene, Roland Rex crossed the treacherous stream, and came to the apricot orchards of Gomboro.

*　　*　　*　　*　　*　　*　　*

Stretched upon the green turf in the moonlight, Roland nursed his wound, whose ache, with the fiery events of the day, kept him from sleep.

He mused upon the cipher. The darkness of the letter and the darkness of the deed conspired; and there was light. "Austria to John!" Aha! Ivanhoe!—his thought burnt up —"The devil is unloosed. Look to yourself!" Then he must mean—oh! but that is too impossible. Let me consider.

And his mind ran back to the strange history of his family.

CHAPTER III

THE DOOM OF ERCILDOUNE

Ewan, fourth Marquis of Ercildoune, was riding alone through the park one drear November day, some eighty years before the beginning of this story. A proud man was he, tracing his descent from True Thomas, the holiest of the ancient Scottish Bards. Of his own house he had predicted glory and earthly power, yet closed it with the weird:

> "A red star and a waning moon
> Rede me this true rune.
> A Gray Sun and a bastard loon
> Ding doun Ercildoune."

High in favour with King George and his ministers, his name renowned in Wellington's campaigns, his power absolute as God's for many a mile beyond the eagle-sight from his castle, his wealth well-nigh boundless, four stalwart sons to bear up his age, and lift his honoured coffin to its grave, no man was more enviable in all the realm that the brave sun controls.

Yet his face was dark, and his hand closed convulsively upon the dagger that lurked at his hip. Also his mouth worked strongly.

Presently he dismounted, and, tying his horse to an oak, plunged deep into the glade. Familiar was the way, though obscure; yet even a stranger would have taken the self-same track, for the steady music of a cascade allured the step. High from its narrow channel it tumbled far out into a rock-bound pool, which overflowing rolled forth into a less dominant music among lesser obstacles. Here the Marquis paused a moment, then blew shrill upon a whistle. Instantly, as by enchantment, the volume of the falling water whitened and glowed, shot through by some interior light; then all was dark again. But the Marquis, seeming satisfied, probed his wary way around the base of the pool; the slippery rocks, the mossy knobs and treacherous fern-roots lent an ambiguous aid. He passed behind the water, and the path grew easy. Up into the cave he pressed, and after many twists came to the central hollow. Fashioned more by man than Nature, the room was large and nearly square. A curious table of brass stood in the centre, and a blue flame burnt variably thereon. Behind it stood a man of great stature, his face hidden by a monkish hood.

This man addressed the noble.

"Who art thou?"

"Ewan Dhu, Marquis of Ercildoune."

"Where is then thy brother the Marquis?"

"Under the heather." A second pause. "Shame!" the Marquis added, "have I come here that you should twit me with this paltry scandal? I never slew him."

"Not with the sword, but with the pen. Where is the Marquis, his son?"

"Who are you, to press the claim of that bastard brat?"

"I wished to see if the coward who did it was coward enough to lie to me about it."

The Marquis controlled himself with courage.

"You come to me," continued the other, "because your foolish dabbling in the false science of the stars has given you fear. You see a baleful planet threatening your house; you invoke the aid and counsel of the Brethren of the Rosy Cross. With unclean hands you come, Ewan Dhu," cried the adept, raising his voice, "and the mire that you have played with shall engulf your proud head. For once your ignorance has taught you all that knowledge could. This is the doom of Ercildoune; your sons shall die before your eyes; your house shall fail utterly, and all your rank and wealth pass to the King. Solitary and silent I see you dying, dying through long months, and no man to take pity."

"I came to you," replied Ercildoune, "that you might aid me, not that you might curse me. I withdraw."

"Stay!" cried the adept, "what do you offer me for freedom?"

"Penitence, sincere penitence."

"You will make amends?"

"Never!" flamed he out, "for the boy is the vilest of mankind. Before God I say it, I will not believe him of my brother's blood."

"Then you must suffer the doom."

"Then be it so! Farewell."

And he turned to go.

The adept strode swiftly forward. "Now are you a man, Ewan Dhu!" he cried aloud, and grasped his hand. "The doom you must dree, for doom is doom; nor you nor I avail; but in—the right—you shall not suffer, and the End is with Him. Vale! Frater Rosae—"

"Et Crucis!" answered the nobleman.

Silently and gladly they parted.

The fulfilment of the curse is matter of history.

Taking shelter in a storm during a hunt, Malcolm, the

187

eldest son, died by the lightning flash before his father's eyes. Duncan, the second, plunged into the sea, while they all strove to save a shipwrecked crew, and was drowned. Ivan, the third, racing his horse against his father, was thrown and died. Angus, the fourth, surprised some knowledge of the doom. Maddened by the fear of it, he hanged himself from his own window, even as the Marquis returned from London town, and cried his name to greet him. Then the old man turned melancholy, and shut himself into a Trappist Monastery, where in silence and solitude he died.

Title and estates passed to a cousin, one Lord Barfield, not yet to the King. This doom remained undone.

   *   *   *   *   *   *   *

This Lord Barfield, who had succeeded to the title and estates of Ewan Dhu, was an elderly man of recluse and studious habit. Many years in India had given him the secretiveness and cunning of that strange congeries of nations. He was a widower; his wife had borne him three sons and a daughter; the last had married a Mr. Rex, and Roland was the only issue of the marriage.

The Marquis had brought up his sons to follow the colours. Nothing had stirred his placid life until the Mutiny in India, where his eldest son, the Earl of Bannockburn by courtesy, was killed before the walls of Delhi.

Hard upon the news followed a curious box of ebony and silver from the East. Within he read the carved inscription, "Lord Barfield, with the compliments of the Marquis of Ercildoune," and, lifting the tray, discovered, wrapped and embalmed in costly spices, the head of his best-loved son. This was all mystery, and he sought the clue in vain.

188

ERCILDOUNE

Three years later Lord Arthur, the second son, who was studying Russian in St. Petersburg, wrote wildly home that he was stricken by a terrible disease, and the old man, eagerly seeking aid from the Government, learnt that "studies in Russian" meant little more to Arthur than the acquisition of the gilded vices of that barbaric society. Hastily he dispatched his doctor, a wise old friend of the family, if haply skill and counsel might avail; but in vain. The next month's mail brought irretrievable disaster; Arthur was dead by his own hand.

But oh! strange horror! Clad in fantastic jewel-work, there came a little casket. Within was an empty poison-bottle and the diamond device, "Lord Barfield, with the compliments of the Marquis of Ercildoune."

The old man, mastering his grief, was roused.

He devoted his whole time and intelligence, his wealth, and influence, to the discovery of who had woven this chaplet of hell's vine for his grey head.

Who was this devil dressed in the grand name? Why did he pursue and faint not? If human power, and power of prayer, might serve, he would know.

But these availed him not. In the end, an accident lifted the veil. As duly shall follow.

CHAPTER IV

CONTINUES THE DOOM

'TWAS a pleasant morning in early October, and the birds were plentiful and strong. The old Marquis, in the joy of his skill, was half forgetting the misfortunes of his family ; dwelling rather on the splendid appetite that his morning's pleasure had given him, and the glorious lunch that awaited the party at the corner of the next spinney.

The guests were few. Lord Adolphus Dollymount was an ass, but his friend, Guy Pendragon, was as fine a young man as England can show. Breeding without snobbery, intelligence without pedantry, marked him for a great place in public life. He had been brought up on the Continent, where (it appeared) his family, notorious Jacobites, had long lived in exile, and had, as it were, taken root in the strange soil. But, he explained, we had had enough of that. England for him, and to serve her was the only life worth living. Besides these were Lord Marcus Masters, the last of the sons of the house, two peers, a cabinet minister, and a famous surgeon, Sir John Bastow.

Guy Pendragon was in the line next to the Marquis, and as they walked, from the fault of one or the other, drew a shade too close together. On a sudden, birds rose, and one fine low-flying cock-pheasant whirred between them. Both swung round, but Pendragon, unable to get a fair shot without danger to his neighbour, withheld his fire and lowered his gun. The Marquis killed his bird.

Then the young man tripped and fell. His gun exploded, and the charge struck the old nobleman in the body. Instantly arose a mighty hubbub. All sprang to his aid ; the despair of Pendragon was dreadful to witness. Yet he had sprained his ankle in the fall.

Sir John hurriedly examined the wounded man, pronounced the injuries grave, but not hopeless, rendered first aid, bound

190

up the luckless sportsman's ankle, and saw to the improvising of an ambulance.

The two invalids were carried into the house. The Marquis, in pain as he was, could hardly refrain a smile, as one of the old keepers, boiling over with rage, shook his fist in Guy's face, while he hissed, "Ye damned fool!"

The fidelity of the servants of a great house like Ercildoune is a thing to restore confidence in human nature.

Soon, too, the old man declared that the accident had shaken him sadly; he would like to spend his last years with his brother's son in far Virginia. The Marquis gave him leave, and in due time he departed.

Pendragon, too, recovered, and went off to Monte Carlo.

    *   *   *   *   *   *   *

So much for Man; but Fate stepped in, and the carefully skinned poker hand was flung wide on the table by a sudden gust of the Everlasting Wings.

It was left to a nameless Anarchist to save the house of Ercildoune. His brain, tortured and diseased by famine of food and surfeit of cheap philosophy, conceived that the death of a few harmless folk would ease the evil of the Universe.

So he dragged a log of wood across the path of the Marseilles Rapide, and screwed it to the sleepers.

The train staggered, left the line, tore up its universe, crashed into a chaos of blind, foolish agony.

From among the wounded and slain young Guy Pendragon extricated himself.

"Here!" he called to another man, uninjured like himself, "help me to save my father—my father!"

Stolid and self-possessed, the stranger set himself steadily

191

—for all his rabbit's face and meek shabby-gentility—to the task, and in an hour's hard work that part of the wreckage was cleared. Nigh unto death, they dragged out an old grey man, and bore him to the relief train.

Then the stranger returned to the work of rescue, musing.

What was this man to Guy Pendragon? Father. How father? For this man was the old keeper from Ercildoune!

He knew it all; since long he had been chief of the detectives employed by Lord Ercildoune to track the murderer of his sons. Yet now? Inscrutable. Not altogether, perhaps: a seed-thought had sprouted in his mind; he smiled grimly, seeking amid the tangle of the train for further clues.

He found at last a small pocket-book in the wreck of Guy's portmanteau. The little therein was enough for his trained intelligence; the whole infamy lay bare.

He set wires to work; the authorities came in; and, torn howling from the yet warm corpse of his father, Guy Pendragon faced the rigours of an English court of justice.

Grayson, alias Lord Guy Masters, alias Pendragon, alias Schmidt, alias Laroche, etc., was informed by the Judge that the claim of his father to the Marquisate of Ercildoune was of no importance in the eyes of justice. It had been clearly proved that he did feloniously of his malice aforethought attempt to kill and murder one of his Majesty's subjects, a gentleman of high rank and dignity, who stood to him moreover in the position of host; further that he did conspire with his said father to commit the said murder; further, that all the sentimental considerations which his counsel had so eloquently urged were balanced by the fact that the accused had for years lived by fraud and robbery; and though he (the Judge) regretted

192

that counsel for the Crown had seen fit to try and connect accused with the deaths of Lord Ercildoune's two sons, yet the main charge was abundantly clear, and he had no hesitation in sentencing him to Penal Servitude for Life.

The prisoner had but time to say: " I am Lord Ercildoune, my Lord, and you shall live to repent it," before he was removed.

*   *   *   *   *   *   *

Nine days, and London had forgotten.

CHAPTER V

DERELICT CORRESPONDENCE

LONDON had forgotten! yes, even Roland Rex had forgotten in the intensity of his three years' wandering in Central Asia. Now, as he lay in the moonlight in the apricot orchards of Gomboro, the whole history rolled its sinister waves upon him.

That devil unchained? Marcus dead? Was there a link between these evil-omened happenings? What of this strange sahib who travelled nine thousand miles, and risked, lost indeed, his life in the hope of meeting Rex or stealing his letters? As the Bralduh roared below, bearing high the funeral dirge of that murderous man of mystery, Roland echoed its eternal restlessness, its unmeaning wail. He could have plunged into the river, and wrested out the heart of that dead mystery. . . .

So came the dawn at last; so, sleepless and stiff, weak from the loss of blood, he and his faithful shikari bent themselves to the endless track that leads through that desperate valley at the end of the world to the green glories of Shigar and the whirlwind-haunted circuit of Skardu.

Two days of hellish agony; the torture of the wound, the torment of the sun, the atrocious thirst upon the bare rock walls through which the path winds up and down, and above all the agony of doubt. What should he do? Two years had passed and more. He knew nothing of affairs. To go home as Roland Rex might be the blindest walking into the trap. What might not have happened since? "Look to yourself" had said the message.

Just then a native passed, giving no salute. Roland started. There was the missing word of wisdom. A native he seemed, a native he would remain. Nothing would be easier; he need not even lack money. He could draw small cheques to his new self as Habib Ju, the first name that came to his mind; he need lack nothing. And it should go hard but he discovered much ere he reached England, and came secretly to his grandfather's house of Ercildoune.

Now they got a raft of swollen goat-skins, and sped down the rushing stream to Skardu. There he wrote a letter to the Tehsildar, stating his intention to remain in the Bralduh Nala for some weeks, and that the native stories of his disappearance were to cause no anxiety; their origin was quite inexplicable.

Thus he calmed official curiosity, and killing one horse on the Deosai Plains and two more between Burzil and Bandipur, came to Baramulla before alarm, either on his account or that of the other man, had yet disturbed the nights of the Tehsildar, a man naturally lazy, incredulous, and slow to action.

When alarm arose, indeed, it diminished almost as quickly. It was only necessary to construct a plausible, probable story of the death of the two sahibs. So the Tehsildar manufactured an avalanche, and was so thoughtful as to include among the victims not only the two white men, but also those of their servants who might possibly be implicated in any inquiry, and therefore thought that it would be best to lie low for awhile.

Thus, six months after, news came to England of the death of Roland Rex.

Meanwhile that worthy was ostensibly engaged in the pilgrimage to Mecca. But he slipped off at Jeddah and took passage in a coaster up the Red Sea. At Cairo he disclosed himself with all due caution to an old schoolfellow at Head-quarters, and was able to continue the journey with a bronzed face, a trim foreign beard, and a suit of Greek-cut serge. Here, too, he was able to telegraph to his grandfather that all was yet well. He had only dared to send one other, from Bombay, and that expressed so cautiously that even the recipient might have been pardoned for failing to guess at its meaning.

Roland had not called for his letters at the agent's there, else he would not have missed the following epistle, which had lain awaiting him for more than two years.

" My dear Roland," wrote his grandfather, " heavy news, heavy news ! I fear grievous trouble. Young Grayson has escaped. It seems that while a working party were out in the fog he made a sudden dash for liberty. The whole affair must have been devilish well arranged, for no trace of the fugitives has ever been obtained—save one, of course. A month after the escape I received a parcel from Leipsig which, on being opened, revealed a convict costume with the inscription, beautifully embroidered in silk :

" ' Lord Barfield, with the compliments of the Marquis of Ercildoune. Merely a memento.'

" As usual ! Leipsig is of course worse than no clue at all but one thing we know at least : there is a woman in it. I hope to send more and better news very shortly. I have wired Arkwright, the man who caught him before ; he must do it again.

" Your affectionate grandfather,

" ERCILDOUNE.

" P.S. I am advertising you daily in many papers as your movements are so uncertain ; it is but a chance if this letter reaches you.—E.

" P.P.S. For God's sake, dear lad, take care of yourself. Three years since Marcus married, and no child."

Receiving no answer to this, the Marquis did not write again. Shut up in Ercildoune, he read deep into the night, and always on the one subject. As a criminologist he had no rival ; from his castle he directed a vast army of detectives.

Yet with no result. Grayson was lost again.

CHAPTER VI

FATHER AMBROSE

NOT only did Ercildoune seek Grayson to avenge his dead sons, but to save his heir.   Lord Marcus Masters was a soft youth of a religious turn of mind.   Only at his father's urgent command had he married.   Even so, he married out of his class ; it was the niece of the parish priest of Ercildoune that led him at last as a sheep to the slaughter.   Meek and pious, like the hybrid of a praying mantis and a mouse, she had but little thought for worldliness.   And that caused no grief to the old Marquis, who thought Marcus safer in the chapel than in the ball-room.

So sped their placid sheepish life ; no bucolics were theirs to be disturbed by some such fiery line as " Formosum pastor Corydon ardebat Alexin."   The idea of passion was foreign to them.   Their idea of love was verbal ; Caroline Masters would have resented the pressure of her husband's hand.

This indeed would have maddened the old noble, had he guessed it.   But Arthur's debauches in Petersburg had determined him to keep Marcus innocent, and the frigidity of Caroline was a rare accident such as the wisest might fail to foresee.

As maturity grew, so religious ardour took the place of virile fervour.   Day by day Marcus and his wife grew closer to Christ, so that in the end no hour of the day but was given to some devotion or another.   Their guests were itinerant evangelists ; their friends converted Atheist cobblers ; their enemies imaginary Jesuits.

THE EQUINOX

It so happened one fine summer that the fame of a certain Father Ambrose went abroad. He gave himself out to be a renegade monk from the Benedictine Monastery at Fort Augustus. Convinced of Protestant Truth, he had (it seemed) suffered a martyrdom comparable only to that of Polycarp, and had eventually made his escape in circumstances only paralleled by those of Paul at Damascus.

The statement of the Lord Abbot that the said person had never been a monk at all carried little weight with those who, like Lord Marcus Masters, were acquainted with the depths of the Duplicity of the Devil in particular and the Roman Communion in general.

From town to town the fame of the young convert, who lent piquancy to his personality by retaining semi-monastic garb and traces of the tonsure, leapt like a beacon. He who at Glasgow was starving with a dozen draggle-tailed hearers, was dining well at Manchester, and, under the wing of a leading Elder, addressing some thousand enthusiasts in the local Bethel. At Birmingham the largest hall in the city overflowed. At London all the cranks of all the sects combined to welcome him; the new revival was in every mouth. Even the street-boys whistled the refrain of his famous Redemption Song, which ran :—

> " There's salvation in Jesus!
> in Jesus!
> There's salvation in Jesus for you!
> for Me!
> There's salvation in Jesus for all of us!
> There's salvation in Jesus, salvation in Jesus,
> Salvation in Jesus for you—
> and for Me!"

The very numerous other verses differed by substituting for the word "salvation" such words as "redemption," "grace," "resurrection," "immortality," "glory" and the like, I rejoice to say with little consideration for so purely pagan a matter as metre.

No society is so easily carried away by its cranks as London Society. "Father Ambrose" might have stayed with almost any Duchess in the Kingdom; but when at the end of a long and glorious season, with a ragged throat and a record bag of sinners, his medical adviser insisted on rest, it was the invitation of Lord and Lady Marcus Masters that he accepted.

Absolutely perfect rest! was the doctor's last word; positively *no* society!

So we lose this interesting trinity for a moment and return to the Albert Hall at the close of the last of his meetings.

"Had the man a brother?" asked a rabbit-faced little nondescript of a man with a meek voice.

"I assure you he had not," replied his interlocutor—who might have been a dog-stealer out of work.

"But it is he himself then!" insisted the first. "I cannot mistake the voice and the gesture. The face is all wrong, I know, but . . ."

"Of course; what's in a face? But I went close, I tell you. I went to the 'glory form,' as they call it, and he prayed with me for twenty minutes."

"In full light?" asked the first.

"Quite full; yet I can't swear to it that the face is made up."

"Come, come!" interjected the first speaker, reproachfully.

"I can't, sir!" he insisted. "But what I can swear to is the eyes; a man can't fake his eyes."

"Well?"

"Our man's were grey, pale grey. This man's are a strange dark iridescent purple—very catlike."

"That settles it, of course. But yet—I wish I could feel satisfied."

A third man touched him on the arm. "News, sir!" he said: "strange, grave news!"

"Yes?" turned the other, swift as a snake.

"Father Ambrose is leaving London to-morrow."

"I knew that, Smithers;" he snapped.

"—with Lord and Lady Marcus Masters."

"Damn your eyes!" he yelled in excitement—"sorry, Jackson! I mean the evidence of *his* eyes; there's something up, depend on it. Follow to the office; I must work out a new plan to-night."

They moved off separately, the man Jackson cursing his superior for a dreaming fool who preferred intuition to plain fact.

CHAPTER VIII

LITERALISM IN PRACTICE

DESPITE the merry detective and his gallant men, or possibly because of their unceasing vigilance, nothing whatever happened. Yet Lord Marcus grew ever more pious, and gloomier; he had strange fits of weeping which alarmed his gentle wife; curious blushes would come over him without apparent cause. He grew morose, unkind to village children, who lacked the accustomed smile. He began to neglect his appearance. "If thy right hand" (he cried one day, reproached for cruelly beating a dog—how unlike our gentle Marcus!) "offend thee, cut it off! For it is better for thee to enter into Life maimed, than having two hands to be cast into the lake of fire. How much more then, if my dog offend me?"

Father Ambrose was genuinely distressed by these scenes. His influence, and his alone, seemed to calm the unhappy pietist—yet these interviews, beneficial as they seemed at the time, left a deeper irritation behind. Lord Marcus began to treat his wife with contempt and aversion; his temper grew daily more uncertain.

One day his wife took Father Ambrose aside, and suggested that medical treatment would relieve the strain. But the good man forbade all profane interference with "the wonderful workings of the Lord with the soul."

"Believe me, dear lady," he would say, "in His own good time the dear Lord knows how to bring our dear Marcus into His marvellous light."

And she was fain to be satisfied.

So far no open scandal.

What brought matters to a climax was this.

One fine holiday, Lord Marcus, in his aimless way, was wandering in the village. Children were sporting in one corner with their big sisters and brothers; some game of forfeits was being played. Lord Marcus looked on moodily, hardly seeing, save to regret that these children were not all groaning over Sin in some damp Bethel.

A great clapping of hands. A buxom wench had broken

some rule, or failed in some test; and must pay forfeit. The judge solemnly condemned her :—

> " By Peter and Andrew and Mary and Anne
> You must go and kiss the prettiest man ! "

They all laughed shrill. But the wench, with a snigger, slyly approached the unconscious Marcus, threw her arms round him, and kissed him loud upon the lips.

Marcus started from his reverie, struck her fiercely in the face, and, crying "Accurséd! accurséd! accurséd!" fled up the street.

The shrieking girl, with her lip bleeding from his signet-ring, stared after him—as one who has seen Satan. Sobered, the children ceased their game, and fell to weeping. Some of the lads threw stones at the maniac; some started to follow, with coarse oaths. But he ran like a hare, and shut himself into his house. For three days he would see nobody; at last Father Ambrose, who was going to America to start a great revival there, insisted on bidding him farewell.

The good man found his noble patron in bed, looking like death, yet with a strange light in his eyes.

What passed none knew; but the ex-monk, pale as ashes, came to bid adieu to Lady Marcus. He was deeply moved. "Do not intrude upon him!" he said, "the crisis is over. Your husband is a great saint!"

But the American crusade never caught fire. Or the preacher lacked the flint, or his audience the steel, and after a futile fortnight the revival fizzled out. Ambrose gave notice that he must seek counsel of the Lord; something (he thought) was the matter with his personal holiness that the dear Lord no longer saw fit to use him. He disappeared, and none knew whither.

But the Marquis?

One day by post from Lagos came to him a shameful, an atrocious, an abominable packet—a nameless horror. And on the wrapping there was written:

"Lord Barfield, with the compliments of the Marquis of Ercildoune."

CHAPTER VIII

THE CHAPEL OF REVENGE

MARCUS MASTERS never rallied from the shock.

Tubercle caught his enfeebled frame in its grip; in less than a year he shrivelled to a corpse.

With the aged Marquis of Ercildoune the enemy had become a nightmare, an incubus, an obsession. The poor old man trembled at every whisper. Why did they whisper? What did they wish to hide from him? Some new misfortune? What did this stranger want at the house? Who was he? Lord Barfield feared even his own detectives.

Surely the shadow of the curse lay heavy on the House of Ercildoune.

A certain trusted valet, an old man whom he had known and loved from boyhood, long ere he took on him the fatal marquisate, was his daily companion. Deeply did he scrutinize each visitor to the once great house, now fallen and neglected. What did the Marquis care? Even his giant fortune-tree was somewhat lopped by the maintenance of what had grown to practically a standing army. In every country of the globe his men sought ceaselessly for traces of the escaped convict. Grayson had Ten Thousand Pounds upon his head; yet he seemed safe as Prince Charlie was among his Highland hearts.

Some men doubted nine-tenths of the history. At the worst Grayson must have died somewhere. A desperate life and a desperate death. Why not ere now? He had not been heard of assuredly for years. Wise men remarked that Father Ambrose was certainly not young Grayson. The Marquis was a madman who saw family feuds in stones, and Grayson in everything.

The detectives would joke about it. When one took cold, he would laugh, "Grayson getting at me again." A funeral in the force was called a "Grayson."

Grim laughter must have filled the soul of that strange man, wherever it was that he lurked.

Ay! the great house of Ercildoune was hushed. Men did not care to pass those portals. Even as the ivy gripped the walls of the castle, so the curse clung upon all the hearts of great house.

Long and earnestly, therefore, did the old watchdog of the Marquis gaze into the eyes of the strange bearded turbaned man that stole to the side gate one night and asked for admission.

Even so, he refused him. Then the Indian drew off his sandal, and from between the leathers took a scrap of paper. In the well-known cheirograph of Roland Rex, of late so longed-for, were the words, "Good news of me by mouth."

The suspicious old man was not yet convinced. This

devil Grayson of all devils was most clever to disguise himself as an angel of light.

But the Marquis thought otherwise. "Bring him in!"
he cried. Some intuition told him that the words rang true.

Yet the obstinate old servant took his precautions like a
wise general. He led the messenger through a dark passage,
and, stumbling, took care to feel him for a hidden weapon.
Nor, leading him into the very sight of Ercildoune, did he
fail to cover him with his own pistol.

The old man lifted up his head. "You bring news of
my grandson?" he asked in Hindustani.

"The best of news," was the answer in English, and
Roland Rex, shaking off his turban, stepped forward and
kissed his grandsire's trembling hand.

Like a stone god, steeled against all emotion, the ancient
noble told in chill bleak words the hideous story of Marcus.
Then he rose.

"Come!" he said.

At one end of the apartment was a tall door concealed
by curtains of black velvet. Beyond lay a strange chapel.
Here hung upon the walls the portraits of those dead
Ercildounes. Above the altar with its lighted candles
flaming was the terrible face of God, a God of Wrath and
Vengeance, the awful God of Judgment, who visiteth the
sins of the fathers upon the children.

Upon the altar, draped all in black, stood the ghastly
trophies of the curse, each in its casket, each with its
sardonic inscription.

And on the empty monstrance was the scroll, "How long,
O Lord, how long?"

THE EQUINOX

Roland started. The terror of the place ate like a cancer into his soul. The curse came home to him. Unreal, in a sense, these old catastrophes had been. These monuments of infernal hate meant little. Now he saw himself as the very target of those frightful arrows, and utmost fear smote him. He feared even lest his old grandfather were an enemy, some appalling avatar of his unresting foe.

Roland sank down before the altar and abased himself, reaching his hands up to Heaven.

Awhile he prayed; then he arose and swore that by God's help he would root out this monster from the fair earth polluted by his infamy.

The old man followed him in silence, approving. Together they left the chapel, with the echo still afloat in their ears.

The pair spent hours of dreary, profitless talk, wasting days in interviewing detectives, and drafting new plans of campaign. The only profitable work done was the reading of all the reports by Roland, afraid lest he should miss one clue.

At the end he shrugged his shoulders. "Accident helped us before," he said, "and may help us again. But before all let no man know that I am still alive, and I will enter that dark hall of namelessness where Grayson lives. There is, I fancy, one man that may help us, the man that sentenced him—Mr. Justice Laycock."

CHAPTER IX

MR. JUSTICE LAYCOCK

MR. JUSTICE LAYCOCK was a capital whip, and his four-in-hand was one of the sights of the Park in the season. If, during the off-season, he chose to keep his hand in by practice in St. John's Wood, at midnight, and indoors, well—it was his business, and not ours.

And a very merry old gentleman he was.

Roland Rex just missed him at the club. There was nothing for him to do. He was big and strong, and very tired of tragedy ; he had not tasted the over-ripe fruits of London for four years ; nor indeed had he the disposition to set his teeth in a hard sharp apple.

He lounged off, with a tired man's eagerness for pleasure, rolled in and out of the Pavilion, stood speechless on the brink of Scott's for minutes that passed like hours, too stupid to go anywhere.

To one who has fallen so far there is but one refuge :—the Continental.

Put your foot on the rung of *that* ladder, and you are safe to reach the bottom !

In sooth, a little past midnight he got away from the drunken turmoil—himself a little enlivened by the light and the laughter and the wine—at the cost of having pledged himself to protect from molestation a beautiful maiden with cheeks far too natural, teeth far too regular, hair far too well-groomed, shoulders far too white, breasts far too well-shaped

207

dress far too well-cut, to be anything but a hideous monstrosity in the eyes of the healthy man.

The chivalry of his conduct melted the frosty hesitation of the fair one ; on arrival at her house she asked him in to rest for a few moments.

The sound of childish laughter from within assured him that he need not fear to disturb the household ; so he followed the lady, who took her latchkey and slipped in.

Like an adder he darted back. " For God's sake, Kissums," he whispered, catching her by the priceless Mechlin sleeve of her, " there's the very man I want to see—and if he sees me now there's an end of it ! "

For within the door stood Mr. Justice Laycock. He had harnessed four pretty girls in reins of blue ribbon, and was driving them gaily up and down the stairs with a whip, while he occasionally blew on the horn that hung from his neck.

It is said that Archimedes, having discovered the principle of the lever, leapt from his bath, shouting " Eureka" as his sole contribution to the usual toilet of a philosopher ; and an equally brilliant idea must, one may believe, have seized the learned judge with equal intensity and suddenness. But if in this respect his costume as coachman seemed incongruous, the same complaint could not have been laid against his steeds, who reproduced the normal costume of a horse with the most scrupulous fidelity.

In the event, Roland suitably bestowed his fair charge at a great West-End Hotel, and repaired early in the morning to try and interview the judge in chambers.

But he had not appeared ; and after an hour of useless

waiting Roland strolled back to lunch at the Savoy, and a little later to his rooms.

About four o'clock the posters caught his eye—

MYSTERIOUS DISAPPEARANCE
OF A
JUDGE,

and a brief notice—vilely padded out to trick the public into the idea that the paper possessed some information—told him that it was Mr. Justice Laycock that was missing.

"Asses!" chuckled Roland from the height of his superior knowledge. " Somebody has run off with the old boy's clothes for a lark! Oh! won't I roast him over this!"

By ten o'clock the affair had grown fearful and wonderful. One paper had it that he had been seen at Folkestone: another said that he had received an urgent call to his sick son in Paris; and so on. All to be squelched by the official statement that he was not missing at all, but confined to his room by the very slightest of all possible indispositions, and would almost certainly be at work as usual on the morrow. So simple was this admirable lie that even Roland believed it. Two days elapsed, and he learnt only that " the indisposition of Mr. Justice Laycock had proved more severe than was at first supposed, and his medical advisers had recommended perfect rest for a week. There was no cause whatever for any anxiety."

But a few noticed that all this did not explain why he was at first reported missing; it did not explain why numberless strangers called at the judge's house: it did not explain the extraordinary activity of Scotland Yard in certain parts of the metropolis.

On the following Sunday *Reynolds's* asked broadly in fat type "WHERE IS LAYCOCK?" and Roland was still far from an answer when his bell rang, and an Inspector from Scotland Yard, accompanied by a little rabbit-faced man, asked for a private interview.

"It's about this business of Mr. Justice Laycock," began the Inspector. "I must ask you to keep it absolutely private, sir, but he is not ill at all. He is really missing; he left his club at nine o'clock last Friday and has not been seen since."

"Oh, yes, he has!" Roland cheerfully retorted. "I saw him myself at one o'clock the following morning—I must ask you to keep it absolutely private—driving a very pretty four-in-hand up and down the stairs at 40, Roumania Road, St. John's Wood.

The Inspector whistled. "That's the biggest lift yet," he said.

"Well, this gentleman"—indicating the rabbit-faced man—"will have it that there's some connection between this case and——"

"This," said the rabbit-faced man, coming forward.

"What makes you think so?"

"This parcel is addressed to Lord Ercildoune, sir, and I think I know the writing." He really trembled as he said it. "You are fully responsible to his Lordship," he went on, "I take it; and between you and me, sir, I fear this parcel may be something of a shock, so we took the extreme liberty of delaying it."

"You did right," said Rex kindly.

ERCILDOUNE

"With your permission, sir, we will open it here and at once."

The Inspector cut the string and tore off the wrapping. A beautiful box of tortoise-shell inlaid with finest filigree of gold lay exposed.

The rabbit-faced man searched for the spring.

"Pull yourself together, sir!" he said sharply.

Lifting the lid, he disclosed a human tongue. To their horrified imagination it seemed still warm and quivering.

"Look! Look!"—the Inspector recovered himself quickly enough. Indeed, the inner lid of the box bore this inscription, beautifully chased in gold—

"The tongue that sentenced me.
"Lord Barfield, with the compliments of the Marquis of Ercildoune."

They stood, rooted to the ground. Upon that stupendous moment the hateful clamour of the telephone broke in. Rex rushed to it, more to silence than to answer it. But the voice came stern and loud—

"Is that Mr. Coffyn?"

"No—yes, of course! What is it?"

It was Rex's assumed name. In that supreme moment he forgot all accidents, stifled with the very breath of hell.

"Is Inspector Maggs with you, sir? May I speak to him?"

Roland handed across the receiver.

"Yes, I'm Maggs. Who are you?"

"Innes. Old Madame Zynscky has owned up: she's here now. Can you come?"

"Right. Ring off, please."

THE EQUINOX

"Will you come round with us, sir? Your evidence may be useful, if only to get the truth from Mother Zynscky."

Roland took his hat. The scent was getting warm.

CHAPTER X

MADAME ZYNSCKY

MADAME ZYNSCKY was the Faubourg St. Germain of the underworld. She had been magnificent, and retained alike the appearance and the pride. She was only too ready, once having taken the step, to throw herself into the arms of Justice, and grease the wheels of the chariot of the Law.

Yet it was a black enough business. There was not only the corpse of one of his Majesty's Judges to explain away, but the corpse of a child to whom the most liberal cynic could not give fifteen summers.

The police had started sniffing around on the very morning of the murder, which she had not discovered till eleven o'clock, when, having no sign of her distinguished guest, she had applied her eye to the peephole of the room, and seen the two dead bodies, and a sickening stream of blood, already chill and clotted on the floor.

So much was easy to tell, even if she risked a dose of penal servitude—one could never tell what these police would do! Somehow, she fancied, the matter would not come into court.

But what the Inspector did want to know was this: Who had been there that night?

This she rolled off glibly, though she risked her livelihood.

212

But the police were a good sort; they would not hurt an honest woman's trade; she was useful enough to them in a hundred ways, God knew!

They would not let her clients know that she betrayed them. Well, thank God, there was one question that he did not ask; what women were there? That is, other than the ordinary.

Did the Inspector know who had done it? She thought perhaps he did. This was no ordinary crime.

Yes! it would be all right for her. They could never bring up the little girl against her; she had her answer for that! She was a cowardly fool not to have come straight to the police on that dreadful first morning, when a thousand expedients worse than foolish jostled each other in her shrewd old skull. No! perhaps it was better to give the man a chance to clear out. The police would prefer that too.

"Mr. Fitzgerald would like a word, sir!" came an interruption at the door.

Mr. Fitzgerald was Laycock's best friend.

"Any news, Inspector?" he whispered.

"The worst, sir, I'm sorry to say."

"Dead?"

"Ay, sir, and worse!"

"Worse? You are mad!"

"Murdered, so that if I had Grayson here in this office, I wouldn't dare to lay a finger on him. I can't bear it, sir; it's a shame to the force. Go, sir, you must break it to his wife— bear up, sir. We must face it all like men. But—look what I've seen to-night, sir!"

And he silently handed over the tortoise-shell box.

213

"Look here, gentlemen," said the rabbit-faced man, who with Roland had joined them at the door. "That man Grayson has never made but one mistake. He loved his father, and it cost him nigh two years in gaol. He won't do a silly thing like that again! He has committed every crime from petty larceny to murder, these thirty years—and tripped but once. Catch him!" and the little man laughed screechily.

It jarred them, one and all. Indeed there seemed a fate about it.

"I shall go to Lady Laycock," said Fitzgerald shortly. "To you, Inspector, I only say one word: there is a God above."

The Inspector shrugged his shoulders.

They went back to the adorable Zynscky, who was now quite at her ease. Indeed, had she been Queen of England for a decade she could hardly have borne herself more majestically.

The physical appearance of all her guests supplied her with an inexhaustible fund of talk. Suddenly the Inspector stopped her.

"By the way," he said, "who was the little girl?"

Madame Zynscky was equal to the occasion.

"Inspector Maggs," she said solemnly, "I pledge you my word that it has nothing to do with the case, and I strongly advise you not to ask."

"H'm"—the Inspector was but half convinced.

"The whole affair will be hushed up—you know it as well as I do! Well!" the placid old voice rippled on, "I will tell you a little story."

"Nonsense!" said the Inspector sternly.

"I knew a very clever policeman in Vienna—never mind how many years ago! who was engaged in a very similar case. That young man had his fingers on a very great criminal—one of the lowest blackguards in Vienna—but the night before he arrested him he had a very curious dream."

"Yes?" said the Inspector, amused. "We don't dream much in London, Madame!"

"You'd better learn," retorted the old woman grimly. "This young man dreamt that he was hunting for a super-intendent's badge in the mud; his fingers closed on it, and—it was a Royal Crown. A red-hot Royal Crown, and it burnt him! 'Twas only the girl with his shaving water that touched his hand with the hot jug to wake him; but while he shaved he thought, and, while he thought, the criminal slipped out of Austria; and the very same post that brought that disap-pointing news consoled him with the news of his appointment to that very 'surintendance' he had dreamed of.

"Now wasn't that funny?" she concluded, with a chuckle.

"The Inspector is a witty man," interposed Roland, "but you go and try the joke on the Most Noble the Marquis of Ercildoune. You'll find, Inspector," he added, "that this affair won't hush up quite as smoothly as all that. I shall see you later. Good-bye!" and he strolled off.

"You may go, Madame," said the Inspector; "we shall always know where to lay our hands on you—and I'll think it over."

"Good afternoon, gentlemen!" and the disgusting creature swept out of the office with the airs of a duchess.

Left to themselves, the two men silently produced their

pipes. They were nearly through the first before the rabbit-faced man opened his mouth.

"Tell you what, Maggs," he said, "if I had Grayson here, I'd choke him right away, and chance what happened after."

The Inspector reached out his hand.

"And not think twice about it," was his only comment.

CHAPTER XI

THE CROWN PRINCESS

THE more Maggs thought about it, the less Maggs liked it. But the certainty of Ercildoune's resentment was bound to outweigh the dubious threats of the old harridan of Roumania Road. After all, she might be bluffing. He determined to go into the case with even more than his accustomed zeal.

But this peculiar case seemed to object to the process.

All his clues were woolly—everybody had a quite straightforward story to tell, and not a soul had heard or seen anything. Of the five or six dapper young men that frequented the house there was not one in the least like the missing Grayson. Every one of them was a fine strapping upstanding healthy clean-living youth, such as England is proud of. Every one of them lived in an honourable way and could be traced back to the cradle.

But they were frankly indifferent to the detective, and had all made a point of seeing and hearing a little less than nothing. Only one, a Mr. Segrave, the private secretary of the Crown Princess (as she was called by every one), offered to assist him.

"Look here, Inspector," he said, "for private reasons of my own I should like to see this matter cleared up. Now you're on the wrong tack altogether. Everybody knows all about old Zynscky's men. You have a look round at the women."

"Well," said Maggs, "I have quite certain information that it was done by a man."

"Or by a woman at his command. You're a smart man, Inspector Maggs; but if you leave out the women, they'll call you Maggots. You have a look round at the women."

"What do you know, sir?"

"I can tell you of two or three who were there that night—but I shan't. You can find out easily enough from other sources, and——"

"Thank you!" said Maggs, "you needn't change my name yet; you've told me."

And off he went.

"There was a Segrave in this case before, too," mused Maggs. "Of course. Captain Segrave, killed with Roland Rex in that avalanche. But, Great Scott! Mr. Rex was not killed. Where is Captain Segrave, then?"

These lying official reports! Perhaps even Mr. Rex himself would hardly know the truth of that story.

Nor did Roland, on being questioned, think the facts of the case good to report, and fubbed off the Inspector with the usual commonplaces of official stupidity.

Rex could hardly have explained this reticence, even to himself. Perhaps the shock of the affair had a good deal to do with it. In any case he held his tongue, and a really priceless clue was lost. The Inspector left young Segrave to himself, and busied himself with other threads. Yet, had he but known it, young Segrave was like a silken skein of Ariadne, to lead him to the hell-heart of the labyrinth.

* * * * * * * *

The young man went over to his mistress, to perform his daily secretarial duties. The Crown Princess was known and beloved all over England. The infamous conduct of her vile husband was perhaps but guessed; yet the one shameful bargain, the refusal to accede to which had cost her a throne, was well enough understood to make her the idol of that mean and obscene class of English people that love to think themselves generous and pure.

Divorced though she was, she commanded the esteem and affection of fhe Court as of the crowd; and if, as a few blackguard busybodies hinted, she sought elsewhere that solace which our beautiful social system had denied her, it was surely her own affair. Not that any decent person listened for an instant to the breath of scandal; in fact, one or two men had been soundly horsewhipped for something less than a whisper to her discredit.

The secretary found his mistress awaiting him. She lay on a magnificent divan of tigers' skins, seriously smoking a cigarette with long deep inhalations. There was more Eastern blood than Austrian in her veins; nay! but the naked Tartar showed clear as noonday in her supple gestures and savage face.

She rose as he entered. She was a woman of full six feet, her body strong and lithe as a leopard's; too slight almost to support the weight of her marvellous head. Of the semi-

218

ERCILDOUNE

Mongolian type, with long sleepy eyes, and eyebrows bushy and black as a raven, the nose more snub than straight with the nostrils jutting like an animal's, the mouth a scarlet slit with thinnest lips crowned with a black down, the teeth strong and projecting, the jaw square and portentous. The cheeks were hollow, and they and the whole face glistened with that coarse dead blue (only enlivened by the purple of two moles upon the chin) that one only sees in Eastern Europe. All this was on a mighty model; its poise on the slight shoulders served to accentuate its great size; so did her lustrous hair. Of gleaming dead blue-black, it rolled and twisted tightly about her in innumerable coils. One would have said Medusa with her snakes!

Yet all the wonder and horror of the head was instantly blotted out when she spoke. 'Twas like some gentle far-off silver bell borne down on the Zephyr to one's listening ear. 'Twas of no great volume, but most utter sweet.

So also the sleepy nectar of her long oblique eyes set deep in the rocky fastness of cheekbone and eyebrows stole out to give you of the nectar of her soul.

Verily a marvel! That all the tenderness and truth of a Madonna should force itself to expression through so dark a veil! Yet it did so. Little children ran to kiss the ugly face. When she smiled, it was a world of beauty—and she always smiled.

A marvellous artifice of beauty thus to hide itself in repulsion! She stood upright on the tiger-skins, her body draped in a clinging cascade of scarlet and silver sequins in the half-light against the deep azure tapestry of the wall, and waited.

CHAPTER XII

MISS ARUNDELL

" MR. SEGRAVE," she said at last, " I have no letters this morning ; but I have a task of some difficulty for you : well, of absurdity rather, but I assure you that it is of the last importance to my interests. You will please go out and buy at the first ironmonger's a hammer and three long French nails ; with these proceed to Guildford Street near Russell Square. You will perceive upon a hoarding a poster bearing the words ' APPLE SOAP.' Kindly drive a nail into the centre of each letter P. You had better leave the motor at the corner of the street. Return, instantly and without looking round, to the car, drive to Brighton, and drop the hammer from the pier-head into the sea. Then leave this cipher message on the ground, and return. You may wait on me to-morrow morning at the same hour."

The secretary bowed and withdrew. " Send Miss Arundell to me as you go out," she added : " I wish to be read to."

In a few moments the door opened quietly, and Eileen Arundell appeared.

What a difference to her mistress was this true-hearted English maiden ! Neither tall nor short, but of a graceful habit, the supple beautiful body was crowned with the daintiest face in the world. A shade piquant in expression, yet the glorious sincerity of her fearless eyes stamped her as no coquette. The lips were not too full, not too red ; curved, yet not curved too much ; and deliciously tiny was the whole mouth, set in the delicately chiselled face with its blush ever flaming over the creamy languor of her cheeks. The eyes were grey shaded with blue ; the hair was of that fine gossamer gold of which the angels make their harpstrings.

She and her mistress loved each other like twin sisters ; the gentle innocence of the one matched well with the sagacious kindliness of the other, and the subtle fascination of the ugly Princess was a splendid foil to the frank appeal of her lovely companion.

Princess Stephanie greeted her with an affectionate caress ; then sank back upon her rugs. "Je suis énervée ! read me of Flaubert—no, of Balzac. Ah ! but not that horrible *Peau de Chagrin*, my beautiful. Read me *La Fille aux yeux d'or*."

Eileen knew the mood. Silently she found the book, and seating herself at the edge of the divan, close to the exquisite feet of the Princess, interpreted in her low melodious voice the inspired words of the great magician of Touraine.

"Eileen," said Stephanie, after an hour had passed, "old Mr. Jukes will be here this morning. I expect very important news of this projected loan, and I shall require to be quite undisturbed. You must lock the double doors, and see that nobody approaches. You understand quite clearly that a single whisper in the City at this juncture would ruin the whole scheme—and then where would your little fortune be ? " she added playfully.

"Do you really mean it, Stephanie darling ? " murmured the timid child. " You will really give me a thousand pounds of stock ? I hardly believe there is so much money in the whole world."

" You have earned it well, kitten ! " laughed the Princess. " You have been very useful to us, I assure you. Who would

221

suspect my beautiful kitten of negotiating a scheme that will startle four capitals when it is made public? Go now, darling one, and see that Mr. Jukes enters unobserved."

The fair girl kissed her mistress, and glided out of the room.

Left to herself, Stephanie gave rein to a tempest of warring passions. She rolled to and fro on the divan like one in grievous pain of body; she lighted a cigarette, and threw it away again; she tried to read, and was revolted by the stupidity of the author in not casting a dazzling light upon her immediate perplexity. She even tried to pray before the dim-lit icon in the little eastern niche; but the Madonna had no message for her.

The paroxysm was luckily soon cut short; the door moved slowly inwards, and the old financier stood before her. The door closed behind him, and Stephanie heard the swish of Eileen's dress, and the turning of the key in the outer lock. She herself made fast the inner door, and turned to greet her visitor.

Mr. Jukes was a bent old man of a pronounced Jewish cast of countenance, with bright eyes gleaming from under his shaggy eyebrows. He walked somewhat lamely, and leant upon his serviceable oaken staff.

Stephanie drew the curtains over the window.

The consultation was prolonged and intense. It seemed that the Princess was torn by the claws of many conflicting emotions, those vultures that scent the carcass of the dead soul from afar.

What awful grief had stunned her? What dreadful passion moved her?

ERCILDOUNE

How should the cold concentration of high finance admit elements so incongruous?

Nor was the old Jew unmoved by the strange episodes of which she had to inform him. Anger and fear held the situation in a fiery grip. Only the most dazzling brilliance of imagination could inspire dull ingenuity.

Long they talked loud; their voices slowly lessened in volume as the minutes passed; but it was an hour before the conversation sank to confidential whispers. The fusion of these two great intellects, triumphing over personal interest, had produced a gigantic masterpiece of intrigue.

Silently and secretly as he had come, the old Hebrew departed; and Eileen returned to her mistress and friend to find fresh vigour and delight replace the apathy and ennui of the morning.

"You have read me Balzac, dear," she said; "I in my turn will tell you a stranger story than he ever imagined. First, I have good news for you. A certain young gentleman we know of is not dead at all, but in London."

Eileen flamed all over with joyful blushes.

"Ah, but there is ill news, too. There are enemies of him and his family; desperate, powerful enemies—and they may seek his life."

The fair girl paled, but kept her courage.

"I am your friend," the Princess said, "and we will try and find a way to defeat them."

Warmly the two women embraced; the child nestled into the strong white arms.

The tale of family distress that she unfolded has already been in part disclosed.

223

THE EQUINOX

Some of the earlier, some of the most recent events were yet dark.

Indeed, the long tale which the Princess told to her dependant was but a partial and distorted view of the events.

We shall understand it better if we look on the affair from the impersonal standpoint, if we go back in time a hundred years, to the generation before Ewan Dhu.

CHAPTER XIII

THE ROOT OF THE MATTER

LONG years before, John, third Marquis of Ercildoune, had begotten two strong sons upon Margaret his wife. The elder, Dugal, had proved but a wild lad, and cared more to wander with the gipsy folk and run for lace and French brandy with the smugglers than to acquire the artificial polish of a noble, and to bow and scrape in the gilt flunkeydom of Court society. The old Marquis cared little; 'twas the wild old blood. If he risked life, what care?

But the wildness grew; the heir went wandering for a year and more at once; still the old Marquis went his way, and took but little heed.

Yet suddenly his folly's crown came on him.

Dugal, after an absence of some months, returned one Lammas Eve with a black-browed wench from Brittany for his wife.

Here was a tangle not to be cut; the devout Catholic was bound to respect the blessing of the Church. He could but

224

pray for death to take her. A week they stayed in the castle; the woman sickened of the fine food and fair clothes; she bore herself like an harlot—as indeed she was—bold and impudent and free with the very lacqueys. Nor did her husband care; all day he drank in the great hall, and shamed his father's roof-tree, while his lady, almost as drunk as he, romped with the scullions.

Then the old man, hard stricken, drove them forth to their mates, the outlaws, and set a curse upon his house that he should never enter it.

A year passed. Ewan, a sober goodly lad, did what he could to assuage his father's shame. But that was little. Still, he rode among the people, and sought to fit himself for the duties of a good magistrate.

One winter's night, as he rode homeward, he saw the red flame glitter over the fisher-village by the sea. He set spurs to his horse, and rode in. A band of smugglers, it seemed, had landed their cargo that night, and were carousing in honour of success. Merriness turned to madness, and in their frenzy they set light, for laughter, to some fisher's cot. The flames spread; the fishermen took alarm, and when the smugglers fought against their attempts to extinguish the fire, attacked them. When Ewan arrived, he saw the riot in the darkness lit by the fitful glare of the blazing huts. He joined the fight, and his long sword turned swiftly the issue. The smugglers fled, save one who wheeled a burning brand caught from the fire, and smote therewith lustily about him. The two champions faced each other, knew each other. Ewan let fall his sword. "Dugal!" he cried. "Jacob!" answered the other; then laughed: "But your hour is come, man Ewan!"

and lifted his club to strike. But a fisher lad darted in, and with his clasp-knife struck him in the throat. The wild Lord Dugal fell without a sigh.

Death sobered all the storm; the winds and clouds joined in to aid the peace; a clamour of great rain rushed down and quenched the last of the fire. Ewan knelt by his dead brother in the darkness.

Death atoned for all; he bore him to the castle, and they buried him lordly; his life was forgotten, only his birth remembered. Four years passed by, and the old Marquis slept with his fathers; Ewan Dhu inherited the fiefs of Ercildoune. Again twelve years; Ewan was married, and bright sons were born to him.

All was at peace; the land prospered exceedingly. Yet trouble was in store. A hundred miles away in the hills lived an old witch, a miser. News came that she had been robbed and murdered. The runners were hard on the track of the murderer, and but a day after this news arrived Ewan, riding lonely through the park as was his wont, was held by an old woman and a youth. "Save me, mine uncle!" was his cry.

Then Ewan knew his brother's wife. "This is Lord Dugal's boy," she wept, "Lord Dugal's, foully slain when facing you in fight!" She wove a web of falsehood as to the cause for their plight; and he, always accusing himself of his brother's misfortunes, must haste to hide them in that cavern under the waterfall where, later, he was to meet the Rosicrucian, his master. But he had cherished snakes. The hue-and-cry after the murderer died away; Ewan conveyed the fugitives safely to America. Then they turned and struck.

226

By force of law they sought to oust their benefactor from the Marquisate. But Ercildoune had learnt that it was the murderer of an old woman (though a witch) that he had hidden from the gallows ; he determined to hold what he had. " Wild and foolish was Dugal," he exclaimed, " but never sire to this hell-brat, born in wedlock though he may have been." He sent a trusty servant to the priest who had married his brother, and by money and finesse obtained the mutilation of the register. With his wealth and influence he fought them to the death ; it was held not proven that the boy was Dugal's son. It was held proven that two years before his death she had left him for a master-thief named Grayson, whom she had married. This marriage was held good, the former null.

Ewan had triumphed ; but his sensitive nature left him never at ease. He sought consolation in the study of the stars, in the companionship of wise and holy men ; he was admitted postulant to the mysterious brotherhood of the Rosy Cross. This availed him, maybe, to his own soul ; but how could it avoid the Doom of Ercildoune?

As we have seen, he surrendered to the curse, and put his trust in God.

Now even as the third distillation of a spirit is purer than the first, so in evil the thief Grayson was but a watery mixture, and the harlot but a child in iniquity. Their son was murderer and traitor from the breast ; but genius leapt in him. Conquering his early errors, his futile pettiness of murdering an old woman for her hoarded sixpences, he rose to eminence in infamy. While yet young, he amassed a fortune in the New England States by a supreme exercise of the pharisaical hypocrisy and smug dishonesty for which the people of that part of the world have been and still are justly celebrated.

At thirty-five he had shuffled his now useless old mother into the workhouse, had married the only daughter of the richest man in Boston, had gotten a healthy son, and was ready to devote his life to restoring the rights of primogeniture.

A year in London, and the aid of the cleverest counsel, convinced him that he had no shadow of hope in law. Might should make right, he said, and let loose the leashed passions of his boyhood. A hideous plan leapt full-armed from his mighty yet devilish brain.

His achievements and failures have already been recounted, even unto that colossal stroke of irony that Fate so glibly played on the railway just north of Marseille, where this master-Anarch fell by the hand of the meanest of his tribe.

CHAPTER XIV

THE FLOWER OF THE MISCHIEF

THAT which was the dream of the father became the hope of the son. Rich enough to maintain an obsequious band of clever blackguards, it was easy to arrange his escape from prison, and assure himself a hundred safe retreats. Handsome and fascinating, with a subtle brain, he could bend to his will many of those beyond the lure of gold. He was sharp enough to see from the first that his only chance of regaining the lost glory was not only to carry out his father's ghastly revenge and so stamp out the house of Ercildoune, but to gain such domination in the houses of power that it should become the necessary interest of England herself to gloss over his offences, and establish him in the enviable seat.

To this end, therefore, he worked steadily. Many a lady of high rank was ready to throw herself into his arms, under one of his numberless disguises, which, deep as they might be, could never conceal the essential force and genius of the man. But he threw them aside as quickly as he picked them up. A month to subdue them, a month to test their influence and find it wanting, and a day to rid himself of them.

At last he met and conquered one who could answer fully his ambition. What mysterious levers she controlled he knew not; enough that she controlled him. It was through her that he found a man like Captain Segrave to sink himself in the nullity of a number—163—in his accurst band of cut-throats. It was through her that Ercildoune had fallen from favour in the Court; and was openly flouted as a madman.

A prevailing inner sense that Grayson was indeed the rightful Marquis, and likely innocent of all the crimes imputed to him, ruled in the inner circles round the throne. Nor had he failed to bind this woman to him by the deadliest bonds. Little by little he had led her from fair ways to foul; at last he had wrought upon her even to this crowning horror —he had made her commit a crime to serve him. So thought the impostor; but even the most desperate criminal is not always right. Was it possible that for the love of him she had done a deed at whose very contemplation many a hardened ruffian would have blanched? Was it she who had lured Laycock to his doom by the innocent bait, and the knowledge of his hideous greed for maidenhood? Would she not have quailed as she took the knife and did a deed which—had any dared to publish it—would have set the world aghast?

But, whoever had done the deed, none dared to make it public. The newspapers reported all in good faith that Mr. Justice Laycock's indisposition had taken an unexpectedly serious turn; that pneumonia had supervened, and a weak heart had proved his bane. Barely a dozen people knew the dread secret; barely a score of others suspected some guile, they knew not what. And every mouth was sealed by interest or fear.

What was the use of Maggs and his determination to see the matter aired? What could he do to upset the bulletins and the death certificate? He threatened this and that; the holders of the secret smiled. He even forced himself upon Lady Laycock, and begged her to avenge her husband— glossing his crime. She half relented; bade him come again. But before the appointment the too zealous detective received a quiet snub from his official chief, and the same evening found in his mail an offer to go to Milan at a very large salary to organize the police force in that city.

What could he do but throw up the sponge? In vain Roland Rex, with whom he had a last stolen interview, urged him to continue his endeavours. Bribes and entreaties were alike of no avail; Maggs had had enough of the task, and rolled off to Italy easier in his mind.

There was but one hope in the fast failing house of Ercildoune. Roland yet lived, and might avenge. The toils closed fast; only this lion might haply break them. Yet hope might well have staggered, had but Ercildoune once guessed that Roland's escape was known to his pitiless and powerful foes.

Nor had they grasped, even with all the evidence before them, the all-reaching mastery of that awful brain. All they had drunk was but the froth upon the hell-brew; they were yet to come down to the dregs.

For while the bastard Marquis yet lay hidden in London, gloating over his last hideous stroke of vengeance, his wily soul grasped out at an idea yet greater than aught he had yet planned.

One master-stroke, one quintessential draught of utmost villany, and the whole problem should be solved, alike on one side and the other, to complete the doom of Ercildoune not only with death but with disgrace.

How? On what obscure and desperate fulcrum would he lean his lever? What lure or menace could bring him to the grievous end? Hath Euclid proved in vain that two circles which cut one another cannot have the same centre? Ah, but geometry is not life.

Even as Roland in despair reached to his youth's dream as his one last hope, so did the deadly malice of the false Ercildoune spit out the name " Eileen Arundell."

CHAPTER XV

LOVE AMONG THE HOOLIGANS

So far the adventure of Roland had led him no great distance. He haunted all the dens of vice in London; he consorted with the vilest criminals, and flattered with attention all the old ghouls that batten on the grave of England's youth. He even gave himself out in various quarters as one of Grayson's gang; but to no purpose. Soon, too, he saw that so far from tracking his quarry, he was on the contrary being most adroitly stalked. An unpleasant sensation, as any who have followed a wounded tiger into thick jungle may admit.

Thus, one day a load of bricks fell over him from a ladder, but luckily scattered, so that he escaped with a graze; a second day, his hansom took the wrong turning, and whirled him down strange streets before he was aware. In the upshot, he was free at the cost of a scuffle with a bully.

Several more incidents of this sort occurred. It never struck him that these were the clumsiest stratagems, that Grayson, if he were so minded, could probably have put him out of the way with ease. That did not occur to him: he attributed his escape to Providence and redoubled his precautions.

But the long search sickened him. Were it not for the terrific evidence of the arch-fiend's presence, he too could have believed him dead.

" I will take the risk," he said to himself, " and declare myself to the Beloved One."

For, ere the shadow of the Curse of Ercildoune fell on him, Roland's youth had been idyllic. Boy and girl together, he had worshipped Eileen Arundell.

What came between them but this doom ? His grandfather had taken him aside, and told him all the woe; after that day he had withdrawn himself, and gone to the unknown, if haply he might find forgetfulness. And she ? She never

guessed—how could she guess? For he had not trusted himself to say " Farewell!" to her—and so she kept the sorrow at
her heart. Old Colonel Arundell died not long after, and left
her well-nigh penniless. Fortunate that she had so good a
friend as the Princess, who let her lack nothing.

She turned the cold scorn of her eyes on Segrave's
measured passion ; wherein her faithfulness, though 'twere
but a memory—as it chanced—availed to save her lover's life.
How, shall be told in its due place.

But how to disclose his identity to his beautiful without
letting the world into the secret was harder even than his
resolution to trust her had been to take. It might well chance
that her great and holy happiness in seeing him alive again
would be swallowed up in some dire and irremediable catastrophe. Yet he saw no other road. Her influence with the
Crown Princess might restore Ercildoune to favour, and set
once more the engines of administration at work upon his
side ; true ! Yet even more important to himself that her
simple faith and purity might in some inscrutable manner
pierce the awful mask that had so long baffled wealth, intelligence and power.

Of her truth he never doubted ; but his late experiences
had made him distrust even the Post Office, that sheet-anchor
of a Briton's faith.

Even as he sat in his little room in Stepney, where he was
hiding since the numerous attempts upon his life had assured
him that his enemies had discovered the fraud of the avalanche
and were hot on his scent, the problem was solved, and that
most strangely.

From the street came a sudden tumult of coarse laughter

233

and jeers, then a cry of anger and alarm above them, then a growing clamour and clatter. He looked out, and saw—Great God!—the very woman of his phantasy—his own Eileen!—running hard with flushed face towards him, pursued by a yelling crowd of young hooligans, the flower of our wonderful social system, and our masters to-morrow when the ideals of Keir Hardie have triumphed over manhood.

In a second he had reached the street door and flung it wide, at the same moment blowing a police whistle with all his force. "In here, Miss Arundell!" he cried.

She knew him instantly, and obeyed. In another minute some half-dozen of the hooligans lay sprawling on the pavement; the rest sheered off. Roland wasted no more time on them; the police, strolling up sulkily, would attend to them. He found Eileen on the stairs in a dead faint.

Lightly he bore her to his room, and revived her. For awhile nothing was said; the tension of the silence grew and grew. Without a word or a look he compelled her by sheer will. For her, fear held her back, but as she gazed she lost the nauseous disease of personality; rapture suddenly overcame her, and with one intense exclaim: "Roland, ah Roland!" she found herself sobbing in his arms. Closer and yet closer he caught her; his head bowed down—was it in prayer? I believe it—then willed her face to his. . . .

That sun of glory looked up through the showers; the sweet chaste lips kindled, despite themselves; the world was blotted out; they kissed.

An hour later Eileen Arundell, with his mother's ring upon her finger, a new woman by the might of love, was telling her adventure.

234

ERCILDOUNE

The Princess had sent her with a message to one of the many Christian missions, offering her great house for a lecture on the East-End ; she would gather many an exalted, many a wealthy listener.   Eileen had barely completed her errand and turned homeward when far along the street a dozen boys had begun to follow her with insult.   She took no notice; they increased, drew closer, threatened her.   At last one bolder and coarser than the rest tore at her hat ; she turned, menacing ; and at that moment received a cruel blow.   She cried for help, and seeing none, began to run.

Roland began to see.   The clumsy failures to strike him down were to be followed up more subtly.   First, they would perhaps kill her before his eyes.   And a blind anguish filled him ; a sense of helplessness, like that which grips men in some great earthquake, swallowed up his soul.

If they had hope at all, it was surely in the power and intellect of the Princess.   They would go to her and tell the whole strange story ; she could not but be moved ; she would help, she would save.   Yet Eileen hesitated.   Might it not be to bring her into the danger ?   Was any one so strong, so high, as to escape ?   Would the hand that had pulled down a Marquis and a Judge be stayed for a Princess ?

On the other hand, was not the doubt an insult ?   Would not the great lady burn red with shame if she could hear ?   Surely it was a crime to doubt her all-but divinity.   Would she ever forgive Eileen if one sorrow of that child-heart were kept back from her ?   In Roland's absence, her father's death, what sympathy but hers ?   At the false news of Roland's death, had she not held her up with hope, fed her with sister tears, been as it were mother and sister and husband in one ?

235

Had she not already some knowledge of the great conspiracy, and offered her protection?

Then they would go to her. Together, an hour later, they mingled their tears and kisses at her feet, while the royal woman, in a very tiger rage, had sworn by her own soul to save them, to bring them back to happiness, and peace to Ercildoune.

CHAPTER XVI

THE MENTAL CONDITION OF MR. SEGRAVE

UNDER the ægis of this Kalmuc Minerva, Roland Rex enjoyed a measure of safety. The attempts on his life ceased; it seemed that the bloodhounds had lost the trail. The Princess hid him in a small house she had in Chelsea; he was wonderfully disguised by an old Hebrew named Jukes, a very master of the art of altering the human face. Luck was with him from the start; he fell in with one of Grayson's gang, and by nearly throttling the fellow in a certain low opium-den to which they had retired with the purpose of discussing in private various blackguard schemes, had obtained all sorts of valuable knowledge. Grayson had gone away; the Laycock scent was still warm; he would be back (and God knew Grayson would kill him if he discovered who had betrayed him) in some three months' time. Then let old Ercildoune beware of him! With much more of the same sort.

Roland could enjoy, too, now and again,—but not too often! —a stolen interview with exquisite Eileen. Hope and faith and love flowed back into the young man's soul: he felt no doubt as to the issue. When Grayson returned—by God, let him beware of Ercildoune!

It may or may not be true that every pleasure of ours is balanced by some other's pain, but in this instance it was surely so.

The mind of Mr. Segrave needed all his ultra-British hatred of visible emotion to hide its anguish from the world. He knew nothing of Roland's return; but he marked the love-light in the wondrous eyes of his adored Eileen, and knew that the flame was none of his kindling. While she was yet a virgin heart (or so he deemed, for the mask of sorrow hid her love), he could afford to wait, to work quietly, to win at his ease. As a jockey in the straight who should have eased his horse to a canter, and finds suddenly some despised outsider furious at his heels, he lost his head a little and lashed in a frenzy at his horse. One evening he caught Eileen alone, and poured out his whole passion.

Gently she put him by.

He could better have borne contempt. He caught her roughly, bruising her almond arms; he called her by the foulest names. Then, suddenly penitent, he flung himself upon the floor in a passion of hysterical weeping. She pitied him, caring little for her own pain and shame; she left him softly and said nothing. Segrave soon conquered himself, and shut himself up in his old suave mask of gentle courtesy and silent devotion, as from afar.

The Princess never guessed what beast might lurk beneath the cultured gentleman, dull in spite of all his intellect, that she had known so long.

Yet the beast grew in cunning and insight; the more

237

Segrave disciplined and controlled it, the mightier it grew. Just as the discipline of physical exercise makes the man stronger at the end, so the first foolish brute impulse, working in ordered channels, became a force to be reckoned with.

Nor was there any one to reckon with it ; Eileen herself never guessed that it was there. She thought his angry fit a passing flash ; and her innocence slept sound.

Segrave's awakened judgment soon warned him of what was going on. The absences of Eileen became suspicious ; his own foolish missions took on a sinister aspect ; it was certain that the Princess was tricking him.

Even his brother's story (which had before seemed commonplace enough) loomed up as a mystery to his new-found subtlety. He reflected upon the sudden mad infatuation that had seized that straight-living soldier ; the change in his way of life ; the reticence that sat so ill on the frank face ; the sudden senseless journey for a sport he had never affected ; and the tragic end of him.

Young Segrave brooded overmuch upon these matters. He began to lose sight of the endless kindness of the Princess Stephanie ; the fascination of her faded ; he began to picture a monster, a vampire that fed upon the lives of men.

Ah ! but he would be her master yet. And he began to look about him for a weapon. Always he had felt that he had little share in her true thought, that invisible bars fenced him from her soul. Well, he must penetrate. Perhaps Maggs could have helped him ; Maggs knew a deal about most people and their ways. But Maggs was gone abroad. By chance he met the rabbit-faced man one day in Leicester Square. He knew him for an old intimate of Maggs, and the impulse

238

came to him to talk to him. That evening he dined him at his club.

It was a royal pumping-match. During dinner, by common consent, the talk was sterile ; yet each casual futility that passed on politics was meant and interpreted alike as a feeler and a thrust. Over their cigars they turned from the skirmish to the battle, and far into the night they plied feint and attack, till the night itself seemed to weary rather than they.

Yet neither obtained much but the increased resolve of silence, and on Segrave's part, an icier gleam in his hatred of the Crown Princess.

As he walked back through the clear morning he swore again to penetrate her fastness, by whatever loophole offered, and to defeat some plan of hers, however trivial, so that he might not feel his manhood shamed.

If he could utterly rout her, and avenge his brother, whom he no longer doubted to have been a victim, in some ambiguous way, to her designs, so much the better.

Thinking over it, he decided to track down first his rival. He paid a man to follow Eileen to what were doubtless assignations. But the girl was clever at throwing off pursuers, and it was not for some weeks that the truth came out. What, then, was Segrave's wrath to find his rival in the person of Roland Rex.

Like all suspicious and jealous persons, he could put two and two together very quickly. But the sum was never less than five, and often reached three figures. So it took him but a moment to convince himself that Rex had killed his brother. Not so bad either ! That is the worst of lunatic's arithmetic, the law of chance ordains that now and then the answer shall come right.

All threads, then, were but one. He had but to slay Roland, and the Princess was beaten, his loved Eileen set free (maybe his victory would bring her to his feet—and, by God! how he would trample her!), his brother avenged.

Mr. Segrave began to wish that he knew Grayson. That man should have at least one staunch ally. In the meanwhile, he would shadow his victim, even as the silent and terrible man-hunting snake of Yucatan.

CHAPTER XVII

THE HOLY DIRK

LORD ERCILDOUNE kept lonely vigil in his ancient castle, brooding over the past terrors that had whitened his still luxurious locks, the future fears that threatened to overwhelm his house thus utterly. Yet to-night he was more cheerful than his wont. Roland's letters had been uniformly hopeful; he seemed to have felt at last upon his own true steel the hitherto invisible foil of his fiendish antagonist; surely, moreover, there was an end to all. "How long, O Lord, how long?" he murmured with more reverence and confidence than he had felt for many years. Before, the prayer was like a wild outcry for some doubtful justice; now, it seemed that the answer "Soon! soon!" came like a benediction on his brows. Also, the familiar words wooed him to the familiar way, and he moved solemnly into his little chapel, and bent him in prayer at the altar.

Then he was aware—as we all are at times by some strange sensorium whose paths are yet unknown—that some other person had been before him. A thing surely incredible? His first emotion was of fear. Had the murderer found him? Had the last hour of Ercildoune struck upon the clock of Destiny? Yet a glance reassured him. There was no place of concealment in the chapel.

He betook him again to his prayers.

Again the strange sensation caught him, and more strongly. Yes, there was something new. And on the altar—how did this come to pass? Strange, strange.

There lay upon the black cloth a silver-hilted dirk, sheathless. To his amazement he beheld upon the hilt the well-known cipher of the Rosicrucians. They who had befriended his cousin the late Marquis—had they come at last to his aid? The mystery was explained, for the old man credited the Brotherhood with powers beyond the common. He reverently lifted the dirk. On the sharp shining steel he read in tiny letters of gold the legend—

> "Master, ye shall sheathe me soon
> And break the curse of Ercildoune."

With a sudden impulse he glanced once fearfully around, and hid the blade in his vest. Then, lingered long, mingling the accustomed prayer with new heart and hope into strains of praise, such as that gloomy chapel, the monument of so many iniquities and woes, had never yet echoed.

The day broke, and Ericildoune still grasped the dagger, and still prayed.

The days passed, and news increased both in volume and

excellence. The rabbit-faced man had missed Grayson in Vienna by an hour; Grayson was in hiding, in flight; his band seemed broken up; he struck back no more; the little army of Ercildoune was closing on him. Any moment news might come that he was taken.

One day, too, when he chanced to be confined to the castle by a cold, there came a kindly message of inquiry from the King. It seemed he was restored to favour.

He had not lived as he lived now since he inherited the fatal Marquisate.

Surely Fate had tired of her enmity; he should yet go down to the grave in peace. Then a telegram reached him from London. "Grayson trapped. Your presence necessary." It was signed by Eileen Arundell.

All the hope of the last month had strengthened the old man; his virile force came back in floods of anger. "Now is the time to strike!" he thought; "now shall I sheathe the holy dirk in the heart of that devil of the pit!"

And, feeling younger and lighter than he had done for many a day, he hurried off to London.

Imagine his joy on reading the morning poster: "The Scottish Vendetta; Lord Ercildoune's enemy reported under arrest," as he passed Warrington; his positive rapture at Euston when the *Owl* flamed at him—

"GRAYSON SEEN IN LONDON—
"EXCITING CHASE"—

at his hotel when the newsboy followed him with—

"GRAYSON CAUGHT."

ERCILDOUNE

He bought a paper and read the following—

"The mysterious enemy of the Marquis of Ercildoune has, it is alleged, been at last identified. He was seen by one of Lord Ercildoune's private detectives in the act of leaving a famous house in the West-End. As he jumped into a private motor and drove off with all possible speed, it was impossible to arrest him at the moment; but the detective, who was fortunately the chief of Lord Ercildoune's numerous staff, and a man highly esteemed by the police—we break no confidence in mentioning his name, Arkwright, who aided the police so greatly in the recent Elmstead Tunnel Mystery—was able to set innumerable activities to work.

"The motor-car was seen last speeding through Ware, and hopes of an arrest at any moment are largely entertained. It will be remembered that Grayson broke prison some years ago——"

the paragraph trailed off into a washy *résumé* of the whole affair.

In the stop press column—

"Grayson has been caught at Royston."

But as the old man went gleefully down to dinner the tape-machine caught his eye. It clicked out—

"The reported arrest of Grayson is denied. Turning the sharp corner at Royston the suspected motor ran into a hedge and overturned. The chauffeur, arrested, proves not to be the convict at all. He declares that his master, an undergraduate at Cambridge University, can entirely clear him, and is indignant at his arrest. On the urgent demand of London, the man is, however, being detained for inquiries."

So the Marquis enjoyed his dinner but little after all. Much less, though, the rabbit-faced man Arkwright. His story as he told it to his most trusted colleague was as follows—

"I was strolling down Hill Street, thinking of nothing in particular, when I saw the door of a great house open—and out walked my man.

"Grayson in the flesh, I tell you. Grayson as I saw him at Marseille; Grayson as he was in the dock and the prison. There wasn't a doubt of it. Well, my gentleman flipped into a motor and is off. You know the rest."

"No, I don't!" returned the other. "You're keeping back the best."

"For God's sake let us be careful," said Arkwright, "this is the biggest thing for years. I know now what old Zynscky meant."

"What! Whose house was it?"

He whispered—"The Duchess of Eltham! There's his influence and this fool talk of his having been innocent all along! There's his base, and his cash, and his every mortal thing he wants!"

"Oh rot!" said his Thomasian colleague.

"Well, hear what I did! I inquired. Her Grace was ill, had been ill for three weeks. The very time, mark you, when Grayson's plans began to go a bit groggy! Where could I find the gentleman who had just left the house? My boy, they denied the whole affair!"

"Arkwright," said the other, solemnly, "did not one thing strike you as very peculiar about that house?"

"No, by Jove! what?" He was rather annoyed if his usually stolid subordinate had an idea that he was missed. "What was peculiar?"

244

"Why, my boy, the blue rats on the ceiling and the pink leopards strolling up the stairs."

Arkwright was too worried to be angry. He just gave him up.

"My dear man, you're absurd," continued the critic, "Here's one of the first ladies in the land, a lady of stainless reputation—

"Umph!" grunted the rabbit-faced man.

"A lady with the devotion of the handsomest husband, and the three prettiest children in London—I am to believe, am I, that she moves heaven and earth to harbour this convict, on your theory a triple murderer and mutilator and Lord knows what beside?—I'm sick of you! You've talked Ercildoune until you've caught the craze. Why! you ought to be in Parliament! That's the place for *you*."

"Yes," retorted the other, "and I'd make a law to drill your head full of holes and pump a little sense into it. All your argument is *a priori* drivel. Who stole Lady Oldbury's pearls? A prince of the blood royal!"

"Well, but he was mad," said the sceptic, though a little shaken.

"Of course he was mad. So may Lady Eltham be mad! We're all mad—read your Lombroso, you nincompoop!" After which the conversation became profoundly theoretical, its obscurity hardly illuminated by the fact that neither party to the discussion understood the subject in the least.

We gladly draw a veil over so painful a scene.

CHAPTER XVIII

THE CUP FLOWS OVER

ROLAND REX was down in the mouth. For one thing, he had been—so Jukes said—spotted during his morning walk by one of Grayson's creatures, and the whole afternoon had been spent in disguising him as a semi-clerical character. Old Jukes had been particularly careful with the make-up, altering it a dozen times till it exactly fitted his ideal. Which had been tedious. On another side, too, he had expected Eileen on the previous evening, and she had not appeared. The failure to capture Grayson had exasperated him, the more so as he knew his foe could not be far away, and might strike home at any moment. He seemed safe enough, yet—what if his previous surmise were correct, and the villain struck at him through his love? Eileen Arundell could not lurk in an obscure nook as he could do, she must be seen and known; she must wait on the Princess. Ah! there was hope. Would she who had helped him so splendidly fail with her own twin soul? Not much!

And even as he thought it, and laughed, came a peculiar knock, the familiar signal of old Jukes. He rose and admitted him; but the old man, usually so calm and steady, seemed perplexed, distressed. His trembling hand thrust a letter into that of Roland.

The latter tore it open. "Where is Eileen?" it ran. " She left the house to see you last night at eight, and has not returned. I only got back from Brighton this morning, and

246

of course the servants knew nothing. For God's sake, do something, Mr. Rex, I shall go mad.

"Your distracted STEPHANIE."

"I will go to her," he decided without the waste of a moment. "There must be some more facts to learn than these." And snatching up his broad-brimmed hat he ran madly to the great house.

He found the Princess in violent fits of rage and tears. She had telephoned to nearly everybody in London, useful or no. For once the giant intellect seemed to have broken down. Roland strove to make light of the affair, though the blackest certainty blotted out the light of all his hope.

Ten minutes, and the great lady was herself again, though now and then she broke into a moan, calling on her loved companion's name, and upon God. Yet she controlled herself, and sternly set herself with Roland to face the situation, Before she had finished imparting the full details of what had passed, the door opened, and a footman entered, with a small package on a silver tray. The Princess took it and opened it mechanically. A card dropped out. She read—"The Marquis of Ercildoune presents his compliments to ex-Princess Steph-anie" (she stamped her pretty foot with anger at the outrage) "and begs her to hand the enclosed small parcel to Mr. Roland Rex, whose present address he despairs of discovering."

The parcel bore the words: "For Mr. Roland Rex."

He took it in his hand. "I no longer fear," he said, "I know. There is no God. Leave me alone."

"No!" she answered, "you must bear yourself as a man should. I will stay with you, and show you what even a woman may endure."

THE EQUINOX

In the certitude of calamity they had both grown preternaturally calm.

" So be it ! " said Rex, and tore off the wrapper.

A gleam of ivory set with rubies met their eyes. Roland steeled his nerves and pressed the spring : the lid flew open and revealed a little tray beautifully engraved with the fantastic irony as of old—" Mr. Roland Rex, with the compliments of the Marquis of Ercildoune."

He lifted out the tray. There lay, fresh-lopped, the flaming lips of his beloved, in their nest of gossamer gold—the hair, the lips he had kissed a thousand times.

" I think, Princess," he said, " our jester goes too far. I think the occasion an excellent one for putting to the test our little theories about the existence of a God. You shall soon hear——" There was a sinister significance about his words, He kissed the little box and put it tenderly away.

But the Princess never answered. She sat like Memnon in the uttermost desert, and her eyes were hard and tearless.

Roland went softly from the room. " There *is* a God ! There *is* a God ! " he kept on muttering as he walked idly down the street. But for the ashen pallor of his face, men might have thought him a mere curate walking early to his work. A pity that old Jukes had not imagined a more rubicund parson !

His eyes sought out some clue—Nature seemed intelligible to him. He felt that every flag of the pavement was a clue, leading him straight to his enemy.

Or—was he mad ? Was the dear God a heartless mocker as well as a cruel tyrant ? What was this strange hallucination, then ?

248

Across the road, cheerily striding, was the bronzed and bearded figure of—himself! Himself as he came back to England, hardly a year ago.

Then the truth flamed out in him—this was the very man! Grayson's last surprising masterpiece of insolence was to pass as Roland Rex.

"O Lord!" he cried, "forgive me for my blasphemy—for Thou hast delivered mine enemy into mine hand!"

Just then the man jumped into a hansom : Roland into another, ordering the cabman to follow.

Up the Edgware road they turned, and Roland began to wonder whether the pleasure of an interview with Madame Zynscky was to be included in his little outing. Strangely enough, he never gave a thought to his dead love. The horror of his heart had transcended itself, become a compelling purpose, far from the sphere of emotion. He had no doubt of the issue ; God, who had shown the quarry, would speed the bolt. So he laughed gaily. The cabman may have wondered at this clerical gentleman apparently engaged in some joyous practical joke.

They went on into St. John's Wood ; the first cab suddenly stopped at a large house with a garden. The false Roland paid his cab, and swung the gate open. Roland flung half-a-sovereign to his man, stepped up to him, and said gravely, "Mr. Rex, I believe?" "Yes," said Grayson, smilingly, "What can I have the pleasure of doing for you?"

"A few words in private, if it is not troubling you too much."

"Not at all. Forgive me if I precede you." And he led the way round the house to a conservatory, and opened the door. Just then a motor-car came noisily up, and stopped.

"It is nothing," airily explained Grayson, "only my grandfather, Lord Barfield!" Roland's politeness took a little jar.

Yet one more act of self-control, and the wrath of years should leap out and wither this cynical devil. He merely bowed his head at the taunt.

CHAPTER XIX

THE TRAP CLOSES

GRAYSON noticed that the gate did not swing open behind them. It was not the old Marquis. Who was it then? Grayson dismissed so idle a query with a slight shrug.

"A seat, Mr.——? I have not the honour of your acquaintance," he said smiling, and pointing to a chair.

"Thank you, I will stand." He cast his eye around. Heaven was still on his side; there was some loose rope in the corner. "My name is a small matter; I think I have had the honour of hearing from you—from your lordship, perhaps I should say—already this morning."

Grayson laughed out loud. "Yes! I could not deprive you of such treasures."

"Come, sir," said Roland, moved out of all patience: "this is my errand, to hang you with these hands.

"Stir!" he said, as Grayson looked about him for a weapon, "and I will shoot you like a dog."

250

The murderer held up his hands.

"The best way, Grayson, perhaps; for as the Lord liveth and as my soul liveth, I will surely hang you with these hands!"

"Ah!" smiled his enemy, "I am unarmed."

"I take you at your word," said Roland; "do you think there is no God?" And he laid aside his pistol.

"Really, I cannot discuss theology, even with so learned a divine," he sneered, "at this early hour of the morning. A divine?" he seemed to muse.

Roland stood ready. "Ah! I have it," suddenly yelled Grayson in a voice that shook the house. "You are Father Ambrose! Father Ambrose! Father Ambrose!"—then he closed with Roland in a death grip. They rolled over, fighting like cats.

But an answering cry woke in the house. From an inner door appeared two figures.

Ah, Roland, had you seen her! had you seen her!

There stood Eileen in life, scatheless and radiant, yet wild with a strange joy, and by her side the old Lord Ercildoune.

"There!" she cried, pointing to Roland, "is the false priest that murdered poor Lord Marcus."

Ercildoune with a boy's joy ran down, waving the holy dirk. "I sheathe thee," he cried, "and break the curse of Ercildoune!" But as he lifted up his arm the outer door was burst, and Segrave, ever hot on Roland's track, rushed in and struck away the blade.

Roland had Grayson by the throat. He looked up.

"Grandfather!" he cried.

The old man started back in fear and wonder. How did this Ambrose speak in Roland's voice?

Eileen dashed in. " Don't you see," she cried, " they are all wrong? That gasping cur is Grayson."

Segrave cried out in terror. " I have saved the very man I meant to slay," he roared, entirely losing his self-control.

Ercildoune's shrewd old mind grasped the situation.

" Mr. Segrave," he said, " if you would save your skin, be a true witness of these proceedings. But if you move or cry, I fear there is but one retort." He calmly possessed himself of Roland's abandoned revolver. " A chair, Mr. Segrave," he added, courteous and calm even in that headlong hour.

Segrave subsided, scowling. " Eileen!" went on the old Marquis, "you will perhaps be good enough to report to the Princess. She may be anxious about you. I regret to have interrupted you, Roland my lad," he went on, when she had left the room, "you had some business with this gentleman."

" Sit up!" commanded Roland, whom the appearance of Eileen had transfigured with rapture. "You have been con‐demned to be hanged ; we shall execute the sentence in a quarter of an hour ; spend the short minutes in a confession of your sins to God and man."

" Ah! you want a few things explained!" he jeered. " Well, then, what is it?"

" No parley," answered the old Marquis. " Commit yourself to God!"

" You may as well know all," he said wearily. " The whole thing's been a plant right along. The game was to get you—Lord Barfield! to kill your own grandson. Then we should have got you hanged out of the way, had myself declared innocent and my branch legitimate, and—there was I with my rights." He flamed up; it was plain that the man had been utterly sincere. His fancied wrongs had preyed upon his mind, and turned its mere original evil to a masterpiece of criminal genius.

"But how could you build up such a scheme?" asked Rex. "It was Miss Arundell herself who called on my grandfather to kill me."

"Why, you fool, it was our plot from the beginning. We paid the hooligans who threw Eileen into your arms; old Jukes—I have been practically living with you for weeks as old Jukes!" The voice had an ineffable scorn. "I sent that dodderer his ridiculous dirk."

"Those eyes of Father Ambrose?"

"Fluorescein," he retorted; "why don't you teach your detectives just the rudiments of some one thing?"

"How did you get Lady Eltham to lie for you?"

"Not at all; I had a footman in my pay. I waited till I saw that rabbit-faced idiot nosing about and then gave him the trail—and the slip."

"But why bring Miss Arundell into it at all?"

"How else could I get him to the intimacy of the Princess? Through that ass Segrave?" he snarled at the embarrassed secretary. "If I had you to myself for a minute, my boy, I'd teach you something about murder. How did you get here anyway?"

The poor coward winced. "I saw you hanging about," he said; "I thought you were Mr. Rex. I wanted Eileen."

"Pah!" said Grayson.

"But what has the Princess got to do with it?" asked Roland.

There was a rustle behind them, and two women swept into the doorway. "Everything," cried the Princess.

CHAPTER XX

THE CURSE BREAKS

"You must hang me too," said Stephanie, seeing Roland busy at his rope. "Why, I did everything. It was I that lured up the Marquis, and I that arranged for you to think Eileen was killed. Ah! sweet," she purred, "you know I would never have let you come to harm. How it hurt me to sacrifice that lock of your gold hair you gave me!" But the girl turned away in horror. "You plot to kill my lover," she said, "and say you would do nothing against me!" and she laughed harshly and hatefully.

"God! I have lost you too," wailed the wretched woman. "Ah! let me die! . . ."

"Ah! you do not know! Yes, it was I that tore the lying tongue from Laycock, and killed the poor innocent that his . . ." she choked with rage and tears. "Ah! you shall never know what happened in that house! It is between me and God, and I shall not fear to meet Him."

They all shrank back from her. She towered tremendous above them in the throes of her passion.

"My child," she sobbed, "my child!"

Even Grayson gasped. Their loathing turned to mere terror; they were in presence of an elemental force. This was

254

not a woman, but a tempest; they shrank from the right of judging her. The voice of the storm of heaven is louder than man's petty cry.

Only Segrave was so little of a man than his querulous question broke—

"But why did you do it at all? What is this Mr. Grayson?"

She turned on him. Like a tree smitten by the lightning he shrank into himself, withered and dumb.

Swifter than an arrow she launched herself at the doomed Grayson. "Ercildoune!" and her voice was again the gentle far-off bell, "Ercildoune, my darling, what I have done is for you!"

Again they were still. A sort of mist blinded their apprehension. All this was all so new, so impossible. For a moment Roland dreamt that she was acting a part.

So indeed; yet like all great actresses, the part rang true because she felt its truth.

She kissed him. For an instant the whole world was blank.

Lord Ercildoune rose to end the scene. But she was swifter.

With one deft motion she drew a bottle from her bosom and dashed it on the ground. Dense choking fumes arose, and before anybody could recover from the confusion she had disappeared into the house with her lover.

Eileen had been nearest to the bottle when it broke, and priceless moments were spent in restoring her in the fresh air of the garden. When aid came, no trace could be discovered. Before half the rooms had been searched, the house was found to be on fire. When the engines appeared, it was already but a spout of flame.

Nobody had been seen to leave the garden ; it was most sure that they had perished.

*   *   *   *   *   *   *

" Roland ! " chuckled the old grandfather in the smiling halls of Ercildoune. " The curse is lifted from us all at last. Eh, my dear ? You are all the curse we have at present," he laughed across at Eileen, now his grandson's six months' bride.

" Well," answered Roland, with a half-serious shrug, " the Doom says that the lands shall go back to the King."

" How stupid you men are ! " said Eileen. " Where were you at school, Roland, not to have learnt that Rex means King ? "

" By heaven, she's hit it ! " and they all shook hands.

A stalwart ghillie brought in the mail.

Eileen, taking her letter, gave a little wondering cry. The Marquis had a small flat package ; his eye fell upon it, and he groaned and fell forward. Roland raised him. " Wait till you know ! " he said. The packet was addressed—

" The most noble the Marquis of Ercildoune."

Within was an old miniature on ivory.

" With this portrait of the fierce old father of all our mischief," the enclosing letter ran, " I resign the last of the links with Ercildoune. A great sinner asks your pardon for a great wrong."

" Children ! " said the Marquis, " come with me." Again he led them to the Chapel of Vengeance.

But within there was a change. For the fierce God of

ERCILDOUNE

Genesis had gone, and in its place was the loving and compassionate figure of the Christ. The monstrance with its angry reproach against the Master had been removed. Instead was a memorial tablet to the Claimant wreathed in flowers, with these words—

"God willeth not the death of a sinner, but rather that he should turn from his wickedness and live."

"Children," said the old man, with tears running down all over his cheeks, "you see there is a God that answers prayer."

Eileen looked at her letter, short and pointed :

"Forgive and forget my jealousy, dear one, and all the disastrous passions of an unhappy woman. The madness and misery are over for both of us ; we too are married, and all the storm-beacon is burnt out to bliss.

"My love, ever my love !

"STEPHANIE."

Eileen kissed the letter ; and, fondly glancing at her husband, slipped it into her bosom.

*   *   *   *   *   *   *

Arkwright sat still with his dull colleague, and pulled more gloomily than ever at his pipe.

"So the Ercildoune case is over," grumbled the dull one, "and a blessed lot of credit it brought you !"

"Umph !" grunted Arkwright, "'slong it *is* over, I won't complain. I call it a fair sickener."

"Come, come!" returned the other, "'tain't as bad as all that. Come to think of it, you must 'a' made a tidy bit o' money out o' mad Lord Ercildoune, fust to last."

"Well," said the rabbit-faced man, "I suppose I did. Fust to last, a tidy bit o' money. 'Ave another beer?"

FINIS

ATHANASIUS CONTRA DECANUM

ATHANASIUS CONTRA DECANUM

[To comfort him with the thought that a Dean may be damned without being a liar and slanderer, I offer this poem to the Rev. R. St. John Parry, M.A., D.D., Dean of Trinity College, Cambridge.]

I

THE Anglicans (whose curious cult
Still entertains "Quicunque vult")
Boasted a grave and pious Dean
Ecclesiastically lean,
Grey-haired and spectacled, sharp-nosed,
Whose tract on "Truth," it was supposed,
Had in its day done much to stem
The tide of Error among them
Who, though well-meaning, nearly ripped your
Church up by whetting tusks on Scripture.

II

Some men arrive at ruin's brink
By dice and drugs and dogs and drink;
Some drab, some dissipate, some drench
Life through a weakness for a wench!

THE EQUINOX

Our Dean, immune from all of these,
Reached threescore years in honoured ease,
When, controversies being over,
He found no thistles in his clover.
Who sleeps too soft is slow to wake,
And finds himself with limbs that ache.
No wolves were prowling round his fold ;
He noticed he was getting old.
Leisure, the vampire of the earth,
Conceived by Satan, brought to birth
A fiend, who said : " Respected Dean,
You're not as young as you have been.
The time is not far distant when
Six other worthy clergymen
Will put your body in a hole—
And what will happen to your soul ? "

III

The blameless Dean conceived a doubt.
As humble as he was devout,
All he would utter was a trust
That God was good as He was just.
Though he had doubtless been the means
Of saving others, even Deans
(Since St. Paul said it) well may say
" If I myself were cast away ! "
" Ah ! " said the demon, " simple trust
Becomes the ignorant, who must.
But you have means whereby to test
Your faith.   I shall not let you rest,

ATHANASIUS CONTRA DECANUM

Till under cross-examination
You prove your title to salvation.
Let us begin—who runs may read—
With Athanasius his creed."

IV

He got through " neque confundentes "
Gay as a boy is in his twenties.
With sang-froid mingled with afflatus,
He gladly uttered " Increatus."
" Immensus " and " omnipotens "
Were meat to his " divinior mens."
" Tamen non tres dii " he smiled,
" Sed unus Deus," suave and mild ;
Reciting thus the Creed verbatim
To " Quia, sicut singillatim."
He slapped his venerable femur :
" Religione prohibemur."

V

" A haughty sprite," (said Solomon)
" Goeth before destruction ! "
" Pride goes before a tumble ! " we
Learnt early, at our mother's knee.
This was to crush the cleric's crest :
" *Filius a patre solo est.*"
Incomprehensibly, to us,
He boggled at " sed genitus."

THE EQUINOX

VI

The good Dean knitted noble brows
That had been wont at ease to rouse
Solution from the deepest lair
Of whatsoever thoughts were there.
Yet, here he stuck.   If he were walking,
" A patre solo " stopped him.   Talking ?
" A patre solo " dammed the flood
Of discourse, or it made it mud.
" A patre solo " spoiled his sleep ;
" A patre solo " soured his sheep ;
" A patre solo " made him ill ;
His thought-chops burned on conscience' grill.
The grave, acute, enlightened mind
Contemporaries left behind,
Yet was an abscess crammed with pus
Round that sand-grain " sed genitus."
" Non possum " (inquit) " tanquam volo
Credere hoc ' a patre solo.' "
He corresponded for a year
With doctors there and doctors here ;
He wrote to brethren near and far,
To Ebor and to Cantuar ;
He even risked (half fear half hope)
A private letter to the Pope.
These creatures of a clotted church
Left our inquirer in the lurch ;
There was not one could reconcile
By ancient thought or modern style,
Two knights, each fit to lay his foe low,
" Genitus " and " a patre solo."

ATHANASIUS CONTRA DECANUM

VII

" A matre sola " were enough
To make anatomists grow gruff!
Yet he could postulate a post—
" Colomba," scilicet " The Ghost."
A thousand ways of thought he'd trod,
Where God seemed bread and bread seemed God.
It did not ruffle up his plumes
To think that one should open tombs.
He thought it simple work to see
That Three in One was one in Three.
But he thought lost whoe'er affirms
A contradiction in terms :
" Without a mother " (was his reading)
" ' Begotten ' merely means ' proceeding.'
' Begotten ' to my mind implies
Some anatomic qualities.
Seed cannot sprout without a soil ;
Oil fills the cruse, the cruse holds oil.
A Word begotten of I AM
Is nothing but to milk the ram !
We know of things whose modest mission
Is to give life by simple fission.
The hydra, too, where pools are flooding
Gemmates, *i.e.* gives birth by budding.
The earliest forms of sex are seen
Nor male nor female, but between.
Do these ' beget,' may one affirm,
In the strict meaning of the term ?

Even so, did we admit this right,
God would appear hermaphrodite ! "

VIII

This thought so shocked the worthy Dean
Black bile corrupted his machine.
Limbo of many a likely lad,
The Dean went melancholy mad.
It is with sorrow like a sword
Cutting my heart that I record,
In this account I dare not " cook,"
The fatal form his madness took.
By Athanasius still obsessed,
He was The Father, and his quest
To solve the problem that had turned
His spirit's sword-edge, that had burned
His mental fingers, by a means
Fitter for schoolboys than for Deans.
Theology has never lent
Her sanction to Experiment !

IX

At death his sanity's last glimpse
Scattered the cohorts of the imps.
Yet on all hope the door was slammed ;
He knew that he was surely damned.
Despite his gaiters and his hat,
He failed with " Ita " on the mat
" De Trinitate sentiat."

ATHANASIUS CONTRA DECANUM

It said as plain as words can say
" Haec est Fides Catholica,"
Adding a warning of the risk we
All of us run : " Quam nisi quisque
Fideliter crediderit,
Non salvus esse poterit."

X

Horribly frightened and alone,
Before the awful judgment throne
The poor Dean stood, the myriad eyes
Of Wheels and of Activities,
Glitterers, Fiery Serpents, Kings,
Gods, Sons of Gods (and other things)
Fixed on him.   " Waste no time ! " he cried,
" I own me guilty.   I denied—
Or could at least not acquiesce
In—Athanasius.   I confess
' A patre solo ' hard for throats.
' Genitus ? '—put me with the goats ! "

XI

" Is this recorded ? " asked the Lord.
" No," said the angel.   " Yet Thy sword
Of wrath avenging is his meed.
Alas ! he played the goat indeed.
The life Thou gavest him, full store
Of opportunities galore,
He wasted all and brought to naught.
Ass-feeding thistles were his thought.

THE EQUINOX

He used his intellectual hammer
On minor points of Latin grammar,
Ruined an excellent digestion
By brooding on a sterile question,
And went beside himself through fretting
About ' proceeding ' and ' begetting.' ''

XII

Damnation's tones in thunder roll :
Gehenna caught the accursèd soul.

XIII

" Satan," said God, " has always been
Too clever for us with a Dean ! "

ALEISTER CROWLEY.

MY CRAPULOUS CONTEMPORARIES

NO. VII

A GALAHAD IN GOMORRAH

A GALAHAD IN GOMORRAH

IT is very fortunate that even in times when the greatest laxity of morals prevails, in England at least there is always found some austere and noble soul to protest against decadence ; to be a witness in the midst of corruption, that there is a standard of pure and lofty thought, a City of the Soul, fortified against all evil, and whose artillery can overwhelm the savage hordes of impurity.

We do not think any one will accuse us of flattery in saying that Lord Alfred Douglas is just such a person, and this is the more striking phenomenon as it is so rare to find true moral greatness associated with poetical genius. We write thus in order to direct his attention to a little book published some years ago in Paris, but reprinted in an expurgated form in England ; a book of so abominable a character that I am sure it is only necessary to direct his lordship's attention to it to raise a very considerable turmoil. We quote one or two passages :—

> " Their (men's) eyes for beauty are but sightless holes,
> Spurned in the dust, Uranian passion lies.
> Dull fools decree the sweet unfruitful love,
> In Hellas counted more than half divine,
> Less than half human now."

And again :—

> " O, food to my starved eyes,
> (That gaze unmoved on wanton charms of girls)
> Fair as the lad on Latmian hills asleep."

271

There is a good deal about Perkin Warbeck, a poem called "Jonquil and Fleur de Lys," of a very unhealthy character, and really very little else in the book.

Then there is a poem called "Prince Charming," incredibly sickly and sentimental; but, worse than all, the poem called "Two Loves," beginning with the celebrated quotation from Shakespeare—"My better angel is a man right fair, my worse a women tempting me to ill." In a vision the "poet" sees two people; the first is joyous, and sings; the second walks aside :—

> "He is full sad and sweet, and his large eyes
>   Were strange with wondrous brightness, and staring wide
>   With gazing; and he sighed with many sighs
>   That moved me, and his cheeks were wan and white
>   Like pallid lilies, and his lips were red
>   Like poppies, and his hands he clenchèd tight,
>   And yet again unclenchèd, and his head
>   Was wreathed with moon-flowers pale as lips of death."

This poem ends with a controversy between these two persons :—

> " . . . I pray thee speak me sooth :
>   What is thy name?' He said, 'My name is Love.'
>   Then straight the first did turn himself to me
>   And cried, 'He lieth, for his name is Shame;
>   But I am Love, and I was wont to be
>   Alone in this fair garden, till he came
>   Unasked by night; I am true Love, I fill
>   The hearts of boy and girl with mutual flame.'
>   Then sighing said the other, 'Have thy will,
>   I am the Love that dare not speak its name.'"

But the great joke is a tragedy in one act entitled "When the King comes he is welcome." There are two characters in it, Giovanni and Francisco. Francisco cannot sleep, having a presentiment that something unpleasant is about to happen. Then there is a knock, and at his private door. It cannot be Giovanni, for "that honey-bee is hived in Florence." It is Giovanni, however, and they slobber for several pages. It turns out that Giovanni had written to Francisco, but the letter had miscarried. It was an important letter. Giovanni had written to say that he was betrothed unto a noble lady. On learning this, Francisco remarked :—

> "Blood of Christ—
> Betrothed!—What word is that? Curled flame of Hell!
> Thou art betrothed? Giovanni! thou, my friend!
> O! five red wounds of God, and Mary's mouth!
> How hast thou dared it?"

A mock-terrible scene follows, in which Giovanni tries to persuade his friend that it will make no real difference to their relations. Francisco pretends to be convinced, but determines to poison himself and his friend. So Francisco proposes to drink the health of Death as a kind of joke, saying :—

Giovanni: "I will drink to our love and Death and thee."
Francisco: "Nay, nay, I favour not that toast,
> Sweetheart,
> What have we two to do with Death?"
Francisco: "Sweet feather!
> How soon hast thou forgot thy troth of faith.
> Consider, chuck, the toast has but this weight,
> That thou and I are friends, and that King Death
> Is friend of both, and will not harvest us
> Before the time of our ripe harvest comes."

We have surely said enough to establish clearly the abominable character of this book. We are sure that the moment it is brought to the notice of Lord Alfred Douglas he will take the proper steps to crush the perpetrator.

The title-page discloses, as might be expected, both the title of the book and the name of the author.

The former is " Poëmes," and the latter is Lord Alfred Douglas.

HOW I BECAME A FAMOUS MOUNTAINEER

BY

PERCY W. NEWLANDS, P.R.A.S., P.R.B.S., P.R.C.S., ...
. . . . . . P.R.Y.S., P.R.Z.S., ETC., ETC.

HOW I BECAME A FAMOUS MOUNTAINEER

I WILL open this little paper for "The Billionaire" [The "Billionaire" has nothing to do with it. But it hurts Mr. Newlands to talk about things that cost less than a guinea. ED.] by remarking that mountaineering fame shares the great advantage of the Order of the Garter—there is no d——d merit about it.

Speaking personally, I took it up because in the first place the dear King likes to hear me chat about mountains, which he himself, dear old chap, is hardly the figure to climb; and in the second place there is a certain curious pleasure in the art of writing in a very even flowing continuous style, like a placid river whose banks are adorned at due intervals by the flowers of felicitous quotation. [We have cut two-and-a-half miles of said flowers—mostly Greek and Latin poetry—with which Mr. N. had embellished his manuscript. ED.] Of course I have always had such a number of friends that mountaineering has been very easy. All my relations are very highly placed in the various services all over the world,—it facilitates things immensely. Our family has always been very well, and it is a great advantage to have friends and relations in high places. At the same time it gives me real pleasure to say that I have become

277

sincerely attached to many simple Swiss peasants, which shows conclusively to any unprejudiced mind that I am far from being a snob, and though some have thought, no doubt, that I lose dignity by addressing François Dévastation (for example) as "vieux chameau" or "mon coco," have we not the very similar instance of the touching friendship between the late dear Queen and John Brown?

I have never had any ambition to climb mountains, but accident (as it were) has at one time and another brought me to the top of a good many. It is really a very pleasant and exhilarating mode of mild exercise. A skilful guide never jerks the rope or slacks it suddenly, so that there is one long even strain upon the waist—not at all unpleasant, but, *au contraire*, rather suggestive of the embrace of a mountain-spirit.

No: I have never taken any active steps to become a famous mountaineer, except to make it my habit to speak authoritatively on all these questions just as if I were one, a most impressive course of action; and to take quite a little trouble to expose all sorts of impostors. What can Mr. Eckley mean (by the way) when he says that this habit of mine shows my strongly gregarious instinct? I grasp it, as it were, you know, and then I seem to lose it again.

It was I that exposed de Rougemont, and Landor, and Graham, and ever so many more. Now this Mr. Eckley is always attacking me; he has not that sense of the *comme il faut* that the dear King (for example) has; his controversial manners have not that repose that marks the caste of Vere de Vere. Why do I not expose him? Why do we allow ourselves (I speak for the Alpine Club) to be called common

278

cheats and impostors in the public press year after year without a word of reproach or denial?

It is the Christian spirit, my dear readers; and when we turn the other cheek, this Vulgarian—nay, hush, hush, I must not use such terms—this charmingly witty controversialist says "No wonder! I couldn't buffet all the cheek you've got from now to the Last Trump." It is disheartening; kindness does not melt that flinty heart; nothing will content him but one thing.

"Let Englishmen climb mountains unaided," he says, "just as they are unaided in every other sport; and with those Englishmen I will shake hands. I think even Mr. Newlands would kick if I hired Hayward to bat, and Haigh to bowl for me; while I, sitting in the pavilion, had their records published as my own, and went about the world as 'the famous cricketer.' Which is exactly what these heroes of the Alpine Club do. They hire one man who climbs rocks, another who can cut steps, and the only thing they do themselves is to take the credit. And because mountaineering (as distinguished from the everlasting repetition of well worn routes) is a sport needing high qualities of brain in a great degree, and high qualities of body in a small degree, therefore the Moral Science Tripos is a better school for the mountaineer than Sandow's, and the English amateur who has studied mountains in mass as well as in detail becomes a very much better man than the Swiss professional who has nothing to guide him but rule-of-thumb. A club of such amateurs might be formed in two years, were it not for the dishonest and unsportsmanlike methods of the Alpine Club in discouraging the production of genuine climbers from the matchless raw material which England can supply. It was the end of Rome when her citizens paid substitutes to fight ; it will be the end of England when professionalism has eaten up all her sports, as mountaineering is already swallowed whole."

These are not his actual words, of course—his method is more lurid—but I think it fairly represents his case. He forgets, like all Radicals, the question of vested interests. The Alpine Club has invested many thousands of pounds in Reputation. If we once admitted that mountains could and should be climbed by Englishmen without aid, all this money would be irrevocably lost—worst of all, lost out of the country. So that Mr. Eckley, under the guise of patriotism, is really sapping the very foundations of our National Wealth : in an earlier sterner age he would have passed through Traitor's Gate and suffered the supreme penalty which awaits the wretch who plots against his fatherland !

The matter is an exceedingly ticklish one ; if we admit the existence of even one guideless climber, our whole position is threatened. We have to get out of it by saying that he was a wonderful genius, and an exception to all rules. But to admit two, three, twenty would sweep us away.

So we have to conceal the existence of the hundred or so first-class amateurs of Austria, Germany, and Switzerland. We have to prevent it becoming known that nearly all first-class climbing is now done by guideless parties. We keep it dark that amateurs hold all the world's records except one ; and we cover with calumny and reprobation the aspiring youth who proves intractable.

We were at one time in most serious danger. Mr. A. F.

HOW I BECAME A FAMOUS MOUNTAINEER

Mummery was an Englishman, and could not be so easily ignored; it had become notorious that no Alpine guide—though he had formerly climbed with guides—could be considered in the same class with him : and unfortunately some of our young bloods who had been investing very largely in that sensitive stock Reputation, had made things much worse by under-estimating his importance, and trying to extinguish him in the usual way by blackballing him for the Alpine Club. Of course one could not openly blackball him because of his guideless propensities; so the inaccuracy—I must confess the inaccuracy—that he was a bootmaker was sedulously circulated, and the result achieved. Luckily, the simple, good-natured fellow accepted our apologies for the " mistake," and consented to join us. Had he found out the real secret of the Alpine Club before his admission we might have been badly off indeed—the value of our securities down to nothing! But his loyalty prevented him from giving us away too dreadfully, though that terrible last chapter of his book came as a great shock to many of us. However, we got out of it by saying "what a brilliant mountaineer he was; and of course one could excuse a little unsound theory in so wonderful an exponent of the sport." And we put it very neatly, I think, and rather turned the tables, by saying that he was an example of the way in which an exceptionally gifted amateur could become after long practice very nearly the equal of the best Swiss guides. However, I have wandered much from my subject. Yet I must flow on—it is the law of my nature—and the truth of the matter is that " How did you become a famous mountaineer?" is answered in a phrase (as above) by referring to my habitual tone of authority; while the question " How do you propose to remain a famous mountaineer, with people like this Mr. Eckley about?" is one which takes all my time and thought to answer. Even my little jokes are turned against me. The other day I said in the Geographical Society that "I think people should say Mount Everest, not Everest *tout court;* for I have just seen in an account of some climbs in Canada, where there is a Mount Newlands, [What incomparable puppies these people are, who give these personal names to presumably dignified peaks! ED.] the phrase:

"Newlands has proved to be rather an impostor. I hope the same may never happen to Colonel Everest."

And the wretched newspaper fellow comments:

"Nobody appears to have laughed. Perhaps they were thinking it over."

[B]

BY SIR MEDIUM COELI

IT was an ingenious thought of my mother's—for I was so unfortunate as never to know my father—to christen me Medium Coeli, for the astrologers [With Reason! ED.] prophesy honour and glory to the lucky children at whose nativity this house is on the cusp of the ascendant. But on no natural grounds should such a prediction have been formulated; for my story—it is nearly a case of "From Log Cabin to White House," though the local colour is wrong—is one long (and stirring) example of the triumphant conquest of difficulties (of course I do not mean mountain difficulties)

282

by persistence, judiciousness, and adroit manipulation of facts. Indeed the "great natural defect" of George Washington, that "he could never tell a lie," has at no time thrust its ugly head in my path. Nor was it, as ordinary people might be tempted to think, such a great drawback that I never possessed the smallest natural gift for climbing or mountaineering, or the wish or ability to learn these (to the dilettante) fascinating subjects.

Even at this day, when my name is practically synonymous with the sport, I am as ever quite incapable of climbing the simplest rocks, or even of descending unaided an unusually rough mule-track, while the ensanguine banner hung out in my cheeks is invariably blanched at the very suggestion of a native bridge. [Brandy does pull one round.] But my intellect was naturally acute, and, on looking round the world of sport, I soon fixed on mountain climbing as the only one in which an absolute duffer can acquire fame. It is quite impossible to pass oneself off as a fine cricketer—people look up your average; but a climber can do his work secretly, and the *Alpine Journal* which seeth in secret will reward him openly. I speak of the man who goes exclusively with guides; for the guideless man has friends who cannot be bribed to silence. Everybody will remember poor Smith, and the trouble he had about that guideless ascent of the Steinbockhorn, which read so well in the pages of the *Journal*, when his honest but deluded companions found out that they had not been to the top of the mountain, and that Smith knew it.

In fact, young Lazarus and his brother deserve a great deal more credit than myself; for they have worked up a reputation in the English hills where an honest body can hardly

283

announce having made a new climb without a yapping chorus of " To-morrow we'll all come and *see* you do it."

In my own case, I had merely to engage competent guides and wander about the Alps. It was easy to do new climbs in those days, once the idea of varied routes was hit upon. My guides pulled me up a few dozen, and in due course I was admitted to the Alpine Club.

To throw a little variety into things—in England at that time it was not good enough to be solely an athlete—I got a little reputation by a really good work on a quite different subject—I forget exactly what ; though, owing to the disgusting conduct of one of her relatives, I have every reason to remember the name of the lady who wrote it. (Of course the title-page would not refresh my memory on the point.) It is a genuine example of actual memory on my part, and I confess to an honest pride in the matter.

I am even prouder of my next step. Merit alone is useless without money, and I was in sore straits. But the distinguished mountaineer was as rare a bird in the 'seventies as the successful general in the days of Venice, and I was able with my tale of moving accidents by field and flood, to swoop down on a stray Yankee heiress, and hustle her into the halls of Hymen before the Hon. Patrick N. O'Flaherty (essentially of Tammany Hall, and incidentally her father) came upon the scene.

I had not bargained for quite such a vulgar fellow ; of course we had to compromise, but his idea of compromise was this : "Waal, young f'ler, I had calculated upon my daughter marrying a peer ; I guess you've done me there ; but every red cent you get from me has got to be honestly laid out in running for the House of Lords, and don't you forget it !"
284

HOW I BECAME A FAMOUS MOUNTAINEER

And I had been looking forward to a quiet life! No more beastly mountains! No more filthy Swiss inns! No more hunting for impoverished persons of talent to write my books! The Club, and the Park, and—— O! my heart is breaking. The worthy Boss mapped out my life from day to day; and before long some silly fool hammered it into his head that the best chance of a peerage for me was that I should go exploring to all the most inaccessible regions of the uninhabitable globe! Useless to point out that I had no scrap of ability in this direction; that plain lump sums to a party caucus would be a more efficient means to the end. He was adamant, and after a week without—my blood boils!—without the very commonest necessaries of life, I gave up and started for New Guinea or some beastly place like that—I forget where, it's all in a book of mine that I never could read —though I have several times honestly tried to do so; people will question one about one's exploits.

So the devil of it was that at the very moment when I was on the top of Mount Thingumbob, I was actually recognized in Coney Island by an Alpine Club man, and, as they have to draw the line somewhere, that did in my chance of becoming President. If Pa found out about that—why, I'm afraid to think about it.

The next few years are a positive nightmare. I was driven from one end of the earth to the other; some of the expeditions I actually had to do, because there were English people all over the starting-point. Then I had to invent the most ingenious explanations about things; one time they actually sent Englishmen with me—that was the most awful experience of all. However, I managed to get rid of one by disgusting him with my mismanagement, and persuading the others that he was bad-tempered. A second I bribed to quit; a third luckily damaged his leg; and I was left with only a fool artist who knew even less about mountains than he did about art, and was easily bamboozled into thinking that the snow-hump we struggled up was a great peak![1] But fate was against me; my faithful guide was "got at" in England by a friend of my very worst enemy, and blurted out the whole story under the influence of alcohol. Oh, the terrible curse of drunkenness! Oh, that man should put an enemy into his mouth to give away my game!

In this heartbreaking manner year after year flew by, and the House of Peers seemed as far off as ever. Pa knew more about England by now, and the wealth of Pittsburg or wherever it was swelled the party chest [I forget which party —I could never understand politics]. We spent thousands— thousands, I tell you! of what ought to have been my money on contesting hopeless seats. At last it was intimated that I might look for my reward. I made all sorts of inquiries in the ermine market, and Benson's sent me a really reasonable estimate for a coronet. Then the blow fell. A Knighthood! A knighthood for the Hercules of the Himalayas, the Charlemagne of the Caucascus, the Attila of the Andes and the Alps! A knighthood. Think of it, dear readers—a knighthood. A common cheap calico knighthood. The sort of thing they give away at Harrod's Stores to all purchasers to the value of over Five Pounds!

[However, when abroad, I may be able to pass as a baronet.]

[1] The author is not quite frank here, perhaps. The natives who were with him have lost all memory of the snow-hump.—ED.

HOW I BECAME A FAMOUS MOUNTAINEER

There was only one advantage to be got out of it—I would settle Pa. I settled him. Of course, I said sarcastically, I *can* go down the crater of Vesuvius if you *like*. But it won't do any good. You haven't bought the British Empire, and you can't, and they've done you, and that's all there is to it. I'm tired; I'm going to sit down a bit, and you let me have a decent allowance, or I'll blow the whole gaff, and show up your silly vulgar ambitions and then where will your daughter be, and that's all there is to *that*.

He consigned me, I regret, to a hotter place than Vesuvius, but he gave in, and there are ripping easy-chairs in the club. If I could only shut that beast Eckley's mouth I should be perfectly happy ; but it don't really cut any ice [I picked up this language to try and appease Pa], for the Britishers are that easy it takes a thousand years to nail a fakir to the counter.

After all, then, I really am an example of a great and famous mountaineer, and let's leave it at that !

[B]

BY THE BROTHERS LAZARUS

I MUST apologize to ladies and gentlemen who read this for using " I " instead of " we " but nobody can distinguish between my brother and me when we write and it's all very confusing but it only makes one mountaineer the two of us. I am born of poor but honest parents in the country so a kind gentlemen said we were both Arcadians like some people in a book because I was so simple-minded sincere and guileless. We never knew why they laughed so when he said it but that doesn't matter what I want to say is we were really nicely brought up, and have always been brought up to be respectful to ladies and gentlemen and I hope we shall never speak rudely that is why I am so much liked by ladies and gentlemen who buy our beautiful pictures. Of course we would not lie about anything for I have been brought up very strictly and the camera cannot lie. I always use the camera to prove our statements for though as we said it cannot lie it can be inclined in all sorts of directions and this is very useful. If a lady or gentleman is lying on a floor and you take a picture of them and then look at it side-ways it looks as if they were climbing up a perpendicular wall or climbing down it head first.

Like all great discoveries (a gentleman told me one day) this is very simple and was made by accident. I once took a picture of a lady climbing a rock needle and we didn't know how to use a level so it all went wrong and the picture came out with the needle all cock-eyed but the lady liked it because it was so much steeper than it looked we mean than it looked when you looked at it. So there was a very nice gentleman called Jones who couldn't climb rocks but was very clever at jumping up them when he caught hold of something he got up and when he didn't he fell down and hurt himself so he was making a tremendous reputation. So I said to him we'll photo you all over all the rocks and we'll tip the camera so that it always looks as if you were on an overhanging precipice. So he said yes and I went into partnership and it was all very famous. But there were rude people who wanted to do new climbs and so we had to prevent them climbing things until we had jumped up them. There are some horrid rocks that you *must* climb because there is nothing to jump at but our partner found a good way to get round that. I used to go out with him (he was a very nice gentleman and treated us quite like friends) and we would stand at the top and let him down by a rope and he would go up and down and up and down and up and down hundreds of times till it was quite easy for him you know it is only a new rock that is difficult because as a kind gentleman told me one day if you don't know exactly where the handholds and footholds are you waste a lot of strength in trying useless things and you get tired and when the pull comes you are too tired to do it. So I kept it all frightfully secret and by and by our partner would say at breakfast " I think I'll stroll over to Gully X to-day and have a look at it." Now everybody would know that Gully X had never been done and was awfully dangerous and all the ladies would begin to cry and say Dear Mr. Jones don't don't go to that awful place! And a gentleman friend of Mr. Jones's (though he wasn't really a gentleman only a farmer) would say " If you climb that place I'll never speak to you again " and everybody would look pale except us and I would try not to laugh. So we would all go to see it and Jones would take his coat off and just cast one glance at the rock as if to take it all in and go straight away up without any hesitation at all and everybody would clap their hands like mad and say what wonderful skill and there would be Mr. Jones at the top not out of breath even and call down it's quite an exhilarating little climb and everybody come up it's quite easy. So everybody would just worship him and when a rude man would say go up that other little gully at the side which would be a much easier place really he would say no it would look like showing off and give the other men a chance.   And get out of it that way.   And everybody would write in the book what wonderful skill and strength and all that.   And the way I would prevent other people doing climbs by climbing was we would make great friends with everybody and say quite secretly I know a gully that hasn't been climbed in such and such a place and we want to do it with you don't tell anybody.   So he would be awfully pleased and treat me quite like a friend and I would say the same to everybody but there would always be a reason why we couldn't actually go and try and I would say the same to everybody and by and by Mr. Jones and us would do it and be famous.   Because having arranged to try with us the others were too honourable to go without me.

There were rude people who said no we always climb by ourselves and your old gully isn't one you found.   It's in the book and was described ten years ago, and the only reason it hasn't been climbed yet is because of your dirty tricks taking advantage of people's ignorance and their sense of honour to run your blackguardly advertising scheme to boom Jones.

These people were not real gentlemen we feel sure though they had been to Oxford and Cambridge and all I can say is if they are we're very glad I'm not.

So sometimes other people would do new climbs and it was horrid but we went and practised them and wrote in the book how easy I wonder people are so vain as to record such silly things.   Anyway we got a lot of new climbs to ourselves and got very famous.   It was very nice for us because I never took any risks and we knew I should have the field all to ourselves soon because I knew Mr. Jones would kill himself one day the way he jumped about instead of climbing and sure enough he did.

We had a dreadful fright one year everybody knows that if you sleep with your window open you go into a decline and die but there was a gentleman who said rubbish you won't and my brother believed him just because he was a gentleman though we know now that a gentleman can be wrong just like common people. So one night he said his prayers twice over and opened his window nearly an inch but it was no good he went into a decline and went to the Alps as a last chance and spat blood and all the ladies said poor poor boy to die so young and he got thinner and thinner. So a medical gentleman said send him to what's his name where there weren't any doors or windows and my poor brother was out in the rain all the time with only a towel on and they fed him on twelve raw sheep a day and he came back so fat I didn't know him and his cheeks flapped against his waistcoat and he broke the weighing machine at the station and we were afraid the railway company would put me in prison.

So then we went to everywhere and tipped the camera more and more every time and learnt to scratch out things in the picture that prevented it looking dangerous and I did a lot more new climbs on the old plan and read Professor Collie's nice articles and Mr. Mummery's nice book which is in very much that style and Mr. Jones' nice book which is a very careful imitation of that style and so we learnt that book by heart and wrote a book in the same style with the same kind of photographs in the same type and the same binding and printed on the same paper and sold at the same price and you can't tell which part I wrote and which part my brother wrote because it isn't our style (*this* is our style) but Mr. Jones' nice style and even that isn't his nice style but Mr. Mummery's nice style, and even Mr. Mummery owes a little to Professor Collie's nice style.

And that is how we became a famous mountaineer.

[D]

By Madame Bock Brune

How sweet it is in the starry morning to set out from some daintily furnished club hut with one's faithful guides! Deliciously primitive, in a strange sad way, to lick the last drops of fragrant olive oil from the slim svelte tin of sardines on the frowning brow of some historic peak, as, lying with one's dark sweet face to the blue azure of the cerulean sky with its cobalt-ultramarine shade of hyacinthine—hang it all! *blue* again; there are no more words—between one's faithful guides one can reflect upon the deep problems of Life and Death, and above all, marriage. [Better have reflected on grammar.—Ed.] Yes! I have been married twelve times; but what is marriage after all? Surely a husband is less intimate, far, far less intimate in many, many ways than one's faithful guides! With a husband, if the rope breaks, one can get another; but there are so few, few faithful guides, none as faithful as mine! Such are my reflections as I lie between—[Possibly. This is not *at all* the kind of article we want. Don't

292

HOW I BECAME A FAMOUS MOUNTAINEER

maunder, tell us how you became a famous mountaineer and I'll make it a dollar.—ED.] Very well, that's talking. I've done some of the commonplace climbs that everybody from cows to Alpine Clubmen has been up millions of times every year, and written about them in the style you don't seem to appreciate. That's straight. [It is. We understand. Here is the dollar. Thank you. Good-morning.—ED.]

[E]

BY MRS. BLOOMER-GREYMARE

CONFOUND and dash these drivelling newspaper donkeys! George! What am I to say, I wonder? George—G-e-o-r-g-e! What the deuce was I about when I married one of these scurvy, feckless, futile, scrimshank, scallywag men? George! Oh, *there* you are! Take that, then! And that! and that! and how dare you come to me with your tie all round at the back of your neck? No, don't speak—nothing but gabble, gabble, gabble all day long—why aren't you some use? I pulled your tie and collar awry, did I? Then why did you *make* me do it? I've told you a thousand times if I've told you once, that I won't have it, you idle gawky good-for-nothing stuck up idiot? Why did I marry you? tell me that! [No answer; but a profound feeling that in a previous existence he must have killed his father and mother, or a holy universal King, or wounded the body of a Buddha!] And on the top of everything the *Daily Mail* wants to know how I became a famous mountaineer. Will you write the article now at once?

293

Mind what you say! Enlarge on the natural timidity of woman, and the wonderful courage—What! speak up! and don't stare and yammer like a dropsical owl! O! Of course!—an appointment in the City? Oh, yes! I know what men do in the City—you can't deceive me. But you'll write the article in the afternoon, eh? Will you? Yah! you idle silly gowk. What? Do you want me to take the *stick* to you? I see you remember! Oh, *you're* no good—I know the sort of wishy-washy muck you'd ladle out to the public—leave it to me! I'll show them what a good true tender beautiful woman can do. Oh, you men! Why, you even kicked at calling the silly mountain Bloomer-Greymare after me! And you positively wouldn't call the other one Lavinia though I beat you till the very coolies ran away for shame! I know you did climb them and I didn't but what's that got to do with it. What the public wants is the Poetry of Married Life and the spectacle of a timid shrinking woman doing what has beaten all you hulking bullying brutes of men—see? you pasty-faced monkey jumping about like as if you were on hot bricks. Stop it now or take that! and that! Get out, can't you? How the blazes can I write my article with you maundering about all the time muddling my mind with your cackle cackle cackle. . . . . .

[And that is how *she* became a famous mountaineer. ED.]

THE TANGO

A SKETCH

BY

MARY D'ESTE AND ALEISTER CROWLEY

PERSONS OF THE PLAY

FISCHER, *proprietor of a night café in Paris*
PAUL, *a young man about town*
A LORD, *about to marry* JAJA [1]
" NEGRO," *a bully*
JAJA, *the Tango dancer*
MADELINE, *engaged to be married to* FISCHER
LILLIE, *in love with* " NEGRO "
       Guests, Waiters, etc.

[1] Pronounce Zhá-zha.

THE TANGO

SCENE: *Fischer's Café.*   TIME: *Midnight.*

[*A waiter is laying the tables for supper, in a lazy manner, whistling. Enter* FISCHER *silently, and observes him. The waiter does not see him.*]

FISCHER. Hurry up, you lazy dog. [*The waiter, startled, springs to attention and bustles about.*] I am expecting a lot of big people to-night. Aha! I have a fine new song for them! [*Hums tune of " The Tango."*]

Enter PAUL.

FISCHER. Good-night, Paul, how goes it? Glad you managed to turn up.

PAUL. Madeline will be here in a minute.

FISCHER. Ah, do you envy me?

PAUL. Devil a bit. She's a dear, though. I suppose you'll have a crowd of Americans to-night?

FISCHER. Yes; I've got a new song.

PAUL. Queer lot, those Americans. Lord, but it's dull here without the Tango. That *was* dancing, if you like! She was an American, wasn't she?

FISCHER. Half-French.

[*Enter* PIERETTE *with three young men; they sit and take up the menu, attended on by the waiter.* PIERETTE *is drug-drunk, and acts unseemly. Enter* MADELINE, *runs to* FISCHER, *and kisses him.*]

MADELINE. Who's half-French?

FISCHER. Jaja.

MADELINE. Oh, the Tango girl? Half-devil and half-child, by my reckoning.

FISCHER. Well, she's reformed now. Going to take up the White Man's Burden!

MADELINE. So she's really caught that millionaire lord after all. Whew! I'm sick of millionaires. Any one can have mine.

PAUL. But not his money.

MADELINE. Bah! Now we've got all we want for the Café. What do you think money means to us women when we love?

PAUL. Yes, when you *do* love. But when do you love anything but money?

MADELINE. Perhaps you think we can't love. Why, it's the only thing we live for.

FISCHER. And if women must have money, it's only to look their best—to hold their love the longer.

MADELINE. And to give it to their love.

FISCHER. You saw how Negro threw Jaja over the minute Lillie turned up in a Poiret frock!

PAUL. Well, Jaja never cared for anything but dancing.

MADELINE. And Negro.

PAUL. Perhaps.

MADELINE. I suppose you think she's only marrying this fool lord out of pique.

FISCHER. Anyhow, she's got money enough. The idiot is trying to buy Paris for her! They're to be married to-morrow.

PAUL. Ass!

FISCHER. He thinks her an angel who has side-slipped.

PAUL. Ho! ho! ho!

FISCHER. And believes that she'll give up the life here for Mrs. Grundy's drawing-room!

PAUL. Poor fool! It can't be done; I've tried it. Once you come here it's for better or worse, for richer or poorer, in sickness and health, till death do us part.

MADELINE. You don't understand what love can do.

PAUL. Oh, love!

MADELINE. Perhaps it's true that after having loved one of us there is no other love.

FISCHER. Absolutely. Marry or die you may, but the soul clings to the old love.

[*During this conversation the café has been filling up with girls and men. Enter* LORD *and* JAJA. *Some, recognizing her, begin to beat on the tables, and call out welcomes.*]

JAJA. I've only come to say good-bye; to-morrow we sail for America.

LORD. She's finished with all this.

FISCHER. One never finishes; it's in the blood.

PAUL. Tell the truth, Jaja; you just couldn't keep away a minute longer.

JAJA [*Nervously*]. For me, it's finished for ever; I've decided to be a Society Bud!

MADELINE. Ah, but you bloomed here!

JAJA [*Spitefully*]. There are some who have never bloomed.

MADELINE. I, for instance. That's why I have kept my perfume!

PAUL. And what a perfume!

THE EQUINOX

FISCHER. Ladies and gentlemen, I will sing you my new song [*Sings*]—[1]

"What is money to the bliss
    Of the honey of a kiss?
What are rank and fame and fashion
    To the ecstacy of passion?

Chorus.
Give me dancing!
    Give me wine!
Bright eyes glancing—
    Yours in mine!
Kisses sucking
    Up my breath—
Give me passion!
    Give me death!

Were the town of Paris mine,
    Its renown should drown in wine.
I would pay the land of France
    For a day and night of dance.
                    Chorus
Dreams entrancing float above
    Music, dancing, wine and love.
Sober sinks the sobbing breath;
    Smiles the sphinx of sleep and death."
                    Chorus.

[*All applaud vigorously.* LORD *begins a conversation with* FISCHER].

JAJA. Bravo! [*To Madeline, aside.*] Has *he* been here?

MADELINE. Who, Negro? [JAJA *nods.*] He's coming; he's trying to teach Lillie to dance the Tango in your place.

JAJA. No one can ever take my place.

MADELINE. So you're really going to marry the young English millionaire?

[1] This song, music by Bernard F. Page, is sold by Wieland and Co. Price 1s. 6d.

300

JAJA. Yes ; to-morrow morning.

MADELINE. You're not happy, dear.

JAJA. Oh yes, I am. Once I get into the new life——

MADELINE. You will begin to weary for the old. You will come back to us.

JAJA. Never ; it's finished, I tell you.

FISCHER [*To Lord*]. But—one never marries this sort of a woman !

PAUL. As if there was any other sort of a woman !

LORD. Ah, you don't know her real self ; she's an angel who fell by accident.

PAUL. Did she fall or was she pushed ?

FISCHER. I know them all ; it's always by accident.

PAUL. [*Singing*]—

> "Give me passion !
> Give me death !"

LORD. But she's not French.

PAUL. Ah, you have the English idea of the French. But that's not nearly as bad as the French idea of the English !

LORD. Well, I'm gambling on her· I am sure my love will keep her straight.

FISCHER. What's rank or fortune after a love among us ? There's nothing else ; all other love is pale and sick.

PAUL. Don't you know the difference between old brandy and ginger-pop ?

LORD. Oh, that's all over. She doesn't love *him* any more.

FISCHER. I tell you it's never over, never !

JAJA. What are you men talking about ?

FISCHER. Love.

JAJA. Oh, talk of anything else ! Bring some more wine !
[*She dabs her face with rouge and powder, and reddens her lips.*]

MADELINE [*To Lord*]. So it's marriage ?

LORD. Yes ; this is the last night of the old life.

MADELINE. Take good care of her ! It's not often one gets away from here.

FISCHER. Shall I marry you, Madeline ?

MADELINE. You're mine, silly ! What more ?

FISCHER. You see !

PAUL. When you've saved enough, you'll marry and do the fine folk from Paris in your château !

[FISCHER *and* MADELINE *shrug their shoulders. Enter* NEGRO *and* LILLIE.]

MADELINE. Hullo, Lillie ! Have you learned the Tango yet ?   [LILLIE *makes a gesture of disgust.*

PAUL. Cruel ! If you understood how we all love it.

NEGRO. She loves only her Negro, and nothing else on earth.

[*She puts her arms round* NEGRO'S *neck.* PAUL *whistles like a railway train, running round the room with his head between his hands.*]

MADELINE [*To Negro*]. Jaja is here ; she is going to be married to-morrow ; that's her best young man ; and aren't we going to be good—I don't think !

NEGRO. Silly cow ! I don't care a pink wart if she's here or in Timbuktu.

LILLIE. Oh, do let us go, dear ! Where you like ; only do let's get out of here. I've got a headache.

PAUL. And I've got cold feet !

302

THE TANGO

NEGRO. Rot ; you've got to dance the Tango.

[LILLIE *points to* JAJA, *and makes a face.*

NEGRO. That was not real love, anyhow ; I've forgotten it, and you'd better forget it too ! The other was nothing.

MADELINE. Lillie wishes she had been that nothing.

NEGRO. Women are never content.

JAJA. More wine, waiter ! Come and drink farewell, Madeline ! Here's the dear old life ! Fischer, sing " The Tango " again !

LORD. No ; please come away, my darling ; you're getting excited.

JAJA [*Impudently*]. And for why ? Because ?

LORD. You're not yourself. I don't understand you. [*He takes her by the arm to lead her away.*

PAUL [*Sings*]—

" They talk a lot o' loving
But what do they understand ? "

JAJA. [*Shaking* LORD *off.*] Let me be ! You promised me this one night, and it's mine !

LORD. A man forgives the past, but never the future.

PAUL. When you're as old as I am you'll know that the past *is* the future.

JAJA. Oh, hang it ! No moralizing to-night ! Let's drink !

[FISCHER *sings.*

JAJA [*To Pianist*]. So you no longer play the Tango now that I am not here to dance. [*She jumps on a table and waves her glass.*] The Tango !

ALL. We are all true to you. [*All rise and clink glasses and drink.*]

JAJA. And I to you ! In heart, I'm always here, always,

always! How the blood aches! How the heart leaps for joy! What other life is so gay, so entrancing? The reek of the smoke is sweeter than all the flowers of the earth and the incense of heaven.

PAUL. Yes! but what price Patchouli?

LORD. [*At table below* JAJA, *looking up, and consequently very ridiculous*]. I beg of you to come away. You no longer know what you are saying. If you are to bear my name you cannot talk so.

JAJA. This night is mine, mine, mine, mine. Fill my glass! . . . So the Tango is dead. Oh, how I'd love to dance it just once more!

ALL. Bravo! Come, Negro, the Tango!

NEGRO [*To Pianist*]. The Tango! [*He moves towards* JAJA *from old habit;* LILLIE *rushes to him and smacks his face, and makes him lead her out. They dance.*] Don't be so nervous. [*She trips.*] If you make another mistake I'll kill you; dance for your life! [*He strikes her. She winces.*] Damn you! You're not doing your best.

JAJA. [*Jumps off table, and tries to drag* LORD *into the dance.*] Come, come, come, dance!

LORD. I cannot.

JAJA. Oh yes, you can! I'll drag you round all right.

NEGRO [*To* Lillie]. Do you hear? Dance, I tell you.

JAJA. [*Mocking* Lillie.] I hate her; I hate her.

[LILLIE *trips.* NEGRO *throws her aside to the ground as* JAJA, *throwing her glass down, cries:* "Then I'll dance alone," *and begins.* NEGRO *joins her in the dance; as he clasps her she cries:* "Give me passion." *All have jumped on tables to watch the dance, except* LILLIE, *who*

THE TANGO

is stunned by her fall, and LORD, *who wrings his hands piteously, and makes little feeble attempts to rush in and drag* JAJA *away. Finally he gives it up, and throwing* JAJA'S *gloves on the table, walks out.* LILLIE *picks herself up, takes a knife, and flings herself on* JAJA *and stabs her.* JAJA *falls as* NEGRO *catches her, throwing* LILLIE *aside with his free arm.*]

JAJA. O God! I am dying. Negrito, Negrito, my own, you have at least saved me from the hell of boredom and respectability. Give me your lips! Kiss me Good-bye!

[*She dies in his arms.* LILLIE *picks herself up, and tries to flee, but* FISCHER *catches her.*]

FISCHER. One moment, if you please!

[*Every one stands spellbound with horror, except* PAUL, *who walks to the front of the stage, and lights a cigarette.*]

PAUL. Never dull at Fischer's!

CURTAIN.

THE BIG STICK

REVIEWS

SCIENCE AND THE INFINITE. By SYDNEY E. KLEIN. William Rider & Son.

WILLIAM RIDER and SON have moved from Aldersgate Street to Paternoster Row, but unless they are very careful they will find themselves in Carey Street. What can have come over the firm that it publishes a book written by a man who knows his subject?

For *Science and the Infinite* forms the most admirable sketch of what should surely be a great and important work. Mr. Klein shows clearly and simply the nature of what we call the Infinite, and proves that the great step to be taken is for the soul to recognize its oneness with that. But in Book 4 this conclusion is given as the result of definite experience. *See* pp. 80 and 87. Mr. Klein however, seems to prefer a sacramental solution of the problem, and advocates in almost too unveiled a manner the cult of the Phallus, which he understands, evidently enough, in its best form.

We could have wished that he had given us twenty diagrams instead of one. We could have wished that his English were less latinized and his sentences shorter, and—most of all—we could have wished that his book had been published in a more important form. The world is deluged with cheaply-got-up books of this kind, and it is difficult for the outsider to distinguish the corner-stone from that which should be "heaved over among the rubbish." Now a book should be a very holy thing. If it be truth, it is that which we most reverence, and it is impossible to expend too much care and lovingkindness in its worthy presentation. Considerations of the cost of production are the death of literature. Publishers are so ignorant of the value of books that they issue any quantity of worthless stuff. They have no idea of what will catch on with the public. They produce things as cheaply as possible, with the American philosophy, "It's a good bet if I lose!" Such a book as Mr. Klein's loses immensely by this vulgar presentation. Rising as it does to heights of sublime poetry, it is a shock to be constantly brought back to the twentieth-century illusion, which is the very sham he is trying to expose with its rage for hurry and cheapness, by the inferior paper and inferior printing. A book of this sort should have been produced, if not quite like the Medieval Books of Hours, yet in a form which represents the highest developments of the particular art used in its production. These things do not seem to matter now. They will matter enormously in a hundred years, and it should be for that part of the Now which we stupidly call the Future that books should be produced.

This is particularly the case with a book which deals with science. It is the common idea that science is practical. It does not occur to the average man that science is holy. He does not see that the microscope is a magical instrument in the truest sense of the word, as it assuredly is when its use leads one to such results as Mr. Klein has attained. Science has appeared principally practical. People say, " Look, it has given us the telephone and the motor-car ! " They have not understood that science may be a religion. To most people, especially so-called religious people, God means one in their own image, the shadow of themselves thrown, enlarged and distorted, upon the background of their own ignorance—not the image of themselves as they really are, but the image of those vile insects which they think themselves to be. The evangelical Christian asserts God to be mean, revengeful, cruel, huckstering—a small tradesman in a provincial town. A single blade of grass is sufficient contra-diction of the existence of such a monster. Even where the people have had no God their Great Man was fashioned in the same way. Buddha is only a magnified Buddhist. In their fierce life calm seems the only good, and so their Buddha sits eternally smiling on a lotus. Even the most elevated thinkers seem to cling to the idea of a personal God. This is because they are them-selves enmeshed in the illusion of personality. It is the personal and temporary self to which they cling. They have perhaps got rid of the idea that the body is real, but the highest ideas in their mind still appeal to them. They say (in the best cases) that God is Light, Love, Life, Liberty, but they still suppose him to be a person possessing these attributes. Hardly ever, save by virtue of spiritual experience of a high order, is that conception transcended. Personality is a limitation. As long as one thing is distinguished from another there are two things ; and there is only one thing. Such a conclusion Mr. Klein faintly foreshadows. I am not certain whether it is his reticence or his ignorance which prevents him from adumbrating the further conception which we have set forth in Book 4 and elsewhere.

It is very well that these conclusions, such as they are, should be restated. There is, of course, nothing new in them. They were stated by myself in almost the same language in a good deal of the poetry which I wrote when I was nineteen years old. Such perception is the birthright of the poet. But even immediate intuition of such truth is of less value than the knowledge obtained by conscious experience. The rediscovery of these truths much later in life had for me all the force of a new creation.

310

REVIEWS

We wish that Mr. Klein had gone deeply into the means of attainment. He seems to be of that school which holds that such attainment is the result of miracle, perhaps of accident. He does not seem to realize that there is a perfectly simple and straightforward method of arriving where he has arrived—a method which is good enough for all, and about which there is no doubt and no difficulty beyond the essential one of sticking to it. I hope that the perusal of Book 4 will enlighten him on this point, and enable him to write a Second Part to his book which shall detail this method in language which may reach those minds to which Book 4 does not appeal.   A. C.

THE BLUE GROTTO. ARTHUR H. STOCKWELL. London. 2d.

IT is monstrous and iniquitous that a person, however bearded, however resembling Bernard Shaw in name and form, should purport to translate a Rune Stone dealing with the Phrygian Mysteries—and scan Pandion wrong. The masterpiece of this anonymous author is full of false quantities, but I don't care if it is, for he has some very beautiful lines and a sense of the musical value of words. He writes:

> " The lovers of a night appear
> In the unravell'd atmosphere.
> Phantasmagoria crisp to gold
> Under Apollo. . . ."

And again:

> "Caduceator for thy knees'
> Ophidian caryatides."

And again:

> " And the red ibis in thy grove
> Feeds poison to the sucking dove."

And again:

> " Under the brown sea-furbelow
> Anguilla slimes; . . . ."

He tells us:

> ". . . Crassicornis seeks to grab
> The streamers of the coral-crab.'

He says:

> " I hear the triton-music swell
> Love-laden in the vulva-shell.'

And speaks of:

> ". . . Corybantes o' the storm
> Leaping coruscant-capriform."

311

I could hardly have done better myself, and Shelley would have been put to it to do it as well.

If the ingenious though fatuous author of *The Blue Grotto* will get a big idea and work it largely out, he will indubitably produce a worthy contribution to the language whose poverty he now enriches with so many admirable new words. A. C.

THE CLAY'S REVENGE. By HELEN GEORGE.

> ". . . equal purged of Soul and Sense.
> Beneficent high-thinking, just,
> Beyond the appeal of Violence,
> Incapable of common lust,
> In 'mental Marriage' still prevail
> (God in the garden hid his face)"—

AND well He might!

It is on these lines that Bertha and Leonard Hammersley agree to lead their married life. The husband is a delicate, refined, over-sensitive, under-vitalized creature, and the arrangement suits him admirably. For a time Bertha is content, her intellect is satisfied, her senses are slumbering. She is not only content; when she looks around at the married lives of her more carnally-minded friends she feels immensely superior, and prides herself on the purity of the relationship existing between Leonard and herself. She wilfully closes her eyes, and if an inner consciousness whispers to her that this vaunted happiness is incomplete, she refuses to listen. The whisper becomes loud—insistent. Mrs. George very cleverly shows us Bertha's slow, almost shocked, awakening. Starved Nature revengefully, triumphantly asserts herself. After three years of the Higher Life Bertha changes the joys of the Intellect and Spiritual Love for the joys of the Flesh and Human Passion.

But it is to the Man as Father, not as Lover, she at first yields.

When, in due course, the Man returns to West Africa, she sees him go without a pang. He has fulfilled his purpose, and she has no further use for him.

It is only later, after the birth of the child, that she desires him as a Lover.

This change in her attitude is depicted with masterly strength and skill.

He returns after two years' absence.

Her first feeling is one of annoyance and faint fear rather than rapture.

He takes it for granted their old relationship will be renewed, and so she drifts back and changes from the passive Mother-Woman, submitting to the Man's love only as a means to her own and Nature's end—to a passionate

REVIEWS

exacting Woman, demanding Love for love's sake and love's sake alone, and putting the plan before the child.

How the child dies, and how the Lover in terror and revolt flies from his too-exacting mistress, we leave it for Mrs. George to tell in her own vivid and unflinching way.   E. G. O.

LES FRÉQUENTATIONS DE MAURICE. By SIDNEY PLACE. One vol.:
    3 fr. 50 c. Dorbon, Paris.

NEVER before has the androgynous male been treated with such cold, cynical, non-moral impartiality.

The " hero " is an empty-headed young fop, and concerned only with the fit of his clothes and the colour of his necktie. " We cannot steal, to work we are ashamed " ; but though he stops short of actual stealing, he slips through life in luxurious sleekness—living by his " wits " and a kind of spurious system of blackmail. When he is not concerned in getting money, this mannikin of straw trips from one tea-party to another, lisping the latest scandal and wafting the newest scent. Sydney Place leads us a fantastic dance with these mincing demi-reps. He deals with flimsy people, but his study is neither flimsy nor wanting in interest. It is, we say it with regret, painfully true to life, and represents a sex which is largely on the increase in London Society of to-day.
                                                                                    E. G. O.

Richard Clay & Sons, Limited,
Brunswick Street, Stamford Street, S.E.,
and Bungay, Suffolk.

A. CROWLEY'S WORKS

The volumes here listed are all of definite occult and mystical interest and importance.

The Trade may obtain them from

"The Equinox," 33 Avenue Studios, South Kensington, S.W. (Tel.: 2632 Kensington) and

Messrs. Simpkin, Marshall, Hamilton, Kent & Co., 23 Paternoster Row, E.C.

The Public may obtain them from

"The Equinox," 33 Avenue Studios, South Kensington, S.W.

Mr. Elkin Mathews, Vigo Street, W.

The Walter Scott Publishing Co., Paternoster Square, E.C.

Mr. F. Hollings, Great Turnstile, Holborn.

And through all Booksellers.

ACELDAMA. Crown 8vo, 29 pp., £2 2s. net.

Of this rare pamphlet less than ten copies remain. It is Mr. Crowley's earliest and in some ways most striking mystical work.

JEPHTHAH AND OTHER MYSTERIES, LYRICAL AND DRAMATIC. Demy 8vo, boards, pp. xxii. + 223, 7s. 6d. net.

SONGS OF THE SPIRIT. Pp. x + 109. A new edition. 3s. 6d. net.

These two volumes breathe the pure semi-conscious aspiration of the soul, and express the first glimmerings of the light.

THE SOUL OF OSIRIS. Medium 8vo, pp. ix + 129, 5s. net.

A collection of lyrics, illustrating the progress of the soul from corporeal to celestial beatitude.

TANNHAUSER. Demy 4to, pp. 142, 15s. net.

The progress of the soul in dramatic form.

BERASHITH. 4to, China paper, pp. 24, 5s. net.

Only a few copies remain. An illuminating essay on the Universe, reconciling the conflicting systems of religion.

THE GOD-EATER. Crown 4to, pp. 32, 2s. 6d. net.

A striking dramatic study of the origins of religions.

THE SWORD OF SONG. Post 4to, pp. ix + 194, printed in red and black, decorative wrapper, 20s. net.

This is the author's first most brilliant attempt to base the truths of mysticism on the truths of scepticism. It contains also an enlarged amended edition of "Berashith," and an Essay showing the striking parallels and identities between the doctrines of Modern Science and those of Buddhism.

GARGOYLES. Pott 8vo, pp. vi + 113, 5s. net.

ORACLES. Demy 8vo, pp. viii + 176, 5s. net.

Some of Mr. Crowley's finest mystical lyrics are in these collections.

KONX OM PAX. See Advertisement.

Collected Works (Travellers' Edition). Extra crown 8vo, India paper, 3 vols. in one, pp. 808 + Appendices. Vellum, green ties, with portraits, £3 3s.; white buckram, without portraits, £2 2s.

This edition contains "Qabalistic Dogma," "Time," "The Excluded Middle," "Eleusis," and other matters of the highest occult importance which are not printed elsewhere.

AMBERGRIS. Medium 8vo, pp. 200, 3s. 6d. net. (Elkin Mathews.)

A selection of lyrics, containing some of great mystical beauty.

THE WHIRLPOOL

BY

ETHEL ARCHER

With a Cover specially designed by E. J. Wieland;
a Dedicatory Sonnet by Victor B. Neuburg; and an
Introduction by Aleister Crowley.

PRICE ONE SHILLING NET

"This is a whirlpool, and no mistake; a witches' cauldron wherein suns and stars and souls, and Lilith and Sappho, and 'whispering hair,' and corpses and poppies, jostle one another in a heaving brew of iridescent, quasi-putrescent, ultra-modernity. Quite good reading all the same. Take p. 44:— . . . . And we must thank the mysterious V. B. N. for a really inspired line—
'Thou lyric laughter of the enfranchised male.'
. . . . The naughty new 'male,' smashing our windows with his inverted commas . . . . unless, indeed, as Mr. Aleister Crowley authoritatively hints in his sacerdotal preface, . . . But the time, we think, is hardly ripe for such disclosures, although the more intelligent among us may have seen a certain Writing upon the Wall, setting forth, in clearest language, that $1 + 1 = 3$."—*The English Review.*

"Poems by a new writer who possesses imaginative gifts of unusual quality. Miss Archer's poems are both mystical and realistic, and they bear traces of having been to some extent influenced by the work of Mr. Aleister Crowley, but without losing an originality which is entirely their own."—*T.P.'s Weekly.*

"This book has all the defects and none of the qualities of Mr. Crowley's work. . . . Miss Ethel Archer misses everything. There is no *élan* in the work. She has none of the happy fluency of her master, and it requires much to carry off the cumbrous apparatus of esoteric epithets with which she is burdened. Miss Archer's mechanical abnormalities are ridiculous; she has mistaken jingle for music and incomprehensibility for passion. . . . The world will not willingly let it die."—*Vanity Fair.*

"On the cover a naked woman is riding a bat over a whirlpool; craggy white mountains are behind her and a red sky behind all. There is a fine fierceness of movement in the design; it is certainly good. Mr. Aleister Crowley introduces Miss Archer briefly but splendidly, with phrases of this sort: 'We find such rime-webs as abaaab-babbba . . ., more exquisite than all the arabesques of the Alhambra.' . . . It is all very splendid. . . . We feel drearily sensible of our outer darkness. Coming to Miss Archer's poetry we are obliged to notice her debt to Swinburne, yet we find it, on the whole, good. . . . The colour is very strong; the shades of thought are clear, and often subtle. . . . The uninitated may certainly recognise great strength of conviction in Miss Archer, even if they cannot or do not wish to appreciate it."—*The Poetry Review.*

"Several of these unpleasant phantasies are reprinted from the *Equinox*, and there is an introduction by Aleister Crowley, in which he says this book is the hell of sterile passion glowing in the heart of the hell of desolation."—*Times Literary Supplement.*

"There is a resemblance in much of Miss Archer's verse to the sensuous school of English poetry, and it has the same lyrical power. Love in its various forms is the theme of her songs, and she expresses her thoughts in vivid words. The portrayal of the intensity of personal feeling with an unguarded freedom, is that which a student of pre-Raphaelite poetry would naturally acquire. (Our reviewer's guarded remarks lead us to suppose he means that 'The Whirlpool' is rather 'hot water.'—Ed.)"—*Publishers' Circular.*

"Moralists with no pretensions to severity will frown at the sentiments conveyed in the poem 'To Lilith. . . .' 'Reverie,' 'Midsummer Morn,' and 'Sleep,' are really beautiful poems. . . ."—*Westminster Review.*

"Full, at any rate, of high artistic endeavour is Miss Ethel Archer's 'The Whirlpool.' There is a strong sense of classical beauty and of form in these passionate and exotic verses. 'The Felon Flower' is an extraordinary rhapsody, and the 'Song to Leila' is delicate and highly wrought."—*The Commentator.*

"The verse is musical and the ideas profound. . . ."—*Light.*

MR. NEUBURG'S NEW VOLUME OF POEMS

Imperial 16mo, pp. 200

Now ready. Order through **The Equinox,** *or of any Bookseller*

THE TRIUMPH OF PAN

Poems by VICTOR B. NEUBURG

This volume, containing many poems—nearly all of them hitherto unpublished— besides THE TRIUMPH OF PAN, includes THE ROMANCE OF OLIVIA VANE.

The First Edition is limited to Two Hundred and Fifty copies; Two Hundred and Twenty on ordinary paper, whereof less than Two Hundred are for sale; and Thirty on Japanese vellum, of which Twenty-five are for sale. These latter copies are numbered, and signed by the Author. The binding is half-parchment with crimson sides; the ordinary copies are bound in crimson boards, half-holland.

The price of ordinary copies is Five Shillings net; of the special copies, One Guinea net.

EXTRACTS FROM PRESS NOTICES

"Not every one will care for Mr. Neuburg's tone in all the pieces, but he is undoubtedly a poet to be reckoned with, and a volume so original as this is should create no small stir. It is superbly produced by the publishers."—*Sussex Daily News.*

"When one comes to the poems . . . it is evident that they are written in English. . . . In a certain oblique and sub-sensible sense, eloquent and musical. . . . Distinctly Wagnerian in their effects. . . ."— *Scotsman.*

"It is full of 'the murmurous monotones of whispering lust,' 'the song of young desire,' and that kind of poppycock."—*London Opinion.*

"A competent master of words and rhythms. . . . His esoteric style is unreasonably obscure from an intelligent plain poetry-lover's standpoint."—*Morning Leader.*

"A charming volume of poems. . . . Pagan glamour . . . passion and vigour. . . . 'Sigurd's Songs' are commendable for dealing with the all too largely neglected Scandinavian theology . . . A scholarly disciple. . . . The entire volume is eminently recommendable."—*Jewish Chronicle.*

"A gorgeous rhapsody. . . . Fortunately, there are the police. . . . On the whole, we cannot help regretting that such splendid powers of imagination and expression are flung away in such literary rioting."—*Light.*

"Sometimes of much beauty of rhythm and phrase. . . ."—*Times.*

"Poets who have any originality deserve to be judged by their own standard. . . . A Neo-mystic or semi-astrological pantheist. . . ."—*Liverpool Echo.*

"Love-making appears to have an added halo in his eyes if it is associated with delirium or blood- shed. . . . Mr. Neuburg has a 'careless rapture' all his own; the carelessness, indeed, is just the trouble. His versification is remarkable, and there is something impressive in its mere fluency. . . . So luxurious, so rampant, a decadence quickly palls. . . . On the whole, this book must be pronounced a quite grievous exhibition of recklessness and folly."—*Manchester Guardian.*

". . . We began to be suspicious of him. . . . Hardly the sort of person we should care to meet on a dark night with a knobby stick in his hand. . . . This clever book."—*Academy.*

"A vivid imagination fostered by a keen and loving insight of nature, and this allied to a command of richly adorned language . . . have already assured for the author a prominent place amongst present-day poets. . . . An enthusiastic devotion to classic song . . . sustained metrical charm. From first to last the poet's work is an important contribution to the century's literature."—*Publishers' Circular.*

"This [book] contains the answer to a very well-known riddle propounded by the late Elizabeth Barrett Browning. You remember she asked in one of her poems, 'What was he doing to Great God Pan: Down in the reeds by the River?' Well, Mr. Victor Neuburg has discovered the answer, for he was obviously wandering near the river if he was not hidden in the reeds. . . ."—ROBERT ROSS in *The Bystander.*

"There is no question about the poetic quality of much of Mr. Neuburg's verse. . . . We are given visions of love which open new amorous possibilities."—*Daily Chronicle.*

"Sheer ennui is apt to say 'morbid,' and have done with it. . . . But here is Mr. Neuburg, with real literary and temperamental gifts . . . but it is not honest to deny that he is actually straying here and there upon the borders of a definite region of consciousness; that the evil and power he acclaims and fears have a phantom existence. . . ."—*Westminster Gazette.*

EXTRACTS FROM PRESS NOTICES—*Continued*

"A volume of no ordinary ability . . . real beauty."—*Advocate of India.*

". . . His poems are a mystery beyond the comprehension of the uninitiate. But we can appreciate the beauty of their sound, and envy those lovers in distant countries who will apparently enjoy the meaning. . . ."—*English Review.*

"By a big Pot, no doubt."—*John Bull.*

"'The Triumph of Pan' contains poems alive with music and rich in thought. Mr. Neuburg writes with distinction, and the book, from first to last, is one which lovers of poetry will appreciate."—*Standard.*

". . . full of the throbbing fever of life which one cannot confine into measure on all occasions.

"'The Triumph of Pan' is full of sonorous lines, with wonderful word pictures and poetic imagery which has seldom been excelled. . . ."—*American Register.*

". . . Many beautiful passages in the volume . . . strange allusions to unpleasant gods, and the imagery is occasionally repellent.

"The tremendous conception of that 'world so wide' . . . at his best in some of the shorter poems . . . stirring rhythm.

". . . we linger with delight over the splendid line—

"'The murmurous song of the morning star, aflame o'er the birth of day.'

". . . Melodious and plaintive with a haunting rhythm . . . vivid and pictorial . . . a painter's vision as well as a poet's ear . . . a fine simile in 'Osiris' is all his own."—*Co-Mason.*

". . . a delirious music . . . the majority of them (the poems) trouble the reader by giving the impression that a deep meaning lies behind the embroidered veil of words to which he is unable to penetrate ; others again seem to suggest events of too intimate and personal a nature to have a general application or interest . . . mixed metaphors—erratic visualisation. . . ."—*Theosophy in Scotland.*

"Passion and pain, 'red desire' and 'red roses' are frequent *motifs* in Mr. V. B. Neuburg's 'Triumph of Pan' ('The Equinox' Office), much of which merits the ambiguous distinction of being unusual. Though by no means deficient in originality, vigour or imaginative power, his verse is too often cumbered with the fantastic symbols of a species of erotic mysticism, into which we feel no desire to probe ; while the lack of reticence consistently displayed constitutes an artistic blemish not lightly to be excused. The author's serene confidence in the immortality of his lays would be better justified were he to make some attempt to discriminate between the gold and the rubbish, and, incidentally, refraining from penning such grotesqueness as is contained, for example, in 'The Sunflower,' where we are informed how, among other portents—

"'a greater god arose,
And stole the earth by standing on his toes
And blowing through the air.'

"It is difficult to believe that the persons to whom certain poems are inscribed will experience any very lively gratification at the compliment."—*Athenæum.*

". . . really notable fluency and fecundity of expression. . . . He gives us little of that boring stuff that is usually termed 'strong meat.' . . . his dedicatory poem is the one that fascinates me most. It is a tender little lyric, delicate, iridescent, fragrant as a summer dawn. I take the liberty of quoting it in full. . . ."—*New Age.*

"Fie, Mr. Neuburg ! . . . a most regrettable collection of songs that deal with unrestrained affection. . . . There's no denying they are first-rate verse."—PERCY FLAGE in *The Equinox.*

". . . We are dizzied and dazzled by a foaming rainbow-hued torrent of impassioned words. We are struck by the wealth and boldness of the imagery, and the facility of mechanical execution. . . . It is brilliant work . . . one is bound to admire the cleverness of it all."—*Literary Guide.*

". . . In the author of the present collection of poems . . . we have a veritable twentieth-century mystic and apostle of ecstasy who, according to his dedication, gives his songs—

"'By the sign that is black and forbidden,
By the word that is uttered no more.'

"'The Triumph of Pan,' from which the book borrows its title, is a remarkable sequence of some forty 'philosophic and ecstatic' stanzas . . . He would also seem to 'hold opinion with Pythagoras,' although we question if even Nietzsche himself could quite fathom the undercurrent of the lay. . . . Despite occasional extravagances in thought and in diction his work is that of a cultured scholar, his verbal artistry undeniably inspired with the true spirit of poetry. Whether he sings of 'Violet skies all rimmed in tune,' of red ravens, of purple kisses, of silver stars 'crested with amber melody,' or of the 'rhythmic sway of the idle moon,' he is always musical albeit, like Wagner, whose effects he now and then distinctly recalls, often utterly unintelligible. . . . In striking contrast to the chaste and serenely beautiful 'Diana Rides' . . . are no less than twenty-two audaciously passionate love-lyrics inscribed not only to one Olivia Vane, but also, curiously enough, to her 'other' lover."—*The Gambolier.*

"He has arrived. . . .

"Mr. Neuburg's work is partly mystical and partly of the flesh. . . . Quite frankly, some of his work we do not at all understand. This applies notably to his 'Music-Pictures,' which 'were obtained under the direct influence of music.' 'This,' the poet naïvely tells us, 'may explain their apparent inconsequence.' . . . he is much more than a minor poet. He can and will yet accomplish great work. . . . His ingenious rhyming capacity sometimes almost startles one. In the choice of some of his subjects he is daring—greatly daring. . . . His genius is undoubted ; and the world has a lot yet to hear of and from this gifted singer."—*Greater London Illustrated.*

"If he rejects this mask, Mr. Neuburg may become a poet."—*Rhythm.*

The Star in the West

BY

CAPTAIN J. F. C. FULLER

FOURTH LARGE EDITION NOW READY

THROUGH THE EQUINOX AND ALL BOOKSELLERS

SIX SHILLINGS NET

A highly original study of morals and religion by a new writer, who is as entertaining as the average novelist is dull. Nowadays human thought has taken a brighter place in the creation: our emotions are weary of bad baronets and stolen wills; they are now only excited by spiritual crises, catastrophes of the reason, triumphs of the intelligence. In these fields Captain Fuller is a master dramatist.

KONX OM PAX

THE MOST REMARKABLE TREATISE ON THE MYSTIC PATH EVER WRITTEN

Contains an Introduction and Four Essays; the first an account of the progress of the soul to perfect illumination, under the guise of a charming fairy tale;

The second, an Essay on Truth, under the guise of a Christmas pantomime;

The third, an Essay on Magical Ethics, under the guise of the story of a Chinese philosopher;

The fourth, a Treatise on many Magical Subjects of the profoundest importance, under the guise of a symposium, interspersed with beautiful lyrics.

No serious student can afford to be without this delightful volume. The second edition is printed on hand-made paper, and bound in white buckram, with cover design in gold.

PRICE TEN SHILLINGS

WALTER SCOTT PUBLISHING CO. Ltd., and through "The Equinox"

SOME PRESS OPINIONS

Dr. M. D. EDER in *The New Age*

" Yours also is the Reincarnation and the Life, O laughing lion that is to be !

" Here you have distilled for our delight the inner spirit of the Tulip's form, the sweet secret mystery of the Rose's perfume : you have set them free from all that is material whilst preserving all that is sensual. ' So also the old mystics were right who saw in every phenomenon a dog-faced demon apt only to seduce the soul from the sacred mystery.' Yes, but the phenomenon shall it not be as another sacred mystery ; the force of attraction still to be interpreted in terms of God and the Psyche? We shall reward you by befoulment, by cant, by misunderstanding, and by understanding. This to you who wear the Phrygian cap, not as symbol of Liberty, O ribald ones, but of sacrifice and victory, of Inmost Enlightenment, of the soul's deliverance from the fetters of the very soul itself—fear not ; you are not 'replacing truth of thought by mere expertness of mechanical skill.'

" You who hold more skill and more power than your great English predecessor, Robertus de Fluctibus, you have not feared to reveal 'the Arcana which are in the Adytum of God-nourished Silence' to those who, abandoning nothing, will sail in the company of the Brethren of the Rosy Cross towards the Limbus, that outer, unknown world encircling so many a universe."

John Bull, in the course of a long review by Mr. HERBERT VIVIAN

" The author is evidently that rare combination of genius, a humourist and a philosopher. For pages he will bewilder the mind with abstruse esoteric pronouncements, and then, all of a sudden, he will reduce his readers to hysterics with some surprisingly quaint conceit. I was unlucky to begin reading him at breakfast, and I was moved to so much laughter that I watered my bread with my tears and barely escaped a convulsion."

The Times

" The Light wherein he writes is the L.V.X. of that which, first mastering and then tran- scending the reason, illumines all the darkness caused by the interference of the opposite waves of thought. . . . It is one of the most suggestive definitions of KONX—the LVX of the Brethren of the Rosy Cross—that it transcends all the possible pairs of opposites. Nor does this sound nonsensical to those who are acquainted with that LVX. But to those who do not it must remain as obscure and ridiculous as spherical trigonometry to the inhabitants of Flatland."

The Literary Guide

" He is a lofty idealist. He sings like a lark at the gates of heaven. *Konx Om Pax* is the apotheosis of extravagance, the last word in eccentricity. A prettily-told fairy-story 'for babes and sucklings' has 'explanatory notes in Hebrew and Latin for the wise and prudent'—which notes, as far as we can see, explain nothing—together with a weird preface in scraps of twelve or fifteen languages. The best poetry in the book is contained in the last section—'The Stone of the Philosophers.' Here is some fine work."

To be obtained of

THE EQUINOX,

33 Avenue Studios, 76 Fulham Road, South Kensington, S.W.

TELEPHONE: 2632 KENSINGTON.

Crown 8vo, Scarlet Buckram, pp. 64

PRICE 10s. net

Less than 100 copies remain. The price will shortly be raised to one guinea net

A.·.A.·.PUBLICATION IN CLASS B

BOOK

777

THIS book contains in concise tabulated form a comparative view of all the symbols of the great religions of the world; the perfect attributions of the Taro, so long kept secret by the Rosicrucians, are now for the first time published; also the complete secret magical correspondence of the G.·.D.·. and R. R. et A. C. It forms, in short, a complete magical and philosophical dictionary; a key to all religions and to all practical occult working.

For the first time Western and Qabalistic symbols have been harmonised with those of Hinduism, Buddhism, Mohammedanism, Taoism, etc. By a glance at the Tables, anybody conversant with any one system can understand perfectly all others.

The *Occult Review* says:

"Despite its cumbrous sub-title and high price per page, this work has only to come under the notice of the right people to be sure of a ready sale. In its author's words, it represents 'an attempt to systematise alike the data of mysticism and the results of comparative religion,' and so far as any book can succeed in such an attempt, this book does succeed; that is to say, it condenses in some sixty pages as much informa- tion as many an intelligent reader at the Museum has been able to collect in years. The book proper consists of a Table of 'Correspondences,' and is, in fact, an attempt to reduce to a common denominator the symbolism of as many religious and magical systems as the author is acquainted with. The denominator chosen is necessarily a large one, as the author's object is to reconcile systems which divide all things into 3, 7, 10, 12, as the case may be. Since our expression 'common denominator' is used in a figurative and not in a strictly mathematical sense, the task is less complex than appears at first sight, and the 32 Paths of the Sepher Yetzirah, or Book of Formation of the Qabalah, provide a convenient scale. These 32 Paths are attributed by the Qabalists to the 10 Sephiroth, or Emanations of Deity, and to the 22 letters of the Hebrew alphabet, which are again subdivided into 3 mother letters, 7 double letters, and 12 simple letters. On this basis, that of the Qabalistic 'Tree of Life,' as a certain arrangement of the Sephiroth and 22 remaining Paths connecting them is termed, the author has constructed no less than 183 tables.

"The Qabalistic information is very full, and there are tables of Egyptian and Hindu deities, as well as of colours, perfumes, plants, stones, and animals. The information concerning the tarot and geomancy exceeds that to be found in some treatises devoted exclusively to those subjects. The author appears to be acquainted with Chinese, Arabic, and other classic texts. Here your reviewer is unable to follow him, but his Hebrew does credit alike to him and to his printer. Among several hundred words, mostly proper names, we found and marked a few misprints, but subsequently discovered each one of them in a printed table of errata, which we had overlooked. When one remembers the misprints in 'Agrippa' and the fact that the ordinary Hebrew compositor and reader is no more fitted for this task than a boy cognisant of no more than the shapes of the Hebrew letters, one wonders how many proofs there were and what the printer's bill was. A knowledge of the Hebrew alphabet and of the Qabalistic Tree of Life is all that is needed to lay open to the reader the enormous mass of information contained in this book. The 'Alphabet of Mysticism,' as the author says—several alphabets we should prefer to say—is here. Much that has been jealously and foolishly kept secret in the past is here, but though our author has secured for his work the *imprimatur* of some body with the mysterious title of the A.·.A.·., and though he remains himself anonymous, he appears to be no mystery-monger. Obviously he is widely read, but he makes no pretence that he has secrets to reveal. On the contrary, he says, 'an indicible arcanum is an arcanum which *cannot* be revealed.' The writer of that sentence has learned at least one fact not to be learned from books.

"G. C. J."

WILLIAM NORTHAM
Robemaker
9 Henrietta Street, Southampton Street, Strand

TELEPHONE—5400 Central

MR. NORTHAM begs to announce that he has been entrusted with the manufacture of all robes and other ceremonial apparel of members of the A∴ A∴ and its adepts and aspirants.

No. 0.	PROBATIONER'S ROBE	. . . . . .	£5	0	0
1.	,, ,, superior quality .	. . .	7	0	0
2.	NEOPHYTE'S	. .	6	0	0
3.	ZELATOR Symbol added to No. 2	. .	1	0	0
4.	PRACTICUS ,, ,, 3	. .	1	0	0
5.	PHILOSOPHUS ,, ,, 4	. .	1	0	0
6.	DOMINUS LIMINIS ,, ,, 5	. .	1	0	0
7.	ADEPTUS (without) ,, ,, 0 or 1	. .	3	0	0
8.	,, (within)	. .	10	0	0
9.	ADEPTUS MAJOR	. .	10	0	0
10.	ADEPTUS EXEMPTUS	. .	10	0	0
11.	MAGISTER TEMPLI	. .	50	0	0

The Probationer's robe is fitted for performance of all general Invocations and especially for the I. of the H. G. A. ; a white and gold nemmes may be worn. These robes may also be worn by Assistant Magi in all composite rituals of the White.

The Neophyte's robe is fitted for all elemental operations. A black and gold nemmes may be worn. Assistant Magi may wear these in all composite rituals of the Black.

The Zelator's robe is fitted for all rituals involving I O, and for the infernal rites of Luna. In the former case an Uraeus crown and purple nemmes, in the latter a silver nemmes, should be worn.

The Practicus' robe is fitted for all rituals involving I I, and for the rites of Mercury. In the former case an Uraeus crown and green nemmes, in the latter a nemyss of shot silk, should be worn.

The Philosophus' robe is fitted for all rituals involving O O, and for the rites of Venus. In the former case an Uraeus crown and azure nemmes, in the latter a green nemmes, should be worn.

The Dominus Liminis' robe is fitted for the infernal rites of Sol, which must never be celebrated.

The Adeptus Minor's robe is fitted for the rituals of Sol. A golden nemmes may be worn.

The Adeptus' robe is fitted for the particular workings of the Adeptus, and for the Postulant at the First Gate of the City of the Pyramids.

The Adeptus Major's robe is fitted for the Chief Magus in all Rituals and Evocations of the Inferiors, for the performance of the rites of Mars, and for the Postulant at the Second Gate of the City of the Pyramids.

The Adeptus Exemptus' robe is fitted for the Chief Magus in all Rituals and Invocations of the Superiors, for the performance of the rites of Jupiter, and for the Postulant at the Third Gate of the City of the Pyramids.

The Babe of the Abyss has no robe.

For the performance of the rites of Saturn, the Magician may wear a black robe, close-cut, with narrow sleeves, trimmed with white, and the Seal and Square of Saturn marked on breast and back. A conical black cap embroidered with the Sigils of Saturn should be worn.

The Magister Templi robe is fitted for the great Meditations, for the supernal rites of Luna, and for those rites of Babylon and the Graal. But this robe should be worn by no man, because of that which is written : "Ecclesia abhorret a sanguine."

Any of these robes may be worn by a person of whatever grade on appropriate occasions.

A GREEN GARLAND

BY

V. B. NEUBURG

Green Paper Cover . . 2s. 6d. net.

WIELAND & CO.

SIGNS AND SYMBOLS OF PRIMORDIAL MAN

BY

ALBERT CHURCHWARD

MR. NEUBURG'S NEW WORKS

IN PREPARATION

SONNETS FROM THE SPANISH
A Contribution to the Personal Note in Literature

THE NEW DIANA
A History. With other Poems, and some Translations

THE CHANGELING
A Fairy Play

ROSA IGNOTA
An Essay in Mysticism

HEINE'S LYRISCHES INTERMEZZO
A Complete Translation, with a Prose Preface

SONGS OF THE DECADENCE
New Lyrics

THE BOOK OF LIES
WHICH IS ALSO FALSELY CALLED
BREAKS
THE WANDERINGS OR FALSIFICATIONS OF THE ONE THOUGHT OF
FRATER PERDURABO
WHICH THOUGHT IS ITSELF UNTRUE

"Break, break, break
At the foot of thy stones, O Sea!
And I would that I could utter
The thoughts that arise in me!"

CONTENTS

PRICE ONE GUINEA

WIELAND & CO., 33 Avenue Studios, South Kensington, London, S.W.

MORTADELLO

OR

THE ANGEL OF VENICE

A PLAY IN FIVE ACTS

BY

ALEISTER CROWLEY

PRICE TEN SHILLINGS NET

"A little masterpiece."—*The Times*.

WIELAND & CO.

33 AVENUE STUDIOS, SOUTH KENSINGTON,
LONDON, S.W.

TELEPHONE : 2632 KENSINGTON

THE WINGED BEETLE

By ALEISTER CROWLEY

PRIVATELY PRINTED: TO BE HAD THROUGH "THE EQUINOX"

300 copies, 10s. net
50 copies on handmade paper, specially bound, £1 1s. net

CONTENTS

www.ingramcontent.com/pod-product-compliance
Lightning Source LLC
Chambersburg PA
CBHW080826010225
21259CB00006B/18